Sex Crime

Sex Crime
Sex offending and society

Second edition

Terry Thomas

Routledge
Taylor & Francis Group

LONDON AND NEW YORK

First published by Willan Publishing 200
This edition published by Routledge 2011
2 Park Square, Milton Park, Abingdon, Oxon OX14 4RN
711 Third Avenue, New York, NY 10017

Routledge is an imprint of the Taylor & Francis Group

First edition 2000
Second edition 2005

ISBN 10: 1-84392-105-7
ISBN 13: 978-1-84392-105-9

British Library Cataloguing-in-Publication Data

A catalogue record for this book is available from the British Library

Typeset by GCS, Leighton Buzzard, Bedfordshire, LU7 1AR
Project managed by Deer Park Productions, Tavistock, Devon

Contents

Preface to second edition

Legal and policy developments towards sexual offending have continued at a formidable speed since this book first appeared. The law on sexual offending has been completely reviewed and a new Sexual Offences Act received its Royal Assent in November 2003; new laws on domestic violence are also expected. A new centralised form of screening workers who will have access to children has been introduced with the Criminal Records Bureau and new multi-agency arrangements created to monitor the 'dangerous' person in the community. New measures have been introduced to tackle Internet sexual crime and in particular the dissemination of child pornography, and new laws put in place to target the 'chatroom' men who 'groom' children for sexual purposes. On the international front new laws have arisen to deal with the cross-frontier 'trafficking' of women and children for purposes of prostitution.

All these developments suggested that a second edition of *Sex Crime* would be appropriate to bring the story up to date. The first six chapters remain as in the first edition with appropriate amendments and additions as required. The second three chapters have involved a restructuring to reflect the 'protection' aims of laws and policies. In broad terms the book now covers the criminal justice approaches to sexual offending (Chapters 4–6) and the civil processes towards greater protection from sexual offending (Chapters 7–9).

General thanks are due to Angela Grier, Jane Gilgan, Eric Janus and Bill Hebenton (again) and to Sheila Milner for word-processing. Special thanks to Lennie for help with the reading of newspapers, and to Jim Wilson for healthy diversion at the 'Drones'.

Terry Thomas
Leeds

Tables of statutes, statutory instruments and cases cited

Statutory instruments cited

Cases cited

Sources cited

Newspapers

House of Commons debates and written answers

House of Lords debates

List of figures and tables

Figures

Table

Chapter 1

Introduction

Sexual offending is often considered as somehow inherently 'different' from other forms of offending and sexual offenders occupy a special place in contemporary society's secular demonology. Sexual crime is a mainstay of the tabloid and broadsheet newspapers, where offenders become 'monsters', 'beasts' and 'sex fiends'. Within prison walls, 'ordinary' offenders see it as normal to harass and bully the sex offender and professionals find them equally difficult to work with because 'those who perpetrate such crimes are hated and despised more than almost any other offender' (Sampson 1994: x). Nash has described the 1990s as: 'the decade of the predatory sex offender, at least in terms of constructing a demon. Across the world a range of legislation has been set in place which seeks to single out this group of offenders for greater punishment, fewer rights and potential exclusion from society' (1999: 1). A particular hostility has been directed at the sex offender who offends against children. Although experts may debate the true meaning of the word 'paedophile', there is little doubt that the paedophile has become the 'hate figure' of our time in the popular imagination.

Despite the demonology and the hatred, the sex offender is also noted for his (and less often her) 'invisibility'. At one time he was the stereotype of the 'man in the grubby raincoat' hanging around street corners, but in truth the sex offender appears in all walks of life and in all guises. Indeed the transformation of the sex offender from the 1970s pathetic, sad individual to today's intelligent, manipulative and dangerous manifestation is remarkable in itself.

The sex offending itself takes many forms: from the man who indecently exposes himself, to the anonymous stranger who abducts,

1

assaults and kills, to the man who possesses illegal pornography; from the man who offends only against his own children, to the men who find employment in children's homes or schools just to give them access to children and opportunities to offend.

In Bolton, a 23-year-old man is convicted for creating child pornography by superimposing photographs of children on to obscene photographs of adult men ('Pervert with an album of child filth', *Manchester Evening News*, 7 November 1998). A 13-year-old in West Yorkshire is convicted of a series of indecent assaults ('Boy aged thirteen is placed on register of sex offenders', *Guardian*, 19 November 1997) and in the south-east a 49-year-old man dubbed 'the M25 rapist' gets life imprisonment when he is convicted for seven rapes ('Violent sexual predator gets seven life terms for ruthless rape campaign', *Guardian*, 5 March 2004).

Intense media coverage takes place when children are abducted. In the summer of 2000 the search for 8-year-old Sarah Payne in Sussex makes headlines day after day and two years later the same happens when Holly Wells and Jessica Chapman, both aged 10, are abducted in the Cambridgeshire village of Soham. The respective trials and convictions of the abductors and murderers of the children are equally high profile ('A cunning and glib liar who should never be set free again', *Independent*, 13 December 2001; 'Beyond belief', *Daily Mail*, 18 December 2003; 'Blunder after blunder', *Guardian*, 18 December 2003).

Information technology and the Internet became a new means of distributing illegal pornography. An ageing rock star takes his personal computer in for repairs and is arrested because of the indecent images found stored there ('Glitter jailed for child porn charges', *Guardian*, 13 November 1999) and an international police operation – Operation Ore – finds over 7,000 UK subscribers to a US-based 'pay-per-view' website in Texas which has 75,000 subscribers worldwide ('Operation Ore: the biggest police probe into Internet paedophilia', *Independent on Sunday*, 12 January 2003; 'How British police officer set trap for paedophiles', *Observer*, 19 January 2003).

Operation Ore reveals users of child pornography from all walks of life, from teachers ('Teacher's child porn shame', *Yorkshire Evening Post*, 20 February 2003) to yet another rock star ('I want to clear my name, says Who star', *Observer*, 12 January 2003; 'Rock star on sex register', *Evening Standard*, 7 May 2003). One of the policemen who had been involved in the Soham murders inquiry is found to be another of the 7,000 subscribers in the UK ('Prison for child porn policeman', *Daily Telegraph*, 29 March 2003).

Internet technology is also misused by child abusers who join 'chatrooms' pretending to be the same age as other young people using the chatrooms. Children are 'groomed' online with a view to meetings and eventual abuse ('The perfect family man who preyed on young chatroom girls', *Guardian*, 10 October 2003). Some Internet service providers became so worried they closed down their chatrooms ('Switching off ... chatrooms proving too hot for children to handle', *Guardian*, 24 September 2003). When the third generation of mobile telephones was developed with a capacity to send pictures and access the Internet, the same thing happened. Abusers found they could use the new technology to target children ('Paedophiles set picture phone trap', *Observer*, 29 June 2003), and the providers felt obliged to move in and protect children ('Child safety fears prompt u-turn on mobile phone porn', *Guardian*, 23 March 2004).

Sometimes a seemingly 'new' sexual offence is 'discovered'. A man who persuaded two 11-year-old girls to undress in front of him but used no threat of violence and did not touch the girls was investigated by the police but not prosecuted because his behaviour did not fit any offences available under English law ('Loophole in law helps man who made girls strip', *Independent*, 16 January 2002). The Sexual Offences Act 2003, s. 8 has now closed this perceived 'loophole'.

Sex offenders seemed thick on the ground and made good copy for a salacious tabloid press. A police officer in Avon and Somerset receives a £20,000 grant from the Home Office to research the safety of children on international holiday exchanges ('Exchange trip pupils in danger of abuse', *The Times*, 21 April 1998) and a tribunal of inquiry takes almost four years to produce a 900-page report on the 'widespread sexual abuse of boys ... in children's residential establishments in Clwyd between 1974 and 1990' (Waterhouse Report 2000: para. 55.10).

At one extreme, the 'sex offender' label is attached to Fred and Rose West, as a country is transfixed by the horrific revelations of what happened at 25 Cromwell Street in Gloucester ('Burn in Hell', *Sun*, 23 November 1995). At the other extreme, questions are asked of Boots the Chemist when they call the police in to look at negatives they have been asked to develop by an ITN newsreader; they turn out to be innocent photographs of her own children ('ITN newsreader in photographs row back on air', *Independent*, 6 January 1995).

The law may tell us in detail what is a sexual offence but an abstract definition remains nebulous. Here we might suggest only that it is the inducement or coercion of adults and children into sexual activities to which they have not consented. This might include the exploitative use of people in prostitution or other unlawful sexual practices, including the production of pornographic material. The absence of a true consent to sexual activities is the overarching feature of sexual offending. The harm caused includes the violation of a person's sexual autonomy, the exploitation of a vulnerable victim, psychological distress and fear.

Alongside this growing awareness is the associated question of what we do about the sex offender. How do we identify him in the first place and bring him to justice? Should that justice involve treatment, containment or straight punishment? How do we monitor the known offender after his treatment or punishment in order to protect ourselves and children from him?

Forms of sex offending

What constitutes a sex offence also varies over time and place. An existing offence may be decriminalised at the stroke of a statute (e.g. homosexual activities in England and Wales in 1967), and existing behaviour may be recognised as needing to be criminalised (e.g. male rape in 1994). What is a sex offence in one country may not be in another.

The exact number of sex offences committed each year is difficult to determine because of the varying forms, the nature of police recording and the unwillingness of some victims to report crimes in the first place. The Home Office recorded 36,690 sexual offences for the year ending September 1998 and 37,492 for the year ending September 1999 (Home Office 2000a); this figure divides into approximately 6,000 rapes and the remainder indecent assaults. Reports suggest, however, that this is a massive under-reporting (see, e.g., 'Hidden toll of rape victims', *Guardian*, 18 February 2000).

More detailed figures from the Home Office show the number of convictions and cautions for specific sexual offences against children to have fallen between 1985 and 1995. Indecent assaults on girls under 16 fell from 2,416 to 2,116 (a drop of 12 per cent) and on boys from 674 to 476 (a drop of 29 per cent). Unlawful sexual intercourse with girls under 16 fell 61 per cent and on girls under 13 by 27 per cent. Convictions and cautions for gross indecency with girls under 14 fell from 206 to 129 and on boys under 14 from 122 to 84 (Grubin 1998: 4). As with the adult figures, cautions and convictions may not reflect the true incidence of these crimes.

The number of males convicted for the offence of indecency between males has also shown a steady decrease between 1987 and 1997. In 1987, 951 males of all ages were convicted for this crime, rising to a peak of

1,503 in 1989; by 1996, however, the figure had dropped to 219 and rose slightly to 237 in 1997 (HC Debs, 9 March 1999, WA 75034, col. 127).

The common theme to nearly all sexual offending is the lack of a real consent, whether by age, by coercion or from consent being given to a 'prohibited relationship', such as between father and daughter. Adults may be coerced into sexual activities against their will by threats or violence, and that will include coercion caused by poverty and economic imperatives that turn women (and men) to prostitution, whether in this country or 'trafficked' in from abroad. Offences may be committed against women with mental impairments who are unable to give a true consent. Violent attacks on women where there is no sexual element can still be seen as sexual assaults simply because they are targeted as women.

Some offences may be committed even when there is consent between the adult parties concerned and most notably when activities are committed in a public rather than a private place, when they are deemed to offend our concepts of public decency.

Children and young people below the 'age of consent' may be engaged in unlawful sexual intercourse, either with or without their consent. Such offending can take place within a family ('intra-familial') or outside the family ('extra-familial'); within a family it will probably be incestuous, or what the law now calls 'familial child sex offences'. Sexual offending outside the family is sometimes referred to as the 'stranger-danger' that children should be wary of.

Allegations have been made that children have been subjected to 'ritual' or 'satanic' abuse, whereby the abuse is subsumed into ceremonies that serve to frighten the children into saying nothing afterwards. The truth of these allegations has been hotly disputed.

Children and young people also attend various institutions outside the family, such as nurseries, schools, youth clubs and sporting clubs; sometimes they require substitute care – when for various reasons their parents are unable to care – which might include a children's home or foster care. The extent of sex offending against children in all these settings has been 'discovered' in the last 10 or 20 years and various safeguards put in place to reduce the risk to children in these 'out-of-home' settings. Some of this workplace sex offending can constitute complex or organised abuse, sometimes referred to as 'rings' or 'networks' of offenders working together in various ways.

Children and young people may be coerced into prostitution against their will and this has been referred to as 'trafficking' in human beings when it involves moving victims (including adults) from one country to another. 'Sex tourists' is the term used to describe men who travel from

North America, Europe, Japan and other developed countries to avail themselves of adult and child prostitutes in developing countries.

Sexual exploitation of children and adults can take place when they are involuntarily involved in the production of pornography which is then disseminated in either paper or electronic format; the latter would include distribution over the Internet.

The idea of outlining the 'forms' of sexual offending in this section is not to suggest a hierarchy of seriousness; all would be experienced as equally serious by the victims, unless, of course, they do not believe it to have been an offence at all. The idea has been to offer a sample of the variety of offending that we consider to be sexual offending; the reader will be able to add his or her own 'forms' to those not covered here.

The law

Although we can talk generally about sexual offending and the law, in practice it will require a criminal court to decide whether or not a particular level of behaviour constitutes an offence. The courts will be interpreting the different common and statutory law for Scotland, Northern Ireland or England and Wales.

In 1985 the Howard League could report that 'the law makes no formal distinction between "sexual" offences and other offences. How one differentiates is therefore largely a matter of individual choice, and the criteria for classification are open to debate' (para. 2.3). Today that position no longer holds.

Within the law various formal 'lists' of sexual offences have been drawn up for different purposes. For sentencing purposes, a 'list' exists in the Criminal Justice Act 1991 for England and Wales (see Figure 1.1) and another in the Criminal Procedure (Scotland) Act 1995 for Scotland (see Figure 1.2); they act as guides to the court that has to sentence a serious sexual offender.

As the criminal law identifies a sexual offence and is used to convict and sentence sexual offenders, alongside it the civil law is increasingly used to try to regulate the activities of the sexual offender to prevent him committing offences in the first place. This pincer movement of criminal and civil law moves forward on the premise of making communities safer and offering better public protection. The two forms of law are linked by the idea that civil orders that are breached may result in criminal proceedings in the criminal courts.

The Sex Offenders Act 1997, which introduced the sex offender 'register', had 'lists' of which offenders might find themselves having to

'Sexual offence' means any of the following:

(a)   an offence under the Sexual Offences Act 1956, other than an offence under section 30, 31 or 33 to 36 of that Act;

(b)   an offence under section 128 of the Mental Health Act 1959;

(c)   an offence under the Indecency with Children Act 1960;

(d)   an offence under section 9 of the Theft Act 1968 of burglary with intent to commit rape;

(e)   an offence under section 54 of the Criminal Law Act 1977;

(f)   an offence under the Protection of Children Act 1978;

(g)   an offence under section 1 of the Criminal Law Act 1977 of conspiracy to commit any of the offences in paragraphs (a) to (f) above;

(h)   an offence under section 1 of the Criminal Attempts Act 1981 of attempting to commit any of those offences;

(i)   an offence of inciting another to commit any of those offences.

Figure 1.1   A 'sexual offence' (England and Wales)

Source: Criminal Justice Act 1991, s. 31(1), as amended by Criminal Justice and Public Order Act 1994, Sch. 9, para. 45

'Sexual offence' means:

(a)   rape;

(b)   clandestine injury to women;

(c)   abduction of a woman or girl with intent to rape or ravish;

(d)   assault with intent to rape or ravish;

(e)   indecent assault;

(f)   lewd, indecent or libidinous behaviour or practices;

(g)   shameless indecency;

(h)   sodomy;

(i)   an offence under section 170 of the Customs and Excise Management Act 1979;

(j)   an offence under section 52 of the Civic Government (Scotland) Act 1982;

(k)   an offence under section 52A of the Civic Government (Scotland) Act 1982;

(l)   an offence under sections 1 to 3, 5, 6, 8, 10 and 13 of the Criminal Law (Consolidation) (Scotland) Act 1995.

Figure 1.2   A 'sexual offence' (Scotland)

Note: For full details see Criminal Procedure (Scotland) Act 1995, s. 120A, as amended by the Crime and Disorder Act 1998, s. 86

register. The Act is a piece of civil regulatory law, but if breached leads the individual into the criminal courts. The 'list' referred to is now to be found in Schedule 5 to the Sexual Offences Act 2003 and is actually subdivided into three 'lists' for England and Wales, Scotland and Northern Ireland (see Chapter 9).

The Schedule 1 'list' in the Children and Young Persons Act 1933 has given us the label the 'Schedule 1 offender' for England and Wales. This is a list of all the offences it is possible to commit against a child, including non-sexual offences such as neglect and physical abuse. The Children (Scotland) Act 1995 (for Scotland) and the Children and Young Persons Act (NI) 1968 (for Northern Ireland) give equivalent 'lists' for Scotland and Northern Ireland (see Figures 6.1–6.3 in Chapter 6).

Other 'lists' exist, such as the one that lists offences which can disqualify a person as a childminder (the Disqualification for Caring for Children (England) Regulations 2002, S.1 No. 635, Schedule); the list of offences which make a person 'automatically debarred' from teaching (the Education (Teachers) Regulations 1993, S.1 No. 543, as amended); and, if we move outside legislation, yet another 'list' of sexual offences was drawn up by the Home Office in a 1996 consultation exercise that we will return to later (Home Office 1996a: Annex A). None of these 'lists' has exactly the same content, which must be a signifier to some of the difficulties of defining a sexual offence.

In 1999 a complete review of the law on sexual offending was initiated by the Home Office with a view to consolidating and reforming it. The review's report was called *Setting the Boundaries* (Home Office 2000b) and this was followed up by the white paper, *Protecting the Public* (Home Office 2002b) and eventually by a new Sexual Offences Act 2003.

Consent

The concept of consent is central to defining sexual offending. Sexual activities are expected to be consensual, and we speak of 'consenting adults'. When one party to a sexual act has not consented, we are moving into the realms of sexual offending. The sexual offence of rape clearly takes place when penetrative sexual activity takes place without consent from the victim, and that victim has been overcome by physical force or immediate threats of violence.

A consent is invalidated if it is given under duress; lawyers talk of the consent being 'negatived' by the presence of 'force, fear or fraud'. It is possible to compare consent here to the consent we give for medical treatment, where patients are said to give 'informed consent' (i.e.

knowing the full implications) or 'real consent' (i.e. where no duress or coercion has been applied).

Consent has also been depicted as a continuum, with a positive consent at one end through to a reluctant agreement or submission at the other end; the latter can also be given without consent at all, which would mean a sex offence has been committed. A growing number of rapes are being reported that have been committed by people known to the victim and are referred to as 'acquaintance' or 'intimate' rapes as opposed to 'stranger' rapes (see Harris and Grace 1999: 5–7); the criminal law does not acknowledge this difference.

Consent to sexual activities is largely gender specific and socially constructed. The law may now recognise the crime of male rape but when it comes to consent we are mostly talking about women saying 'yes' or 'no' to heterosexual activity. Men have been culturally subsumed into being the partners that somehow 'always' want sex and indeed are sometimes said to have a 'sex drive' that is 'uncontrollable'. Such cultural thinking is not immutable and different cultures in different times and places have seen things differently. In Greek mythology the blind seer Teiresias, who had had the advantage of experiencing sex as both a man and a woman, was clear that women enjoyed it more than men on a ratio of about nine to one.

Children and young people are held to be unable to give a full autonomous consent because they lack the 'competence' to make the decision until they have reached a certain age – the age of consent. The age of consent for heterosexual activities in England, Scotland and Wales was fixed at 10 in 1285, raised to 13 in 1875 and to 16 in 1885, where it still stands (Sexual Offences Act 2003, s. 9). The age has been examined from time to time to see if it should be altered (see, e.g., Policy Advisory Committee on Sexual Offences 1981; Law Commission 1995), but it has remained at 16 for some time now, and the review of the law on sexual offences that preceded the passing of the Sexual Offences Act 2003 always excluded any discussion to change the 'age of consent' (Home Office 1999a).

The age of consent for homosexual activities was fixed at 21 for England and Wales by the Sexual Offences Act 1967, s. 1, with the same age being brought into Scottish Law in 1980 and Northern Ireland in 1982. Amending legislation lowered it to 18 in 1994 for all parts of the UK (Criminal Justice and Public Order Act 1994, s. 145).

Campaigners continued to argue that the ages of consent for homosexual and heterosexual activities should be equalised. A case was put together by two men – Euan Sutherland and Chris Morris – with the backing of Stonewall, the homosexual rights group, to challenge the UK law in Europe. In July 1997, the European Commission on Human Rights accepted their arguments and found the present UK law contravened the European Convention on Human Rights. The next step would have been the UK appearing in the full European Court of Human Rights in Strasbourg, but the government managed to broker an agreement to avoid the court hearing by promising to change the law at the earliest opportunity. This was duly achieved with the passing of the Sexual Offences (Amendment) Act 2000 (now the Sexual Offences Act 2003, s. 9).

Sexual activities, of whatever orientation, with young people below the age of consent is a criminal offence even if a form of consent has been given and, in the case of a child under 13, may be defined as rape.

While most people would regard such under-age sexual activities as exploitation or criminal, arguments have in the past been made that there should be no age of consent. Apologists for sex with children have even turned the concept on its head to argue it as a case of children's rights: 'children should have some say in what they do with their own bodies. They should be free to decide, as a matter of right, whether or not they want a sexual relationship' (O'Carroll 1980: 127; see also Brongersma 1988).

British law does accept that older children have a developing competence to make autonomous decisions and that autonomy and competence do not just appear on a given date in the calendar (*Gillick v. West Norfolk and Wisbech Area Health Authority and the DHSS* [1986] 1 AC 112). Discretion in the implementation of the law may be used when young people are only just below the age of consent and the defendant just above. A man under 24 years of age used to be able to use the defence that he had 'reasonable cause' to believe a girl was over 16 (Sexual Offences Act 1956, s. 6(3)); that so-called 'young man's defence' has now been repealed (Sexual Offences Act 2003, s. 9).

Consent is also declared invalid if people are entering into a 'prohibited relationship'. This would be a relationship between parents and their own children or with an adult relative (Sexual Offences Act 2003, ss. 25–9 and 64–5). The 'incest taboo', the fear of in-breeding and the simple revulsion of the idea that those charged with caring for children should seek to have sex with those children are all reasons cited for prohibiting certain relationships.

Teachers, children's home staff and other workers having the care of young people are also prohibited from having sexual relations with those young people. The offence of 'abuse of trust' was created in 2000 to prevent such relationships even if the young person was over 16 years of age (now in the Sexual Offences Act 2003, ss. 16–24).

The opposite side of the coin to 'prohibited relationships' is the idea that some recognised relationships give 'automatic' consent to sexual relations. For many years this was the case for married couples where the man had the relationship itself as a defence against a charge of rape; it was the orthodoxy that a man could not rape his own wife. The Law Lords overturned this common law idea that marriage means a man has a 'continual' consent from his wife for sexual activity at any time (*R v. R (Rape: marital exemption)* [1992] 1 AC 599), and this was later brought into statute law in 1994 (now in Sexual Offences Act 2003, s. 1).

Although there may well be agreement on what constitutes 'prohibited relationships' such as incest, there are still a number of 'prohibited relationships' where controversy persists. The behaviour of two consenting adult males could, for example, be construed as a criminal act of indecency if their behaviour was in a public place and against the common law that declares their behaviour as obscene or disgusting enough to 'outrage public decency'. Here the prohibition was more about whether the act should be in private or public, rather than a reflection on the act itself. The purpose of the law was to ensure that 'reasonable people may venture out in public without the risk of outrage to certain minimum accepted standards of decency' (Lord Simon of Glaisdale in *R v. Knuller (Publishing, Printing and Promotions) Ltd.* [1973] 2 AC 435). The gay rights campaign group OutRage took its name from these common law provisions. The statutory offence of committing a sexual act specifically in a public lavatory has now been added to this common law provision (Sexual Offences Act 2003, s. 71).

The Sexual Offences Act 2003 also tightened up the law on other sexual offences where consent clearly did not come into the picture. Sexual acts with an animal or a corpse were simply considered morally unacceptable (Sexual Offences Act 2003, ss. 69–70).

The Act also put voyeurism on to the statute book. A number of cases of people – usually landlords – installing video equipment to film others without their consent in what would normally be considered private settings, had triggered the need for this change ('Pay up for your toilet video', *Oxford Mail*, 8 September 1998; 'Spy camera filmed girl in bedroom', *Yorkshire Evening Post*, 28 February 2000). The Sexual Offences Act made such activities an offence whether or not video equipment was used (Sexual Offences Act 2003, ss. 67–8).

For many years sexual offending was synonymous with prostitution, which in turn was described as the 'crime without a victim'. The argument was that consent for this financial transaction was forthcoming on all sides, yet it was still circumscribed by laws forbidding soliciting, procuring or allowing premises to be used as a brothel – the public as opposed to the private aspects of prostitution. As we have seen earlier, more recent feminist approaches have argued that the women's consent is often not 'real' because she has been driven to her actions by poverty and lack of income; from this perspective prostitution becomes a form of abuse against women and especially against those under 16, who are legally incapable of giving a 'real' consent.

Consent has had its limitations as a defence exposed elsewhere. In what became known as the 'Spanner Case' (named after the police operation), in 1990 a group of men were successfully prosecuted on charges of causing actual bodily harm and wounding under the Offences Against the Person Act 1861, s. 47. The men's defence, that they all had an interest in sado-masochistic activities and that they had all consented to the acts, was not accepted; the prosecution was based on a home-made video of them that had come into the hands of the police.

On appeal the convictions were held to stand, but the custodial sentences imposed were reduced in length; the law appeared no clearer (*R v. Brown* [1993] 2 WLR 556 HL). With the support of Liberty, the civil rights organisation, the men went to the European Court of Human Rights in Strasbourg, but that court too upheld the rights of the government to prosecute in its role of protecting public health and morals; consent was not relevant (*Laskey, Jaggard and Brown* v. *UK* (1997) Times, 20 February).

Consent as a defence against allegations of sexual offending does, therefore, have its limitations. This legal ambivalence was displayed further when, in line with the *Brown* decision, a man in Wakefield was convicted for 'branding' his wife's buttocks. On appeal the case was thrown out as serving no useful purpose (*R v. Wilson* (1996) Times, 5 March). For most court hearings, however, the presence or absence of a 'real consent' is the turning point for deciding whether or not a sexual offence has taken place.

The private and the public

It has become the conventional wisdom that we live our lives in 'private' and 'public'. We move between these two spheres on a daily basis. Where exactly we draw the dividing line is a matter of some debate and will vary from person to person, at different times of the day and between men and women. We value our privacy and we think we know when it has been 'invaded', even if we cannot accurately define what privacy is.

In general terms, the private sphere is characterised by being the unknown or unobserved area of life and an area in which 'free' behaviour is permitted without interference. It is the areas where individual and small group activities are permitted, including consensual sexual activities. As we have seen, the same activities in public space may well constitute crimes.

When the UK government has looked at the law on sexual offending, it has always paid deference to matters of 'privacy'. The 1984 Criminal Law Revision Committee made out the case quoting verbatim from the 1957 Wolfenden Report:

> the criminal law should not intervene in the private lives of citizens or seek to enforce any particular pattern of sexual behaviour further than is necessary 'to preserve public order and decency to protect the citizen from what is offensive or injurious and to provide sufficient safeguards against exploitation and corruption of others' (Criminal Law Revision Committee 1984: 1.5; see also Wolfenden Report 1957: para. 13).

The review of the law started in 1999 took a similar view:

> Our ... key guiding principle was that the criminal law should not intrude unnecessarily into the private life of adults ... most consensual activity between adults in private should be their own affair, and not that of the criminal law (Home Office 2000b: para. 0.7)

What actually constitutes the 'private zones' of life has been increasingly questioned. The privacy of the family or the household has been accepted to varying degrees since it was decreed 'an Englishman's [sic] home is his castle'. Women victims of criminal violence and sexual assault within the home would ask what value there is in delimiting such private zones wherein crimes against them are committed. The term 'domestic violence' has been questioned for its 'cosy' connotations that suggest this is perhaps a 'different' form of violence from public violence.

The most blatant example, until recently, has been the lack of recognition of rape in marriage (see above). Exactly the same behaviour carried out by a stranger in public would result in a lengthy prison sentence, but in the privacy of the household and circumscribed by 'marriage' it was not a crime at all. Some feminists have started to argue that privacy should only be applied to individuals totally alone in a house.

There is no definitive legal definition of privacy in the UK and consequently no right to privacy. From time to time the courts have been called on to attempt a definition (see, e.g., *McConnell* v. *Chief Constable of Greater Manchester Police* [1990] 1 All ER 423 (CA)), and in turn they have lamented the lack of a statutory definition (*Kaye* v. *Robertson* [1991] FSR 62 (CA)).

UK law in the past has gone so far as to stipulate that certain sexual activities should only be undertaken in 'private'. The law decriminalising homosexual activities at the same time said those activities must be 'in private' (Sexual Offences Act 1967, s. 1). The law made no attempt to define what 'in private' meant, although later legislation has tried to throw some light on the subject (Criminal Justice and Public Order Act 1994, s.143(3)). In 1997, seven men in Bolton were still prosecuted for homosexual activities that took place in a private household, but in the presence of others, which meant that it was considered not 'in private' ('Fight grows for gays in video case', *Guardian*, 23 January 1998).

International conventions and declarations have stated rights to privacy, including the UN Declaration of Human Rights (UN 1948: art. 12) and the European Convention on Human Rights (Council of Europe 1950: art. 8). The European Convention has now been assimilated into the UK's own Human Rights Act 1998 and it remains to be seen if this will clarify the domestic legal definition of privacy; recent rulings suggest not (see 'Law Lords rule there is no right to privacy', *Guardian*, 17 October 2003).

Sexual offending does take place in 'public space' but it is more likely to take place in 'private space', where there are rarely witnesses. For the criminal justice system, lawyers and victims, this has presented major difficulties in bringing what went on, and determining whether or not there was consent, into the public arena of the court.

Dangerousness and risk

The idea that certain behaviour by individuals can be 'dangerous' has a long history. The Victorians thought that whole classes of people – the poor and dispossessed – could be called the 'dangerous classes'. For the most part of the twentieth century, the term was restricted in use to describe the behaviour of some mentally disordered people. In 1977, in a seminal article, Bottoms described what he called the 'renaissance' of dangerousness as the label was increasingly used to describe criminal behaviour. Not only that, but practitioners in the criminal justice system including the police, probation officers and the judiciary were being called on, ever more, to divide criminal behaviour into what we might call 'dangerous' and that which was 'non-dangerous'. Penal disposals could then be decided upon in terms of the dangerousness posed (Bottoms 1977).

The 'renaissance' of dangerousness in this fashion put practitioners into the business of trying to tell who exactly the dangerous person was. The word 'dangerous' having been, up until now, an adjective used to describe certain behaviour, now turned into a noun as we looked for the 'dangerous person'. Psychologists, social workers and psychiatrists were just some of the professionals who now engaged in the search for those attributes within people that would justify them being assessed as 'dangerous people'. Once identified we could go on to assess the degree of risk they posed to other people.

Risk assessment takes a more detailed look at the same phenomenon, but realises that an individual had to be seen, not in isolation, but in the context of his immediate social environment, be that family, household or community. Risk assessment is the process whereby information on the individual and his environment is collated – from various different agencies if necessary – to provide as complete a 'picture' as possible. Once assembled, the information has to be verified, sifted and weighted in significance; any deficiencies in the information have to be identified and that information duly gathered in. Various risk assessment 'instruments' have been developed to assist the risk assessment (e.g. Matrix 2000, Oaysis, etc.).

In making a risk assessment, practitioners are making a prediction about a person's likely future behaviour. Everyone's future behaviour is, to some extent, uncertain and inherently unpredictable. Risk assessment accepts that we have enough information – including 'personal information' – about an individual to make an informed decision on that individual's future behaviour, albeit within a range of probabilities.

Sexual offenders are subjected to risk assessment when brought to court for bail or sentence decisions. They are assessed again at the start of their community or custodial sentence or on release from a period of detention. Multi-agency Public Protection Panels (MAPPPs) make risk assessments on people in the community considered 'dangerous' (see Chapter 9). The assessment of risk is an ongoing process for practitioners working with sex offenders and an ongoing experience for those offenders.

Risk management follows on from assessment and involves the implementation of whatever measures are required to reduce the risk a sexual offender may pose. These measures may be community based through supervision and conditions attached to that supervision, or may involve custodial containment.

Risk assessment and risk management will be a constant theme throughout this book; put together they can be considered under the umbrella term of 'risk analysis'.

Present approaches

This book attempts to introduce the reader to an overview of sexual offending as we have come to understand it today. Chapter 2 explores the explanations and responses made and put forward by the public, the press, politicians and the 'experts'. These different voices are often in competition with each other to try to define and 'claim' the phenomenon of sexual offending, and to say what should be done.

An illustrative history of sex offending is offered in Chapter 3, in so far as it can be distilled from historical sources. Particular attention is paid to themes and responses that have been made in the past which continue to have a resonance today. Such themes include the fear of the 'dangerous' person at large in the community and the need for the 'authorities' to identify him so that protective measures can be taken, and the need for 'experts' to understand what sexual offending is all about.

Chapter 4 outlines the current role of the police as the initial agency brought in to investigate sexual offending and detect those responsible. Chapter 5 carries the story on to the prosecution process and various difficulties encountered in the 'search for justice' where sexual offending is concerned. This 'search' ends with an examination of appropriate sentences for the convicted offender and (Chapter 6) how the agencies charged with carrying out those sentences go about their work.

The remaining chapters (7–9) move beyond the criminal justice system to examine the civil measures put into place to achieve better public protection from the sex offender. Chapter 7 focuses on protection in the home for children and victims of domestic violence. This chapter includes an overview of children involved in prostitution which is increasingly seen as a form of child abuse however much the children engaged in it appear to have freely 'chosen' to be so engaged.

Chapter 8 examines protection in care settings and especially the new developments in pre-employment screening through the Criminal Records Bureau which came online in 2002. Pre-employment screening to achieve safer environments in schools, children's homes, hospitals and other care settings has now become a multi-million pound industry with the full implementation of the Police Act 1997 Part V. Other measures, such as the Disqualification Order introduced in 2001, are also considered.

Chapter 9 looks at the spread of the civil law into a range of other areas of life to try to achieve better public protection in the wider community. Central to this spread has been the sex offender 'register' and its associated measures. The Sexual Offences Act 2003 has introduced other civil measures to help contain the sex offender.

The book concludes with some speculation on future directions and developments, and an assessment of the role of 'personal information' and 'data' as the key to future regulation of the sex offender; that regulation also includes the use of such data for purposes of risk assessment and risk management. Throughout, the book seeks to act as a 'sourcebook' guiding the reader to other references for more detailed study.

Chapter 2

The sex offender 'problem' – and responses

A number of different constituencies are competing with each other to claim and explain the phenomenon of the sex offender and to say what we should be doing with that offender. Criminologists refer to this as the struggle for 'dominion'. In its broadest terms, there are community groups representing grass-roots; public opinion; the press and other media outlets; politicians seeking to be representative and responsible at the same time; and the 'experts' and practitioners in the form of doctors, penologists, therapists, police officers and others. The interaction between them all is complex – this is not a simple stand-off where the loudest voice gets to define what is happening.

The picture is further confused by what has been called the climate of 'popular punitiveness'. This term, coined by Bottoms, refers to the way in which politicians, using the umbrella of the rhetoric of 'law and order', have been 'tapping into, and using for their own purposes, what they believe to be the public's generally punitive stance' (Bottoms 1995: 40). Garland has gone further to suggest that public opinion has now replaced the voice of research and more considered debate:

> a few decades ago public opinion functioned as an occasional brake on policy initiatives: now it operates as a privileged source. The importance of research and criminological knowledge is down-graded and in its place is a new deference to the voice of 'experience', of 'common sense', of 'what everyone knows' (Garland 2001: 13).

The emotive nature of sex offending has often caused the formation of angry street crowds to protest against the crimes and the criminals; the communal anger increases when the victim has been a child. Crowd reactions of this kind can be noted throughout history, with the precipitating event being the arrest of a sex offender, the trial, or the simple knowledge that the sex offender is living in a given locality.

The traditional role of the press has been to report such crowd disturbances. In the UK in recent years, however, we have seen the press as instigators of crowd reactions when they have published the identity and whereabouts of known sex offenders. The role of the police has normally been to ensure public order in the face of crowd violence, but they too have reportedly 'leaked' information on an offender's where-abouts to trigger that crowd into action in the first place. Probation officers and police officers, on the other hand, have complained that the press reporting of sex offenders has prevented them carrying out their duties.

In this chapter, we try to disentangle some of the threads of thought that overlap and pull these different constituencies in different directions: the local neighbourhood with genuine fears to express about the safety of their children; the politicians and press trying to voice those fears and at the same time take a lead in what we should be doing; and the practitioners such as probation officers, police officers, doctors and therapists trying to contain and regulate the activities of the sex offender. The aim is to reflect these different constituencies and their varying explanations and responses, rather than to lay claim to any single explanation and response that carries the imprint of a definitive 'truth'.

Popular explanations and responses

At the Conservative Party annual conference in October 1991, the MP for Littleborough and Saddleworth, the late Geoffrey Dickens, famously advised the government how to combat sex offending: 'If you want to stop child abuse and rape of women, pass legislation and, on the second offence – not the first in case there is a mistake – put it before Parliament that you can castrate the buggers' (cited in Sampson 1994: 45). Dickens' speech was well received and widely reported. It was a popular view-point to be hard and decisive on sex offenders, and it appealed to the crowd and the press alike. It is a viewpoint repeated often, and a viewpoint that challenges the 'expert' view that sex offenders can be helped and treated; it is a viewpoint that wants sex offenders 'locked up and the key thrown away' or simply wants them 'away from here and out of our neighbourhood'. When plans were announced in June 1999 to build accommodation for sex offenders in the grounds of Nottingham prison, a demonstration against the plans ensued; one demonstrator held a placard naming one of the offenders who might live there, saying he was wanted 'dead or alive', but with a cross deleting the last two words (see the photograph on page 2 of the *Guardian*, G2, 21 June 1999).

Communities have a genuine fear for their children and demonstrating is one way to voice it. The press and politicians will represent those fears and add their own motivations for taking up the cause. An intricate three-way relationship builds between these constituencies, which belies any direct power the media has to influence people. In turn, the audience reception of media reports and their own 'reading' of those reports to align them with existing knowledge and attitudes all play a part (see Eldridge *et al.* 1997: esp. pp. 168–79).

The reporting of sex crime by the media and the double-edged relationship the media has with such offending have been well documented (see, e.g., Soothill and Walby 1991) and there is not the space here to go into the subject in great depth. On the one hand is the self-righteous indignation that such horrific crimes take place, and on the other, the knowledge that readers are compulsively fascinated with these stories and circulation figures may well depend on a regular supply of them; witness, for example, the *Sun*'s headline reporting of the conviction of Rose West for the crimes committed at 25 Cromwell Street ('Burn in Hell', *Sun*, 25 November 1995) accompanied by a 24-page special insert on 'the crime of the century'. From the Balkan conflict of the late 1990s came apocryphal stories of reporters moving through the crowds of refugees asking if there were any women who had been raped and spoke English.

The same ambiguity can be seen in the wearing of children's clothes by adult women as the 'latest fashion' (see, e.g., 'School's out', *Independent on Sunday*, 17 August 1997) or by women pop stars deliberately cultivating a schoolgirl 'look': 'Most schoolgirls are aware of the undesirable effect that they have on a certain category of the population … powerlessness, naivete, and the general vulnerability of adolescence still exert an undeniable sexual pull' ('Little girl power', *Guardian*, 5 April 1999). In the last ten years, the overall shift downmarket of newspapers and broadcast news bulletins has also been noted, as journalists and news reporting have been forced to recognise market forces and competition. Franklin has documented this 'dumbing down' of the media's presentation of news, which he calls 'newszak': 'Newszak understands news as a product designed and "processed" for a particular market and delivered in increasingly homogeneous "snippets" which make only modest demands on the audience. Newszak is news converted into entertainment' (1997: 4–5). Tabloid newspapers lead the way, followed by the 'broadsheets' and radio and television news, current affairs and documentaries. Ultimately, the 'fly on the wall' or 'docu-soap' replaces the traditional investigative documentary because they are cheaper to produce and the old-style documentaries that do appear have allegations of 'fabrication' thrown at them. For Franklin, this shift from news reporting as a public service to newszak, driven by market forces and competition, is raising serious questions about the role of the news and current affairs features and their contribution to mature democracies. It is in this world that crime and sex offending is being reported.

Some research found a decline in the quantity of media reports on rape between 1978 and 1992, accompanied by a tendency 'to concentrate on the more sensational cases which provide the most opportunity to titillate or to feed public outrage' (Grover and Soothill 1995). One reason put forward for this fall-off has been 'boredom' and 'reader-fatigue' (Skidmore 1995). Other trends have been noted: 'The continued reporting of such notorious cases as the Yorkshire Ripper and the Moors Murderers is akin to a "sex offender soap". Certainly, tabloid reporting of trivia helps to maintain a public interest in certain well-known cases' (Grover and Soothill 1995). Even the death of one of the Moors Murderers in November 2002 has not stopped her being the centre of continuing stories (see, e.g., 'Myra "confessed to victim no. 5"', *Daily Mirror*, 14 February 2004). And in the investigation of new sex crimes:

[Journalists] have widened the reporting of sex crimes and have found new areas whereby they can titillate readers. This is particularly so in the search for the 'sex beast' in cases where no culprit has been identified and where the media is able to produce speculation in their construction of the sex fiend (Grover and Soothill 1995).

The other trend in the latter half of the 1990s was the media's 'discovery' of the 'paedophile'. An analysis of articles about paedophiles in six leading British newspapers found nothing less than 'an explosion of interest in the topic [of paedophiles] among all these newspapers since 1996' (Soothill *et al.* 1998). Paedophiles were big news; they were 'evil', 'monsters', 'beasts' and 'fiends' – the latter a word surely only ever used by journalists:

They set a sex monster on my children (*Daily Mirror*, 15 August 1994).

Bestiality beyond imagination (*Daily Mail*, 17 May 1996).

Born a misfit, he became a monster (*Daily Mail*, 19 July, 1996).

Monster bailed three times to attack again (*Yorkshire Post*, 23 November 1996).

I'll name the sex beasts (*Daily Mirror*, 9 June 1997).

Cops to unmask fiends (*News of the World*, 10 August 1997).

6 more child sex fiends to go free (*Sun*, 13 March 1998).

Cage him before he kills again (*Daily Mirror*, 14 March 1998).

Having constructed the paedophile in their own terms, the press were not going to engage in any deconstruction of him. It was pointed out, for example, that the press rarely reported successful appeals by sex offenders which, presumably, enabled them to throw off their 'monster' or 'beast' persona and return to being ordinary men again. The only time they were likely to report such appeals was if they could take another angle on it, as in the case of Stefan Kisko, where the police could be criticised for obtaining a confession from a man proved innocent by scientific techniques (Grover and Soothill 1995).

The other effect of this 'name calling' of the individual who committed sex offences was to put them beyond the pale and out of reach of ordinary treatments and civil liberties. It also helped push the country into something of a 'moral panic' about sex offending, especially when that offending was against children.

The social theory of the moral panic as originally put forward by Cohen (1972) is the interaction between events on the ground, and their interpretation by 'primary signifiers' like courts, MPs, and inquiry reports and the media as 'secondary signifiers' in an escalating spiral of concern and outrage accompanied by demands that 'something must be done'. The triggering events invariably involve an element of violence, and that violence is on a scale that has crossed a threshold of acceptability and legality. The transgression of childhood innocence by adult aggressors was one such threshold.

In 1996 and 1997, the UK saw a series of popular 'uprisings' directed against sex offenders. A key element in these crowd reactions was the part played by the press and media reporting of sex crime and in particular the new role the press appeared to have taken upon themselves, actually to identify and publicise the whereabouts of sex offenders in the community. This 'outing' of sex offenders by the press was made against the backdrop of the political debate which had started on whether or not the police and other professionals should tell the public where 'known' sex offenders lived; the practice called 'community notification' or Megan's Law (see Chapter 9). It was as though the national and local press felt a need to go beyond just reporting the news and that it was their duty to protect the community if the professionals were going to prevaricate.

The *Sunday Express* was amongst the first of the national newspapers to enter the fray with its campaign 'Will your child be next?' The paper published five photographs and details of men with a record of sex offending whose addresses were unknown; readers were invited to identify their whereabouts: 'They could be living next to you, targeting your children right now. But you will not know their background – nor will your local police' ('Could these evil men be living next to you?', *Sunday Express*, 19 May 1996). These men were all free citizens who had been punished by the criminal justice system and could be said to have 'done their time and paid their dues to society'. The implication was that these men were 'different', were likely to offend again and were not entitled to the restoration of normal civil rights and duties that anyone else might expect. Not only that, but there was an accusatory tone about the reporting that further implied the professionals had somehow 'got it wrong' and 'we', the public, were going to be suffering as a result.

The *Daily Mail* found a man in Lincolnshire who was on probation when they clearly thought he should have been in custody ('How could this man go free?', *Daily Mail*, 14 November 1996) and the *Yorkshire Post* reported on a man who had committed sex offences whilst on bail because of alleged incompetence by the Crown Prosecution Service ('Why was this monster set free?', *Yorkshire Post*, 23 November 1996). The message was that 'the authorities' were getting it wrong a little too often.

The local press joined in. The *Bournemouth Echo* produced its own register of sex offenders from a trawl of its back editions; the register was available to professionals rather than the public. The *Yorkshire Post* photographed a known sex offender in the streets of Leeds ('Rapist just a face in the crowd', *Yorkshire Post*, 9 October 1996); the *Oxford Mail* found them visiting Chessington World of Adventure ('Mum's anger at pervert outings', *Oxford Mail*, 6 September 1996); and another Yorkshire paper found them at Flamingo Land and Lightwater Valley in North Yorkshire ('Theme parks off limits to sex offenders', *Yorkshire Evening Post*, 24 October, 1996).

These press activities were mirrored by local communal activities involving demonstrations, protests and vigilante action against sex offenders. In Manchester, a group of parents stormed the house of a known sex offender and marched on the local authority housing department to ask how many more there were ('Parents storm sex fiend's flat', *Manchester Evening News*, 7 November 1996). In Leeds, a gang burnt down the house of suspected child abuser ('"Child abuser" flees as vigilantes burn his home', *Guardian*, 8 July 1997) and protests were reported in Birmingham and Essex ('Nowhere to hide', *Daily Telegraph*, 22 March 1997).

Some of these activities were large and got beyond control. On the Logie estate in Aberdeen, a crowd of one hundred, described as mostly teenagers and young women, destroyed a house where they thought an offender was living. They described their estate as a 'dumping ground':

> At first it was disciplined – loud but disciplined. 'Perverts out!' was the most popular chant among the children and parents ... no one knew if the person whose blood they were baying for was inside. The whole affair was based on rumour and speculation. In the end brute force brought all the answers ('The day fury erupted on a city estate', *Aberdeen Evening Express*, 9 June 1997; see also 'Mob smashes up house in search of attacker', *Scotsman*, 9 June 1997).

As with all crowds, the motives for gathering and demonstrating are never clear-cut. Boredom and a search for action and 'something to do' could be as much a part of it as drunkenness and a desire to 'have a go' at authority, let alone demonstrate against sex offenders. Some journalists could see these traits running through the crowd:

> their demonstrations have shades of political rallies, religious ceremonies, union meetings – all those group experiences which used to define people's sense of selves, and which are no longer available to them ... now, people ... organise against paedophiles. In a few years the cause will be something else ('Paedophiles are one of the few groups you can respectfully hate', *Guardian*, 24 April 1998).

In the summer of 2000 more demonstrations and vigilante activity were triggered by the *News of the World* newspaper. In reporting the abduction of 8-year-old Sarah Payne in Sussex the newspaper took it upon itself to start publishing the photographs and details of known sex offenders ('Named, shamed', *News of the World*, 23 July 2000). A campaign was started by the newspaper, for a 'Sarah's Law' comparable to 'Megan's Law' in the USA. For a week demonstrations had to be carefully watched by the police, especially in the Portsmouth suburb of Paulsgrove ('Families flee estate hate campaign', *Guardian*, 10 August 2000). Eventually order was restored after discussions between the newspaper, the police, probation and the NSPCC (Thomas 2001a; see also Chapter 9).

The theme of the crowd gathering against the sex offender has historical precedents (see Chapter 3). The ambivalence of the crowd has also been noted before. At the 1965 trial of Myra Hindley and Ian Brady, for the assault and murder of children in what the press called the 'Moors Murders', the late Jeff Nuttall recalled the reaction of a friend of his: 'A press photographer I know had to be taken off the case, not on seeing the face of Hindley or hearing the tapes but on forming the impression that the crowd stood outside the court ... stood there in envy rather than in indignation' (Nuttall 1970: 130). Phrases like 'lynch-mob' and 'witch-hunt' were used in the reporting of crowd reactions. Paddy Ashdown (then leader of the Liberal Democratic Party) described the crowd in his Yeovil constituency as a 'lynch-mob' when they demonstrated outside a police station at the presence of the released paedophile Sydney Cooke. The crowd were happy to take on the label: 'So? What's wrong with that? We used to burn witches and it worked' (cited in 'Paedophiles are one of the few groups you can respectfully hate', *Guardian*, 24 April 1998).

Demonstrations against the same man outside the Broadway Road police station in Bristol deteriorated into violence which had to be contained by police using riot gear; reports suggested petrol bombs had been used. Home Secretary Jack Straw condemned the violence: 'I understand the concern that people have about paedophiles. But there is no excuse for this kind of disgraceful behaviour, particularly when it's directed against the police who ... are there to protect the public from paedophiles' ('Straw pledges action on paedophiles', *Guardian*, 27 April 1998). Presumably Straw was less than pleased when later evidence revealed the police themselves to have leaked details of 'high profile sex offenders ... to the media and others' and in one case 'disorder [had] occurred resulting in injuries to many police officers' (HMIC 1999: para. 5.30).

When the crowd did get hold of a known sex offender, the term 'vigilante' started to be used. An early example had occurred just outside Edinburgh, when 37-year-old Lawrence Leyden was identified by neighbours as having a record of sex offences against children. Leyden was subjected to verbal harassment, had his car vandalised and the words 'die' and 'beast' written on his front door in excrement; a petition was started to have him re-housed. Leyden himself also requested a move, but it was all too late. He was stabbed to death by unknown assailants who broke into his home. The community was reportedly not very keen to help police with their inquiries ('Closed doors on murder', *Guardian*, 28 February 1995).

The same thing happened to 73-year-old Arnold Hartley, who was also a convicted child sex offender and lived in Redcar. Hartley had been victimised by local people since his return home from prison and was eventually found dead from head injuries inflicted with a heavy object. Three days after the murder the response from the local public to police inquiries was described as 'one of deafening, resolute silence' ('That's one less on the streets', *Guardian*, 2 December 2003).

The *Manchester Evening News* ran a front-page picture of a sex offender named by them a few days earlier sitting in his vandalised car, and ran an editorial in the same edition justifying its actions:

> Once a paedophile always a paedophile ... we are well aware that our action creates a civil rights problem, but we believe the safety of young children over-whelmingly outweighs the rights of a convicted paedophile ... there have been far too many cases in recent years of perverts obtaining jobs working with children ('Why we did it', *Manchester Evening News*, 30 August 1996).

Later the same editor explained the demands being put on him by members of the public: 'The only time we have named individuals is when the public come to us and tell us they have serious concerns about a person living near them ... they were absolutely livid and they contacted us' (quoted in Potter 1997). Frances Duffy, aged 67, was mistakenly identified as a paedophile after another man had had his photograph in the *Manchester Evening News*. Duffy suffered a broken wrist, broken finger and severe bruising. A *Sunday Times* investigation into vigilantism estimated Duffy to be just one of about '30 cases where men wrongly suspected of abusing children have been beaten and humiliated by gangs bent on driving them out of their homes' ('Child abuse vigilantes terrorise the innocent', *The Sunday Times*, 2 November 1997). In August 2000 a paediatrician in South Wales had her house vandalised by people who seemingly confused her title with that of a 'paedophile' ('Doctor driven out of home by vigilantes', *Guardian*, 30 August 2000).

A unique feature of the situation in Northern Ireland was the backdrop of sectarian violence that was present throughout most of the 1970s and 1980s. The police and security forces, of necessity, had to give priority to 'the troubles' which meant that 'normal' policing activities, including the policing of sex offenders, sometimes received a low priority. In turn, the paramilitary groups in the province were able to move into the resulting vacuum left by the police and operate parallel unofficial criminal justice systems and mete out violent reprisals on suspected sex offenders; as one witness told an inquiry:

a lot of it's about the paramilitaries making themselves in-dispensable within the community. Sex offenders is a popular issue. In the past, Sinn Fein would go to another organisation to have the RUC called. Now the paramilitaries are more successful at driving sex offenders out because it's very popular with the local community (HRW 1997: 110).

Not only was the vacuum filled, but the paramilitaries gained goodwill and kudos within their neighbourhoods.

Elsewhere, protest was more low key. On the Seacroft estate in Leeds, a woman distributed leaflets and sent an open letter to residents giving details of a local man's address and conviction record. The project was triggered by the man receiving a community sentence for indecent assaults on children: 'as far as his sentence goes the word justice no longer exists to the people of Seacroft ... we feel betrayed' ('Police called in as mum shames paedophile', *Yorkshire Evening Post*, 27 June 1997).

Some spontaneous protests became more formalised and turned themselves into campaigning 'action groups'. At national level, the 'Parents against Child Abuse', 'Mothers against Murder and Aggression', 'Scottish Parents against Child Abuse' and 'People Power' were formed; at local level there was the 'Child Protection Action Group' (Wakefield), the 'Unofficial Child Protection Unit' (Glasgow), the 'Peterhead Campaign against Paedophiles', 'The White Ribbon Campaign for Justice' (Milton Keynes), and the 'Council for the Protection of Children' (Bradford), to name but a few. Many of these were short-lived but they demonstrate the degree of concern that was being felt.

Although the police had been in the direct firing line of some of the demonstrations, the long-term effect of the press coverage and communal activities started to have an impact on the activities of other practitioners trying to work with sex offenders. In high-profile cases it was impossible for police, probation officers and social workers to do anything that was not in the glare of the media's spotlight. Hostels refused to take sex offenders for fear of hostility from the local community and housing authorities started to do the same. For their part, sex offenders – high profile or not – were fearful of coming forward for help and, at worst, were being 'driven underground' where no one knew their whereabouts. A spokesperson for the Association of Chief

Officers of Probation said: 'there is firm evidence that real damage is being done to innocent children and adults by people taking the law into their own hands. Existing vital and effective supervision and surveillance operations are being destroyed' (quoted in 'Vigilantes "putting children at risk" ', *Daily Telegraph*, 25 April 1998), and the Chief Inspector of Probation added that hostels were refusing to take offenders 'not because they can't handle them but because of the consequences from the local community doing something very stupid and silly to the hostel and staff there' (cited in 'Hysteria toward paedophiles "may increase the risk"', *Daily Telegraph*, 29 April 1998).

In August 1998, the Association of Chief Officers of Probation (ACOP) announced its intention to meet with the Press Complaints Commission. A spokesman for ACOP said: 'We want to get some sort of guidelines and reach more of an understanding with the press so that journalists can cover the stories without scuppering the arrangements made by police and probation services to supervise offenders' ('Call for media curb on paedophile releases', *PA News*, 13 August 1998). Gill Mackenzie, ACOP Vice-chair, said: 'We must keep pressing for a more sophisticated debate to keep things in proportion. We must have a constructive dialogue with community groups without constantly finding ourselves deadlocked in stand-offs and threats of mob action' (ibid.; see also 'Press gag sought to stop paedophile lynch mobs', *Independent*, 14 August 1998). Discussions with the Press Complaints Commission did take place, but the Commission said they needed someone to bring an actual complaint to them for consideration. Nonetheless, these background talks do appear to have made some impact, and probably helped with the talks that followed the *News of the World*'s 'Naming and Shaming' campaign in the summer of 2000. In retrospect Mackenzie felt that that campaign had only hastened things already in the pipeline and did nothing to contribute to the protection of children (Silverman and Wilson 2002: 166).

The public, the media and the politicians have a view of sexual offending and have expressed that view to varying degrees. Other views, which we might call the 'expert' views, can be juxtaposed against it without necessarily saying that one should predominate over the other.

'Expert' explanations and responses

The term 'expert' has been used here to encompass different disciplines, including medical, penal, psychological and feminist. As already suggested, there is a struggle going on between the 'experts' and the more 'populist' explanations of sexual offending; each lays a claim to define the truth. To whom should we give credence? We can only say that the 'populist' explanations appear more subjective and prone to propagating 'mythologies' of rape about victims who 'ask for it' and 'strangers who lurk in shadows' like 'monsters', compared to the – hopefully – more informed and objective research that comes from the various 'expert' disciplines.

The doctors

The general medical profession has a forensic role in helping the police to gather evidence following a sexual assault, but has otherwise made only a limited contribution to understanding why some people commit sexual crimes. Psychiatry is the branch of the profession that might have been expected to throw light on sexual deviance and behaviour, and to some extent it has fulfilled this role. On the other hand there is growing consensus that sexual offending is more often unconnected to mental illness. Recent proposals to change the law on mental health reveal the inherent problems.

The Mental Health Act 1983 had appeared to disconnect the mental health services from sex offenders. Section 1(3) stated that those engaging in behaviour that was only 'promiscuous' or considered 'sexual deviancy' were not covered by the Act. Moreover, people who were diagnosed as psychopaths could not be detained under the Act unless their condition was considered 'treatable' (s. 3(2)(b)). This criterion of 'treatability' could be used by psychiatrists to opt out of engaging with sex offenders who might be psychopaths. In the mid-1990s the term psychopath appeared to become synonymous with the 'personality disorder' which was deemed equally untreatable; in turn 'personality disorder' became increasingly applied to sex offenders. In the courts probation officers described what they saw as the 'classic situation' when psychiatric reports to court would end with the conclusion: 'this person is not mentally ill under the meaning of the 1983 Mental Health Act but has a personality disorder; therefore I cannot offer any treatment. However, he might benefit from a period of probation' (Gosling 2002). Home Secretary Jack Straw confirmed a picture whereby in 'the opinion of many experienced observers of the system … psychiatrists are all too often using the treatability test in the Act as a way of absolving themselves from their duty of providing health care' (cited in 'Treatability row leads to war of words over service funds', *Community Care*, 5–11, November 1998: 1). One way forward was to review the working of the Mental Health Act and find a way of incorporating a service to people with a 'dangerous severe personality disorder' (Home Office 1999).

Such a review started in late 1999 culminating in a white paper (Department of Health 2000a) and a draft mental health bill published in June 2002 (Department of Health 2002). The proposals looked at all aspects of the Act, but for present purposes we should note that 'sexual deviancy' was removed as an excluding provision of the Act, and the definition of mental disorder widened. The definition of treatment was also widened to include 'education, and training in work, social and independent living skills'. In this way it was presumably hoped that the 'severe personality disorder' could be brought clearly within the remit of the new Mental Health Act.

The criticisms of the proposals were severe and fifty campaign groups for mental health came together to protest at this 'fundamentally flawed' bill (Mental Health Alliance 2002); the Royal College of Psychiatrists said it could lead to 'internment without trial' (RCP 2001). The government has baulked at the criticism and in November 2003 effectively went back to the drawing board with the draft.

Some people with a mental illness and in need of treatment may commit sexual offences, but the treatment is for the illness and may or may not remove the propensity to offend. The distinction may not always be clear to a public still confused about the nature of mental disorder and there is still talk of 'sex maniacs' and 'dangerous' people, plus the fact that sometimes mentally ill people do commit sexual offences (see, e.g., 'Schizophrenic rapist given five life sentences', *Independent*, 8 February 1996).

Even if it could not offer explanations, psychiatry still felt able to offer some treatments, and psychiatric skills in 'risk assessment' were still taken into account by courts and parole boards when it came to decisions on a person's civil liberties.

Treatments could include a general medical approach to organic or genetic factors that were in turn leading to sexual offending. Some patients with a 'hormone imbalance' could be helped by being given 'suppressants' to minimise their sexual drive (see, e.g., Fennell 1988). These treatments needed the consent of the patient. If there was going to be a surgical implant of a suppressant under the Mental Health Act, a second doctor needed to approve it, even if consent had been given (Mental Health Act 1983, s. 57).

Castration or 'de-sexing' was, according to Meyers, introduced to England by the Normans, who used it as a punitive measure for rapists (1970: 26). It has not become a regular feature of modern policies on criminal justice in this country, but is permitted in a number of states in the USA.

In the 1920s and 1930s, castration became confused with sterilisation as part of the eugenics debate that, at its extreme, wanted to control the reproduction of people with mental impairments (see King 1999: chap. 3). Fennell recounts the story of actual castrations carried out in the Public Assistance Institution in Gateshead in 1930. A Ministry of Health inspection found three people to have been operated on, including a 14-year-old boy charged with indecent assault. The ministry warned Gateshead that, even with the consent of the boy's mother, these castrations were illegal and could result in prosecution; the medical officer confirmed that there would be no more operations of this kind (Fennell 1996: 86). King cites evidence that illegal sterilisations were not uncommon at this time (1999: 92) and in 1923, in Derbyshire, the county council wanted changes in the law 'to empower a court to order the sterilisation of mental defectives convicted of sexual offences' (Fennell 1996: 81).

The confusion surrounding castration generally has been succinctly clarified by Meyers: 'the cause of, and answer to, the sexual psychopath's abnormal urges lies in his cranium, not in his scrotum. Castration, like sterilisation, ensures neither a reduction in libido nor in sexual act capability. The only certainty of the operation is that its effects are "very variable" ' (Meyers 1970: 46; see also Heim and Hursch 1979). In the past, psychiatrists have involved themselves with 'treatments' such as aversion therapy or covert sensitisation, but, more recently, have left such techniques to the psychologists.

The therapists

Aversion therapy techniques depend on ideas of 'classical conditioning'. A person is exposed to evidence of the deviant behaviour or sex offending at the same time as an aversive stimulus is applied. Thus, a child sex offender would be shown pictures of children to induce sexual arousal and receive an electric shock or chemically induced nausea by way of association.

Covert sensitisation is a form of aversion therapy, but without the external aversive stimulus. The technique depends upon a purely cognitive approach, whereby the patient or offender is asked to produce his own aversive thoughts whenever the deviant or sexual offending thoughts come into his head. Some therapists have suggested a simple elastic band around the wrists which is pulled and released as a sharp reminder whenever deviant sexual thoughts occur.

If aversion therapy seeks to reduce undesired behaviour, other techniques seek positively to increase desired behaviour. Thus, 'aversion relief' builds upon aversion therapy by giving positive reinforcement to benign or socially desired images and thoughts. A further variation is known as 'fading' or 'shaping', whereby deviant images are slowly replaced by more socially acceptable ones to change the subject's erotic fantasies. 'Orgasmic conditioning' relies on the subject learning to switch the theme of his fantasies from deviant to acceptable at the point of masturbatory orgasm (for an overview of these and other behavioural approaches see Hawton 1983).

These crude behavioural approaches fell out of fashion in the 1980s and 1990s, and the treatment method now most favoured is that known as the 'cognitive-behavioural' approach. This approach draws on a variety of social and psychological explanations.

Psychological explanations of sex offending also locate the problem with the individual. Personality traits of the individual, such as an extrovert personality that seeks to dominate others, or a lack of social skills to contain anger and violence, all contribute to the development of a person prone to sex offending. Problem-solving skills with adults are poor or non-existent in these offenders.

Alternative personality traits could be a lack of self-esteem and a poor self-image, which leads on to, once again, poor problem-solving skills with adults and a preference for relationships with children who are seen as 'weak' and 'non-threatening' by comparison. The presence of so-called disinhibitors like alcohol or drugs, or the presence of 'stress' in various forms, then become facilitators of the propensity towards sexual offending.

These personality traits are seen as developing slowly through childhood and are linked to inappropriate parenting or theories of the 'dysfunctional family'. Associated features would include a 'distortion' of thinking that sees offending behaviour as not really offending at all, as well as an accompanying 'denial' of a problem.

The 'cognitive-behavioural' approach to treating male abusers appears to work best with those who offend against children. It is an eclectic approach, drawing on a variety of 'treatments', including some of those we have just looked at as 'behavioural approaches'. 'Cognitive-behavioural' work can be carried out by probation officers, prison officers, social workers and psychologists and can be delivered in either an individual 'one-to-one' format, tailored to the particular offender, or on a group-work basis. It has been posited that a multi-agency approach to this work has the positive advantage of drawing in various perspectives and skills. Beckett has summarised the essentials of cognitive-behavioural treatment: 'these interventions focus on altering patterns of deviant arousal, correcting distorted thinking, and increasing social competence, with educational input assisting offenders to gain knowledge in sexual matters, the effects of sexual abuse and sexual assault cycles' (1994). The sessions with the offenders, whether individual or group work, are linked together by intervening 'homework' sessions which have to be completed: sometimes these programmes are called 'personal change programmes'. We should also note that, although we are looking at treatments here, practitioners such as probation officers and prison officers have other roles to perform in the containment and punishment of sex offenders (see Chapter 6).

'Cognitive-behavioural' approaches take the starting point that the offenders know what they are doing and are making a conscious decision to commit sexual offences. This decision-making is, however, qualified by the fact that the offender bases it on distorted thinking ('cognitive distortion') that becomes 'hardened' into 'fantasies' and 'anti-social personalities'. In the end, they may believe they have done no wrong, or that the victim 'led them on', or they are in total denial about the crimes.

The starting point for 'cognitive-behavioural treatment' – or CBT – is that the offender is willing to accept that an offence has taken place and is willing to enter into a 'contract' with the therapist to uncover the true motivation for the offending and to start confronting some of the distorted thinking that has formed around that offending. Once that has been achieved, an input of 'avoidance' and 'coping' mechanisms can be attempted, as well as general 'social skills training' to improve social competence, and also the developing of an understanding and empathy with the victim of the crimes (Beckett *et al*. 1994; Clark and Erooga 1994).

One technique of 'cognitive-behavioural' treatment is to introduce offenders to the idea of the 'model of change' developed by Prochaska and Di Clemente. Within this model, the offender is seen to move through various phases with respect to his behaviour:

1 Pre-contemplation: the offender is unaware of his 'problem'; in denial; defensive.
2 Contemplation: the offender decides to change.
3 Action: the 'rehearsal' of the change.
4 Maintenance: sustaining the new behaviour.
5 Relapse: giving up and returning to old behaviour.

The model, first developed with alcoholics and drug users, invites the offender to place himself in one of the various phases with a view to understanding his progress. As relapse is built into the model, it can be anticipated and foreseen by worker and offender (Prochaska and Di Clemente 1986).

Another frame of reference used by therapists with a 'cognitive-behavioural' approach is that of the 'pre-conditions' for child sexual abuse identified by Finkelhor. The starting point for this analysis is a person who is motivated to offend against children, but is prevented from doing so by 'internal' and 'external' obstacles. The 'internal' are personal to the offender and, once they are overcome, he looks to circumvent whatever 'external' obstacles exist by way of parents or other adult carers or guardians. If the 'external' obstacles are successfully overcome, there is only the child's own 'resistance' to be worked on before abuse takes place (Finkelhor 1986).

One other aspect of treatment that has come to the fore is the idea of 'early' treatment for young sex offenders. Although the emphasis inevitably falls on adults, the extent of sexual offending by children and young people has long been recognised, with some estimates suggesting it could account for up to a third of all sexual offending (see, e.g., Grubin 1998). Department of Health guidance looks to a multi-agency approach involving education authorities, psychologists and adolescent mental health services alongside youth justice and child welfare agencies and: 'an assessment should be carried out in each case, appreciating that these children may have considerable unmet developmental needs, as well as specific needs arising from their behaviour' (Department of Health 1999: para. 6.33). Specialist agencies, such as G-MAP in the Manchester area, have been developed to take on the treatment of young sex offenders (see also Coombes 2003).

The big question remains – does 'cognitive-behavioural treatment' work? The popular argument is that nothing changes these men and, as we have seen, 'once a paedophile, always a paedophile'. Evaluative studies would suggest otherwise, albeit with caution. The consensus appears to be that sexual offending behaviour can be controlled and contained, if not completely removed: 'whilst no treatment approach is 100 per cent effective for all offenders all of the time, certain offenders do appear to benefit from particular types of intervention, as indicated by reduced recidivism' (Beckett 1994). For Beckett, those 'particular types of intervention' favoured a 'cognitive-behavioural' approach (see also Beech et al. 1998).

Part of the process of treatment has involved the categorising and 'labelling' of offenders into various types. In Scotland, for example, researchers classified child sex abusers into four categories using the acronym RAPID (Random Abusers, Paedophiles, Incest and Deniers) (Waterhouse et al. 1994: chap. 4). Others have categorised paedophiles as 'fixated' or 'regressed'.

The 'regressed' paedophile is described as the less serious offender, who 'drifts' in and out of a desire to have sexual contact with children. The 'fixated' paedophile, on the other hand, is the more dangerous offender, being described by Wyre as 'highly addicted' in a way 'similar to a gambling or drug addiction'. Wyre goes on to explain how these paedophiles molest large numbers of children by being seductive towards them and their parents over a long period of time, in order to impose their distorted thinking on their victims to make their behaviour appear 'normal'. Part of this distortion is the idea that children can actually consent to what they are being induced into. For Wyre, the concept of the 'fixated paedophile' 'helps explain why there are some paedophile offenders who really do want to stop but find it impossible' (1996).

The feminist analysis

A feminist analysis of sexual offending, however, finds the labelling of a man as a paedophile unhelpful. Feminists argue that the label obscures the normality of the male perspective, which sees young girls as attractive and desirable, and overlooks the 'normality' of sexual offending being almost wholly a male activity, and one in which they choose to engage.

Cameron and Frazer, in their book on sexual murder, also indict criminology for overlooking and obscuring the gender-specific nature of murder: 'there are various social constraints on who is a killer and who gets killed. One of these is, quite simply, gender: killers are mostly male, victims mostly female' (1987: 30). Cameron and Frazer have been criticised for overstating their case (Jenkins 1994: chap. 7), but the statistics are on their side. A large study of 500 known child sex abusers in Scotland found 99 per cent of them to be male and three quarters of the abused children female (Waterhouse et al. 1994), and in Northern Ireland, an estimated 95 per cent of serious assaults categorised as 'domestic' were by men (McWilliams and Spence 1996: 49).

Kelly has put forward the idea of male violence and sexual assault as being on a 'continuum' from so-called normal behaviour through to generally recognised deviant and criminal behaviour. Forms of male behaviour at one end of the continuum are jut a different version of behaviour to be found at the other end, and the idea of 'types' of sex offender becomes redundant. Male domination of women thus becomes normalised in all areas of life, as does the expectation of women's subordination and the requirement that they 'fall into line' almost as 'property' of men.

These cultural expectations are supported by patriarchal norms that are to be found in institutions, language and customs wherever we look (Kelly 1988).

The 'continuum' idea explains how women experience male violence in various forms and as being all-pervasive. Male expectations of women are backed up by attitudinal, verbal and actual violence in all areas of life. Thus, women experience violence and domination in the home, in the workplace through limited career opportunities, sexual harassment and actual violence, and on the streets in generalised hostility towards women and the idea that some public places are safer than others. Many of these activities may fall short of being sexual offences as defined by a criminal court, but the 'continuum' provides a cultural context that circumscribes sexual offending.

If women are male 'property' they can be 'objectified' and in turn become 'dehumanised', making offending more likely. As the women's movement has analysed this phenomenon and challenged it, the very challenge has 'threatened' male dominance and led to a renewed effort – including violence – on the part of men to reassert their position.

Within the idea of a 'continuum' of sexual violence and assault, the very word 'paedophile' becomes unhelpful. As Kelly has pointed out, the labelling of a man as a 'paedophile' – invariably by male 'experts' – takes him outside the continuum by focusing on the person rather than the behaviour and marks him out as being intrinsically 'different' from other men. By classifying the paedophile as 'different' it lets all other men and their 'normal' behaviour off the hook. This 'difference' gets elaborated to suggest that the paedophile never has sex with adult partners, invariably prefers boys and usually operates outside the family. All this is distracting us from the 'normality' of men targeting young girls, acting within the family and having adult relationships at the same time. Kelly quotes a worker with child prostitutes in Bradford: 'What is a paedophile anyway? As far as we can see on this project, he's over 30, drives a nice car and has a wife and kids' (1996). An inquiry into safeguards for children in Scotland (see Chapter 8) had a similar experience. The committee of inquiry received various submissions on how to identify 'the paedophile', mostly in the form of 'check lists'. The committee was sceptical: 'There are checklists in existence which would probably allow every adult in Scotland to be seen as a potential paedophile' (Kent Report 1997: para. 6.6.7). The use of the word 'paedophile' implies that the man cannot help his behaviour and actually needs 'treatment' of some kind (see, e.g., 'Paedophile begged for jail, to save children', *Guardian*, 2 March 2004). The feminist analysis challenges this 'need for treatment' by emphasising the normality of the behaviour and by insisting that men could control it if they chose to. This challenge is also made to the 'cycle of abuse' concept – victims of abuse go on to become abusers – when it is pointed out that most victims of abuse are girls, and yet it is the men who are said to suffer most from being abused, when they go on to become child abusers (Kelly 1996).

The devaluing of treatment in this analysis has gained some support from a study of treatment programmes of rapists where the victim has been an adult rather than a child. Cognitive-behavioural treatment programmes were found to be less successful with this group of offenders and 'current research ... offered no clear indication of the most effective approach' (HMIP 1998a: 3.21).

In this way the position of all women becomes one of vulnerability if they allow it to be; as one worker in a Rape Crisis Centre has put it: 'Whether or not we have been raped ourselves, we all share the experience of the threat of male violence, the sense of smallness and powerlessness constructed by the ideology of male authority, and the actualities of male social and economic power' (Anna 1998). Along the 'continuum', specific forms of sexual violence are thus connected to more common everyday aspects of male behaviour that include abuse, intimidation, coercion, intrusion and threat. The continuum is not about the relative seriousness of male activities or the idea of a hierarchy of abuse, but more an illustration of the prevalence of the phenomena (Kelly 1988). In turn it is suggested that: 'Society does not want to hear what women have to say about this subject, and men have a vested interest in keeping definitions of sexual violence as narrow as possible. It is vital that women continue to speak, to tell their stories' (Hague and Malos 1998: 8). Radford and Kelly have elaborated on the experiences of women when 'nothing really happened' to show how women's minimising and discounting of their experiences is effectively a 'silencing' exercise by the mainstream society, which they rename as 'malestream' society:

> Men, who as the perpetrators of sexual violence have a vested interest in women's silence have in a range of ways and in a range of contexts, constructed 'knowledge' about sexual violence, crime and women's sexuality; through institutions such as the law, medicine, psychiatry as much as the 'common sense' that is promoted by the media, including pornography (Kelly and Radford 1990–1).

All the time, women's experiences are coming up against the ascendancy of the male perspective.

Drawing on information from the Equal Opportunities Commission, Gregory and Lees have quantified the male perspective:

> A mere 14% of police officers are women, mostly concentrated in the lowest rank ... a total of 71% of solicitors on the Law Society's roll are male as are 78% of barristers and 94% of Queens Counsel (QCs) ... the judiciary of 90% male and those women who are employed as judges are working mainly as assistant recorders, district judges, deputy district judges or stipendiary magistrates ... the House of Lords judges and The Heads of Divisions are all men. There is one woman Appeal Court Judge (out of 35) and seven High Court Judges (out of 96) (1999: 203–4).

Whether women take this ascendant position or men actually relinquish it, the difficulties of establishing that actually 'something did happen' in terms of a sexual offence are starting from this initial imbalance.

Summary

In this chapter we have sought to find explanations for sexual offending that have been offered by the press, the public and the politicians on the one hand, and by 'experts' such as doctors, therapists and feminist scholars and activists on the other. The former have offered us a simplistic model of 'monsters' and 'beasts' that has sometimes led to direct action to identify and deal with these offenders. The later has attempted to offer a more considered and scientific look at the phenomenon, although the 'experts' inevitably disagree amongst themselves.

Chapter 3

Social responses to the sex offender: a historical perspective

The idea of sex offending as we know it today has evolved slowly over the course of history. The definitive history of sex offending has probably still to be written, and this chapter attempts only an outline of developments to define and counter the sex offender, and the culture, mores and legal provisions put in place at the time. The chapter tries to highlight those provisions from the past that have a continuing resonance today; the perceived need to identify, label and regulate the 'dangerous' person, the competing definitions put forward by the popular crowd, the press and politicians and the later arrival of the medical and penal 'experts' and the move towards public protection. For more general histories of crime and the response to it, the reader is referred to Beattie (1986) and Radzinowicz and Hood (1990).

Pre-industrial times to 1800

Criminal behaviour that was apprehended in thirteenth-century Britain was brought before either the secular courts or the church courts. In general terms, the former examined crimes against property or public order, the latter crimes against morality, including sex offences. We should remember, however, that married women and children were often formally considered as 'property' in those times and marital separations, for example, might not necessarily end up in the church courts. The laws to be implemented were a mixture of common law, statutory law and church law.

The emerging ideas of 'the market' and private ownership of property, to replace that held in 'common', fed into the notion that sex offending was not just rape or sodomy and the crimes we know today, but could also include adultery, fornication, sex outside wedlock and bigamy. One form of regulation was the parish register of births, deaths and marriages. This early form of registration could help decide subsequent property transactions and, according to the historian Christopher Hill, 'declared who had and who had not a "settlement" in any given parish, and so prevented false claims to poor relief ... [and so] the discipline of parish registers and parochial assumption of control over the marriage of the poor complemented the discipline of the market' (1996: 202). The Statute of Westminster 1285 had made rape an offence punishable by death and put the 'age of discretion' (consent) at 10. Children aged 10–12 were given some protection, but claiming consent had been given was a valid defence for a man. The age of consent rose to 12 in 1576 (see also Jackson 2000: 12–14).

Incest was historically an ecclesiastical offence, triable before a church court and incestuous marriages could be declared null and void. Offenders – or sinners – 'were forced to do penance either by public confession in the parish church or in the marketplace ... in bare feet, clothed in a white sheet and clutching a white wand' (Bailey and Blackburn 1979). Ex-communication from the church could be added. Parents who sexually abused their own children might be similarly punished, but, given the poor levels of housing and accommodation and lack of 'policing', such offences rarely came to light.

Sodomy, or anal intercourse, was made an offence by an Act of 1533 and persons – male or female – convicted were sentenced to death. It has been reported that such harsh sentences were reinforced by the belief that sodomy was associated with witchcraft and was, in fact, the way in which witches had communion with the devil 'who with his forked penis committed sodomy and fornication at the same time' (Bancroft 1974: 8).

There is evidence to suggest that women were less in fear of sexual attack and rape than in fear of straight violence in these pre-industrial times. Historians have found few writings expressing such fears, and the conclusion has been drawn by some feminists that male domination was so clear-cut that men had little need to employ the threat of rape to maintain their dominance (Porter 1985).

The natural hazards of life meant that children were always at risk from illness and disease, as well as injury from accident. Risk from adult offenders outside the family seems to have been relatively rare. One early example of a recorded abduction of a child is related, by Heywood, of one Alice de Salisbury: 'who in 1373 stole Margaret Roper, the little daughter of a London grocer, carrying her away and stripping her of clothes so that she might not be recognised by her family' (1959: 6). The abduction was to use the child for begging purposes, but the offender was caught and spent one hour per day in the stocks. In 1645, Parliament was informed that 'divers lewd persons do go up and down the city of London and elsewhere, and in the most barbarous and wicked manner steal away many little children'. Constables were to apprehend anyone stealing, buying or receiving stolen children (Laurence 1994: 84–5). The state of policing through the local constables and 'night watch' was, of course, primitive, and prevention and detection of crimes were difficult. An Act of 1604 required the whole community to assist, when necessary, in the apprehending of criminals.

It is probably at this time also that the spectre of the individual dangerous person – as opposed to groups – first appears as nomadic figures which could threaten communities anywhere. The vagrant was a particular demonised figure of the times. A figure that blends in with mythical tales of demons, werewolves and those, like the 'raggle-taggle gypsies', who would steal your children.

Vagrancy Acts were introduced to impose some order and improve public protection. The Vagrancy Act 1714 identified the mentally disordered person – ' the furiously mad and dangerous' – as requiring restraint as a matter of urgency to protect the community. The Vagrancy Act 1744 allowed for restraint of the mad, along with an element of 'curing' in such establishments as the emerging county workhouses. Children as well as adults could end up in workhouses, where their treatment was quite miserable. Many children in these early institutions 'were the victims of murder, manslaughter, assault and rape' (Heywood 1959: 19).

The mid-eighteenth century saw the vagrancy problem worsen with the influx of many Irish people on to the British mainland. The idea of a register was proposed in 1748 to help deal with the problem:

> Vagrants released from the county workhouses should be made to appear at the Quarter Sessions to be 'registered and recorded' so that their offending might be more easily convicted, which Register, and proving the identity of the Persons, shall be sufficient Evidence for convicting such Vagrant in order for Transportation (cited in Radzinowicz 1948: 19).

Other suggestions of the time included the need to require 'servants and labourers' to have a certificate signed by a magistrate, minister or churchwarden should they wish to move from their place of residence (ibid.: 20).

The earliest attempts at policing, as we know it today, also thought the idea of a register was a positive one. Henry Fielding, the Chief Magistrate of Bow Street (1748–54), started his reform of the police in London in the 1740s with the creation of the Bow Street runners, which included the innovation of the post of 'Register Clerk'. This particular register was to be a record of crimes reported, goods lost and names and descriptions of people both suspected and convicted. Sir John Fielding, Henry's brother, later suggested that one of its purposes was to help identify those who should be shown mercy, instead of being executed: 'Wisdom, policy and humanity dictate that the most abandoned, dangerous people and incorrigible offenders should be pointed out for this melancholy purpose, the knowledge of which cannot be obtained with any degree of certainty but from the valuable register of offenders' (Radzinowicz 1956: 47). The idea of a sex offender register in 1997 has a long pedigree.

A variation on this use of a register for helping to detect crime and for influencing sentencing was the early idea of a register to assist with pre-employment screening. In 1749, the Fieldings established the Universal Register Officer 'as a labour exchange where employers might examine prospective servants and study their character references', and published a bulletin called *The Public Advertiser* providing information on the servant labour market (Linebaugh 1991: 252).

Later developments from the Fielding brothers included dissemination of information through the *Weekly Pursuit*, the *Quarterly Pursuit*, and *Lists of Offenders at Large* (Radzinowicz 1956: 48). Later still, another 'founding father' of early policing, Patrick Colquhoun, developed the register idea and organised 'a continually expanding inventory of all that was noxious in society, so as to serve the purposes of his General Police Machine' (ibid.: 295).

1800 to 1900

The start of the nineteenth century found the UK still without a regular police force yet with an emerging working class being 'created' from the Industrial Revolution, living in rapidly growing cities and in housing that was insanitary and squalid. Criminality was considered endemic amongst the dispossessed 'dangerous classes', where it went hand in hand with the immorality of 'demoralised' communities.

New prisons were being built to complement the bridewells, and the houses of correction and the old debtors prisons were being overhauled after the reforming interventions of such as John Howard, the Sheriff of Bedfordshire, and the Quaker, Elizabeth Fry; the aim was to introduce order into the prison system, which previously seemed only to offer chaos. By the end of the century, the prison system had been reformed, an organised police force was in place and laws protecting children and defining sexual offending had been passed.

Forms of detention for the criminal lunatic were limited. Madhouses, licensed houses or Poor Law establishments existed but this seemed insufficient. The County Asylum Act 1808 permitted the building of local asylums to increase the number of beds for these patients. Later amendments to the law allowed for the transfer of the criminally insane from prisons to hospitals. In 1862, building started on Broadmoor as a special institution to hold the dangerous criminally insane. One novel feature of the laws at this time was the power to fine hospital staff who allowed patients to escape.

The second event to shake complacency in the early decades of the century was the so-called Wapping murders, when two whole families in London were murdered en masse in 1811. Some of the local watchmen were summarily dismissed and special armed patrols appointed to protect the neighbourhood. Neighbouring parishes sent volunteers in for additional night patrolling to take place (Critchley 1967: 40–1).

The ruling class was slowly coming round to the idea that new forms of public policing were needed. People with money might buy their own private policing protection, but it was clear that more was needed. The Peterloo killings in Manchester had shown the shortcomings of the military's ability to keep public order, and the increased vagrancy from soldiers returning from the Napoleonic Wars suggested that new measures were needed. The Metropolitan Police Act 1829 brought into being the first regularised police force on mainland Britain for the London area, to be followed by enactments to create provincial forces across the country. A police force for Ireland had already been established in 1786.

These early forms of policing would inevitably involve the collation of information on people, but it was to be some time before a formal national collection of criminal records was started. There is evidence that in these pre-computer days and the notion of a Criminal Records Bureau on nobody's agenda, employers were already looking to the police for information on the trustworthiness of potential employees, perhaps prompted by the early experiments of Fielding with his Universal Register Office. Emsley reports that:

> In 1857 the Chief Constable of Bedford gave confidential information to a local employer about one of his workmen [and] ... in 1863 the Chief Constable of Lincolnshire protested that his men were 'constantly receiving letters from private enquiry offices seeking information as to the character, respectability, and money value of persons residing in the towns and villages (Emsley 1991: 107).

It is probable that the screening out of sex offenders was not a priority for these employers, but it was clear that in some quarters, at least, police records from an early age were seen as not just being for the police to use for policing purposes, but were legitimate information for others who had to weigh up risks about people.

In 1857, an Obscene Publications Act was passed and the Metropolitan Police formed an Obscene Publications Squad in 1863. The advent of photography had brought a new dimension to this particular 'art' and the term 'pornography' was passing into common usage. In 1870, the Obscene Publications Squad mounted a joint operation with a voluntary organisation called the Vice Society against the sellers of obscene material, but not long after the squad was disbanded until its re-emergence in the late 1880s in response to public demand (Bristow 1977: 47).

Police progress against brothels remained notoriously uneven. Prostitution had yet to be conceived as a form of economic violence against women and was seen rather as a crime without a victim. Bristow reports that the slow progress was due to 'a vexed tale of Home Office delay, badly drafted legislation, unfavourable judicial rulings and police corruption' (ibid.: 57). By the late 1850s, a concerted effort was made for action when the Vice Society joined forces with other campaigners, rescue houses and local authorities in London to press for better policing of the brothels. Together they formed what later would be loosely called the 'Social Purity' movement.

Part of the continuing problem with regulating prostitution in all its forms was the Victorian double standards surrounding sexual matters, and the latent belief that prostitution might even enable 'the family' to exist in a more perfected form. In practical policing terms, there was the problem of obtaining evidence and the overall hostility to the police, especially when they entered brothels. Added to this was an age of consent of 12, which was only raised to 13 in 1875 (objections were raised that young men would be entrapped and blackmailed by girls if the age was raised any higher) (ibid.: 91).

It was the outraged mob who also still saw it as their role to let the perpetrators of sex crime know exactly what they thought of them. In working-class communities in Wales, we are told: 'generally the community, embodied in the mob, intervened on the side of women, upbraiding wife beaters and punishing adulterers' (Jones 1982: 111). In Dowlais, a man who lived off immoral earnings had a crowd of some 500 put his doors and windows through (ibid.), and when two men were publicly hanged for killing their wives because they suspected infidelity, 'it needed all the efforts of the constables ... to keep the angry spectators at a distance' (Jones 1992: 74).

Behind many Victorian reforms of this period were the organisations of the 'Social Purity' movement. The Vice Society, formed in 1802, was a central agency of this movement, but so too were organisations like the London Society for the Protection of Young Females, the Guardian Society, the Rescue Society, the Midnight Meeting Movement and a host of others. Their rise should be seen against the declining influence of the church courts and the desire for something to replace them. Towards the end of the century, they would be complemented – or replaced – by such as the National Vigilance Association, the White Cross League and the Social Purity Alliance (see Bristow 1977: *passim*) and, ultimately, by the rise of the authority of the academic hierarchy and the professional 'experts'.

The 'Social Purity' movement saw their role as being to ameliorate the worst excesses of Victorian high liberalism and laissez-faire, and saw immorality and criminality being closely entwined, with the former usually a precursor to the latter. They campaigned for tighter laws on pornography, prostitution and brothel keeping and sought to enforce the law through private prosecutions or in tandem with the police. For their part, the police seemed happy with this arrangement and to leave these aspects of law enforcement to these vigilant – 'vigilante' – groups who could only enhance the efforts of the police. Bristow offers further explanation:

> Officials left the initiative for law enforcement as well as legal reform to the vigilantes. Did the State acquiesce with a cunning understanding of the function obscenity played in the social system, as was the case with prostitution? Perhaps more relevant in explaining official reticence was the availability of a strong voluntary effort, the tradition of private initiative, the unpopularity

of using the police to entrap people and the very magnitude of the task (ibid.: 45).

The Vice Society, for example, saw a number of legislative initiatives taken which they had campaigned for. The Vagrancy Act 1824, for example, included for the first time 'streetwalking' as an offence; the earlier 1744 version of the Act had left out streetwalkers.

Previously, the prison had been a 'secondary' arm of penal policy that 'held' people for short periods in local debtors' prisons, bridewells and houses of correction; the more serious offenders were 'held' on a temporary basis to await transportation or execution. The loss of transportation and the accompanying reduction in the use of capital punishment caused the Victorians to rethink the role of the prison. Now, the prison would move to centre stage as a 'primary' arm of penal policy and as penitentiaries in their own right. It would no longer be the place where you waited for punishment but would now be that punishment.

The period between 1780 and 1850 had already seen reforms and experiments in prison design and regimes. Sophisticated systems of surveillance were designed, such as Jeremy Bentham's panopticon, which allowed the prisoner no privacy or escape from the all-seeing warders; an actual panopticon-style prison was never built in the UK but the ideas were taken on board (Ignatieff 1978: 109–13).

As the prison became more central to penal policy, the Victorians started to worry about what happened when prisoners came out and went back into the community; a worry that never existed with high levels of capital punishment and transportation for the serious offender.

Within the prisons, a new rising class of prison administrators also saw the need for systems of remission and early release to help control the conduct of individual prisoners and to regulate the growing size of the prison population (McGowen 1995).

The Penal Servitude Act 1853 increased prison sentences and created a system of licensing for discharged prisoners, known as 'ticket-of-leave'. Despite amendments to the law in 1857, the 'ticket-of-leave' system never really worked and the public had little faith in these new arrangements. The press blamed ticket-of-leave men for all manner of crimes and the general feeling was that they were dangerous and had been discharged too early. Letters to *The Times* described them as 'creating terror in the public mind' and said the public was 'becoming thoroughly frightened' (Bartrip 1981: 164).

In 1862, a wave of 'garottings' hit London as a form of street attack that left victims half strangled and robbed; the garotting epidemic was blamed on the ticket-of-leave men (ibid.: 166). In the same year, the failings of the system were revealed most starkly when the Home Office asked the Commissioner of the Metropolitan Police for a report on the ticket-of-leave men; the Commissioner had to acknowledge that 'the police could not find or produce a single man of them' (Radzinowicz and Hood 1990: 249).

The government reviewed the whole system of penal servitude with a Royal Commission in 1863. The report came down in favour of continuing the system, but with a more rigorous supervision of ticket-of-leave men by the police. The new, enhanced supervision was to be based on systems developed in Ireland by Sir Walter Crofton; the argument ran that if it worked on the Irish, it would work on the British (HL Debs, 7 June 1864, col. 1339). The Penal Servitude Bill was published in 1864.

Essential to the new system was the requirement for ticket-of-leave men to report to the police within three days of leaving prison, and thereafter on a monthly basis or within 48 hours if they should change address. The system was immediately criticised as an infringement of civil liberties and for being 'un-British': 'to make it a misdemeanour for a discharged criminal not to report himself to the police was a regulation far better adapted to the police systems of other countries than of our own' (ibid.: col. 1342). Others disagreed. Lord Cranworth thought protection of the public was paramount and he: 'had no sympathy with those who advanced the argument, that to require a convict to place himself under supervision would interfere with the rights and liberties of the subject. The matter properly to be considered was, what system would answer best for the public' (ibid.: col. 1345). In practice even with the new Penal Servitude Act 1864, the ticket-of-leave arrangements did not work. The police found it hard to communicate between themselves and had no central register they could refer to. In 1869, Parliament heard that the system verged on 'absolute failure' (HL Debs, 5 March 1869, col. 691ff; see also Bartrip 1981).

The Habitual Criminals Act 1869 repealed the ticket-of-leave arrangements except for those with two felony convictions who had been given absolute prison discharge; police supervision continued for them. The major innovation of the 1869 Act, however, was to be the compilation of a national register of offenders – the Habitual Criminal Register – to assist the police in general matters relating to crime detection and prosecution, as well as supervising those remaining hard core ticket-of-leave men.

Within the Parliamentary debate on the 1869 Act, cautious voices were raised:

> A man watched at every step and moment of his existence, and becoming more notorious, as he is sure to be before long by the action of the police, and a thousand other circumstances, will find the door of ordinary employment shut against him, and will be driven to the choice between violence and starvation (HL Debs, 5 March 1869, col. 697).

Such arguments were lost and the Habitual Criminals Act 1869 introduced a national register of criminals (England, Wales and Ireland) to be held at Scotland Yard and to be regularly added to and updated by contributing forces. According to one MP, it was to be nothing less than 'a wholesale system of police surveillance, so that another considerable portion of the people would be in a state of out-door imprisonment, tied, as it were, by the leg to the police' (HC Debs, 4 August 1869, col. 1261). The Prevention of Crimes Act 1871 extended the system to Scotland. Ticket-of-leave men were rarely charged for failing to report, although most did, in fact, do so; the strictness of the supervision was always 'greater on paper than in practice' (Bartrip 1981: 172).

The Metropolitan Police were amongst those forces having difficulty with their supervisory role. In 1880, attempts were made to try to remedy the position by the creation of a specialised Convict Supervision Office, made up of a chief inspector and three sergeants. The new office improved the maintenance of the register and dissemination of relevant information to other officers, and also improved the efficacy of home visits to ensure compliance. It also worked more closely with the emergent Societies for the Aid of Discharged Prisoners. The new arrangements were generally considered successful by the police, although offenders at the time could still point out that 'if a man is determined to do wrong all the supervision in England will not prevent it. They cannot always watch a man' (cited in Petrow 1994: 80).

This particular form of police supervision was effectively dismantled in 1910 by the Home Secretary, Winston Churchill. Had it been successful? Some think not: 'On balance police supervision, while theoretically valuable, had been practically useless. It helped the police manufacture a criminal class, without really deterring criminals or diminishing crime' (Petrow 1994: 82).

The Victorians passed laws to help protect children from the worst excesses of child labour and to give them rights of elementary education. The Prevention of Cruelty to Children Acts 1889 and 1894 were also passed, but their implementation was left largely in the hands of voluntary agencies like the NSPCC, formed in 1889, or the Waifs and

Strays Society, founded in 1881; the latter later became the Children's Society of the Church of England. Other notable 'rescue' organisations included Dr Barnardo's Children's Homes, which started in 1870, and the Charity Organisation Society (COS) in 1869. Later, these 'casework' experts would evolve into the child care officers and social work experts of the new century (see also Bartley 2000 for an account of rescue work with women prostitutes). Looking back, one of the founders of the COS, describing London in the late 1860s, saw only: 'a confused mass of poverty, crime, and mendicancy living side by side with the independent wage earners under conditions of overcrowding and insanitation, and baffling all the efforts of authority and benevolence' (Bosanquet 1914: 17). Mrs Bosanquet also noted that one of those involved in the discussions to start the COS was Sir Walter Crofton, the architect of the ticket-of-leave supervision policy (ibid.: 18).

In 1885, the position of children as victims of sex offending was to be given massive publicity by what became known as 'The Maiden Tribute of Modern Babylon'. This was a series of special editions of the *Pall Mall Gazette*, edited by William T. Stead, which highlighted the extent of prostitution that existed in London and the large numbers of young girls being drawn into it. By the third edition in July, 'mobs were rioting at the Pall Mall Gazette offices in an attempt to obtain copies' (Bristow 1977: 110), and although other newspapers and publications were slow to follow, Stead could eventually boast that his revelations had been printed 'in every capital of the Continent, as well as by the "purest journals in the great American republic"' (Walkowitz 1992: 82). (Stead himself was later drowned in the *Titanic* disaster.)

Stead had been briefed in advance of publication by campaigners in London and it was they who continued the agitation in the post-publication phase; the Salvation Army was reported to be particularly active at this time. Overflow meetings were addressed throughout the country. At Manchester Free Trade Hall, for example, the campaigner James Wookey was heard by a crowd of 6,000 when he spoke on 'The Massacre of the Innocents'; Wookey 'harangued against the privileged who abused poor girls but whose own daughters were protected by footmen' (Bristow 1977: 111).

The result of all this public pressure and campaigning was the Criminal Law Amendment Act 1885. The Act, amongst other things, raised the age of consent to 16, and made illegal acts of gross indecency between males (the law had previously only covered acts of buggery and sodomy). To ensure the Act was implemented, 'vigilance committees' started to appear across the country and were ultimately absorbed into the newly formed National Vigilance Association (NVA), which took over the mantle of the Vice Society. The Act was most (in)famously used to prosecute Oscar Wilde.

In 1888, the serial murder of five women prostitutes in the Whitechapel area of London was taken up by the press and public to cause a wave of panic throughout the capital and beyond. The police failure to solve these so-called 'Jack-the-Ripper' murders only added to the sense of awe and mystery.

As the press reporting of the murders intensified, a picture emerged of the squalid conditions of the housing in Whitechapel and the contrast and similarities with other parts of London. The ineptitude of the police in being unable to find a suspect was reported, alongside the grisly nature of the sexual mutilation carried out and the facts of why women had to resort to prostitution as a means of income. The press speculated on possible suspects and one, John Pizer, named by the *Star*, had to turn himself into the police to escape the fury of a mob (Walkowitz 1992: 203).

The respectable citizens of Whitechapel organised themselves into self-protection patrols, and called for the closure of brothels and common lodging houses, described as 'nurseries of crime'. Walkowitz suggests these activities were not just about self-protection but about 'surveillance of the un-respectable poor and low-life women in particular' (ibid.: 213).

The un-respectable poor of Whitechapel contented themselves with violent rioting and the victimisation of Jewish immigrants and doctors (both considered possible suspects, according to the press) as well as police officers (for their inability to find the killer). The funerals of the victims produced large crowds and outpourings of sympathy (ibid.: 216–17).

Cameron and Frazer (1987) have pointed out that a Robert Louis Stevenson story published in 1886 may have fed into the hysteria of this time. *The Strange Case of Doctor Jekyll and Mr Hyde* is the story of a respectable doctor who is transformed by various medications into an evil monster. The story has taken a hold on popular imagination to this day, to support the idea that there is, within us all, an evil side that may come through at any time.

Meanwhile, within the hospital systems, further changes were taking place in the care of the criminally insane. The new profession of psychiatry, having got a foot in the door in 1845 to detain people, was anxious to try to treat as many as possible as early as possible. Arraigned against them were the lawyers, upholding principles of Victorian liberty and due process of law, and conscious that the public was somewhat alarmed at the ease with which people could be detained in hospitals (Unsworth 1979).

The lawyers won out and the doctors had to stand back. The Lunacy Act 1890 eventually put legal safeguards above the doctors' desire to treat. Coercion and therapy did not have to go hand in hand and even the medical journal the *Lancet* agreed that 'no single power is needed by physicians engaged in the medical treatment of the insane which the common law does not give every citizen' (editorial, 7 February 1885).

Violence towards women – including sexual violence – was endemic throughout Victorian times. The philosopher John Stuart Mill joined the campaign to highlight the extent of the problem and, in the 1870s, the feminist campaigner Frances Power Cobbe published her pamphlet 'Wife Torture' (republished 1992). Men who raped their wives could not be prosecuted following a rule laid down as early as 1736 by Sir Matthew Hale, which stated that a wife gave a general consent to all future sexual intercourse when she married him; this common law ruling was only abandoned in 1992. As late as 1915, a London magistrate was still able to say that 'the husband of a nagging wife ... could beat her at home provided the stick he used was no thicker than a man's thumb' (Wilson 1983: 84–6; see also Ross 1982).

The position of children was not much better:

Until late in the nineteenth century, both Parliament and the national press were largely unconcerned with the way in which parents treated their children, regarding even the most barbarous cruelty as beyond public intervention since children were not then regarded as citizens in their own right (Pinchbeck and Hewitt 1973: 611).

It was known that sex offending against children did take place within the home, and references to it start to emerge at this time. Andrew Mearns, who would go on to be a founder of the National Vigilance Association, had produced in 1883 his 'Bitter Cry of Outcast London', drawing attention to the poverty, overcrowding and the moral corruption that inevitably went with it; amongst it all Mearns reported that 'incest is common' (ibid.: 1883). Apart from protection in the public sphere, children appeared to need protection in the private sphere of the home (Jackson 2000).

In 1885, the Royal Commission on Housing reported that incest appeared to be all too common in overcrowded accommodation (RCHWC 1885: 267) and, in 1890, William Booth produced similar findings in his report, deliberately entitled to mock the then fashionable explorers of Africa, *In Darkest England and the Way Out*. According to Booth, 'incest is so familiar as hardly to call for remark' (1890: 65).

There is also evidence to suggest that, however much campaigners might be offended by incest, the same feelings were not always experienced by those who had been victims of it. Beatrice Webb recalls talking to: 'Young girls, who were in no way mentally defective, who were, on the contrary, just as keen witted and generous-hearted as my own circle of friends [yet] could chaff each other about having babies by their fathers and brothers' (cited in Wohl 1978). Webb could only attribute this to the general debasing effect social environment could have on personal character and family life. In terms of legalities, incest was in the anomalous position of being outside the criminal law. Incest was an offence against morality and as such had, in the past, been dealt with by the ecclesiastical courts or bawdy courts and politicians appeared in no hurry to change this situation: 'legislating authority in the home was entirely different from legislating public morality and perhaps if the official policy was to let sleeping siblings lie, it was because "laissezfaire" was preferable to state intervention' (Wohl 1978). The NVA turned its attention to putting this anomaly to right and, in doing so, 'found a valuable ally in the NSPCC' (Bailey and Blackburn 1979). Their continued efforts were to take them into the new century.

1900 to 1970

Moving into the modern era, this narrative divides into: 1) the policy area we now know as criminal justice studies or penal policy; and 2) what starts out as child care policies and becomes a more generalised public protection exercise.

Criminal justice

At the start of the century, the NSPCC and the NVA continued their efforts to get incest made a criminal offence and supported unsuccessful bills in 1900, 1903 and 1907. MPs referring to 'this rather disagreeable subject' thought the policing of the new proposals constituted the main stumbling block (see, e.g., HC Debs, 5 March 1903, col. 1683). A better approach might be through education or moral instruction rather than law enforcement, because even if one caught the offenders one 'might thrash and imprison people, but [still] not make them good' (HC Debs 26 June 1908, col. 288).

The Home Office was eventually won over by the arguments that 'it was exceedingly necessary to add to the law ... [as] the offence was by no means rare' (ibid.: col. 284). A secondary consideration hovering in the background was the eugenics argument that inbreeding led to degeneration and weak mindedness, although these arguments did not come to the fore (Bailey and Blackburn 1979); in 1908 the Punishment of Incest Act became law for England and Wales. Scotland continued to use the common law until the passing of the Incest and Related Offences (Scotland) Act 1986.

Putting a law into place was one thing; enforcement of that law was another. The British police, arguably, only got to grips with sexual offending against children and adults in the last quarter of the twentieth century. No doubt investigations and prosecutions took place in the years following the 1908 Act, but throughout this period sexual offending was perceived more as prostitution or homosexual activities. Even with this focus, police interventions were often seen as callous or indifferent.

A 1928 parliamentary report on soliciting and other street offences had gone out of its way to mention the need for police tact, especially when there was the chance of wrongly accusing innocent people: 'No class of crime requires more tact and discretion on the part of the police and any failure in this respect on their part in dealing with such cases is visited with public condemnation' (Report on the Street Offences Committee 1928: para. 53). The comments of one police officer writing in the 1930s makes the point:

Now and again they brought in a Nancy-Boy as they were then called, and treated him as though he were an inanimate object without feeling. They rubbed his face with toilet paper to procure evidence of make- up, joked and laughed about him as if he were not present and always found the same sized tin of Vaseline in his pocket (Daley 1986: 101).

Or consider the following reflections in a training manual for the Scottish Police, published as recently as 1980:

the terms 'sodomy', 'indecent exposure', 'lewd and libidinous practice' and 'gross indecency' etc. which are used in law give but little indication of the nature of these offences; the manner in which they are usually committed, and the veils they are liable to bring in their train ... the movement of persons of manifestly lewd disposition should always be closely watched as many and varied are the artifices employed by these persons to achieve their evil objectives (cited in Crane 1983: 41–2).

Crane gives a number of examples of poor policing practice against homosexual activities that still breach the law despite the Sexual Offences Act 1967, which largely decriminalised such acts in the UK. These varied from forms of police entrapment, to abusive behaviour towards gay men – 'queer bashing' – or a refusal to take seriously their reports of crime.

At the turn of the century, the police shared concern with the public that all classes of offenders were getting more mobile and more anonymous with the growth of public transport and the expansion of urban conurbations. The spectre of the invisible sex offender moving around at will took up the mantle of the dangerous vagrant.

One response was the merging of the Habitual Criminals Register, the Convict Supervision Office and the new Fingerprint Registry into a national Criminal Record Office; in 1901, the Fingerprint Registry had started using the Henry System of Classification. The *Police Gazette,* which circulated to all forces lists of wanted men, was revamped and relaunched by 1910 with supplements on 'travelling criminals' and details of 'expert criminals' recently released from prison (Petrow 1994: 99–101). The Criminal Record Office remained more or less unchanged until its merger into the National Identification Bureau (NIB) in 1980: the NIB subsequently became the National Identification Service in 1995, by which time the whole national collection of criminal records was being transferred to the Police National Computer.

The Probation of Offenders Act 1907 introduced the modern Probation Service to take over the earlier work of the Court Missionary Service; supervision of offenders to keep them out of prison was a new item on their agenda. The Prevention of Crimes Act 1908 brought in separate custodial facilities for young offenders, named after a pilot scheme in the Kent village of Borstal, and included the new idea of supervised after-care on a compulsory licence basis, with the possibility of recall for any breach of supervisory requirements.

After-care supervision was not totally novel and we have earlier described the ticket-of-leave system, whereby ex-offenders from prison had to report monthly to the police and notify the police whenever they changed address. The new arrangements for young prisoners leaving Borstal combined this straight policing role with a general helping role from probation officers. Any help that the old ticket-of-leave prisoners got did not come from the police, but might come from such voluntary organisations as the local Discharged Prisoners Aid Society.

The Prevention of Crimes Act also introduced the idea of preventive detention (PD). This was to be a measure for tackling the 'habitual' offender – including the sex offender – by not just punishing them for what they had done, but by recognising their previous convictions and to give them longer prison sentences in order better to protect the public (PCA 1908: s. 10(1)). The courts were not really sure about PD and it seems to have had an uncertain start in life. In 1911, the then Home Secretary, Winston Churchill, said it should only be used for the older offender (over 30) who had already had one sentence of penal servitude and had now committed another serious offence. It was not for the public nuisance but for the persistent dangerous criminal.

Despite this guidance, there was variation in the use of PD and arguments emerged that perhaps it was not such a good idea after all. Some judges hardly used it, as it seemed to contradict the principle that an offender be sentenced for the charge on which he or she came to court. After the Second World War, the Criminal Justice Act 1948 restricted the use of PD to the serious persistent offender only, and it was eventually abolished by the Criminal Justice Act 1967 (see also Home Office 1963).

A new sentence was created by the 1967 Act, which had a resonance with PD, and this was the 'extended sentence' which could be passed on people who already had three or more previous convictions. In practice, 'extended sentences' were hardly used and the government decided to repeal the power to pass them: 'to the extent that [an extended sentence] may have been useful for dealing with persistent violent or sexual offenders and protecting the public, it will be replaced by [a] new Crown Court Power' (Home Office 1990a: para. 3.17). The Criminal Justice Act 1991 duly repealed the extended sentence, but within a few years the idea of preventive detention – now in the form of indeterminate sentences for sex offenders – was back on the agenda (see Chapter 9).

Penal policy had started to receive an input from the medical and psychiatric services from the 1930s onwards, premised on the idea that offenders could be 'treated' rather than just punished (see, e.g., East and Hubert 1939). The idea of treating prisoners in 'therapeutic communities' found its fullest form at the prison opened in 1962 at Grendon Underwood in Buckinghamshire. Grendon took sex offenders and other prisoners who suffered from various neuroses or personality disorders; the inmates were transferred there from within the prison service rather than going directly from the courts (Parker 1970).

For all prisoners on discharge from prison, there has always been a tradition of helping the offender and his or her family. This has included voluntary arrangements through the Discharged Prisoners Aid Societies. The concept of the Borstal Licence introduced an element of control and sanctions into custodial after-care, and these two dimensions of both helping and controlling the ex-prisoner have always rested uneasily alongside each other.

The licence system applicable to young men leaving Borstal was eventually adapted for adult prisoners leaving prisons. The Criminal Justice Act 1948 brought in the new sentence of corrective training to run alongside preventive detention, and along with it came new arrangements for release on licence after two-thirds of the sentence or five-sixths of a PD sentence. Further reforms in the 1960s saw the Probation Service move more centrally into the after-care of prisoners field, and a merging of the care and control elements.

In due course, the Criminal Justice Act 1967 replaced the 1948 Release on Licence arrangements with the concept of parole. As Parsloe put it: 'Licence is a right – or an obligation – for certain prisoners but is in almost all cases unavoidable. Parole, however, is widely held to be a state which a prisoner can earn' (1979). The Criminal Justice Act 1967, Part III established the Parole Board to consider the discretionary release of 'Life' prisoners for post-custodial supervision; the formulation of parole policies has to be seen in the light of the abolition of capital punishment for murder which preceded it (see Coker and Martin 1985). Life prisoners, however, could also encompass serious sex offenders and not just murderers. The current position on the sentencing of sex offenders is returned to in Chapters 5 and 6.

Protecting children and the public

The Children Act 1908 consolidated what law there was on child protection and was a public indication that children were important and that their care and protection should be taken seriously, but enforcement of the law at this time was often left to voluntary agencies, such as the NSPCC, when not left to the police.

A parliamentary report in 1925 looked specifically at sexual offences committed against children and young persons, and noted the high number of acquittals that seemed to take place. Overall, it reported a decrease in sexual crime accompanied by violence, but an increase in such crime committed against children under the age of 16 (Departmental Committee 1925: para. 18). The report also noted the wide variety of male offenders who came from all classes of society (ibid.: para. 75) and recommended long prison sentences as the best punishment for them; probation was an alternative to be used with 'caution' and probably worked best with young offenders (ibid.: para. 87).

The report suggested that the police or the courts should notify schools when a pupil had been the victim of sexual abuse. This was to facilitate the teacher giving assistance to a child who was 'unsettled' by the experience and to 'prevent contamination of other children' by the possible spreading of 'debased tendencies' (ibid.: paras. 110 and 114). As for the very young child, it was thought that the experience would be 'quickly forgotten' (ibid.: para. 93).

A similar report the following year on sex offences against children in Scotland came to similar conclusions, but made the wider comment on sex offending generally that it was 'no more than the surface manifestation of the irregular habits and secret moral standards of a considerable section of the community – a mere symptom of a larger disorder' (Departmental Committee 1926: para. 141). As such the real answer was to raise the moral tone of society.

The civil law on child care and protection was consolidated in the Children and Young Persons Act 1933. The Act introduced its Schedule 1, which would pass into the everyday language of child protection workers for the next 70 years and more, being the list of offences it is possible to commit against a child and which, in due course, has led to various prohibitions on activities that can be engaged in by 'Schedule One offenders' if those activities should bring them into contact with children (see Chapter 6). In the same year, the Children and Young Persons (Boarding Out) Rules prohibited anyone from becoming a foster-parent if they had offences which rendered them 'unfit', and this was upheld a few years later in primary legislation by the Public Health Act 1936, s. 210(c), which prevented anyone being a foster-parent who had: 'been convicted of any offence under Part I of the Children and Young Persons Act 1933, or Part 2 of The Children Act 1908'. Presumably, some form of criminal record information disclosure took place to ensure these requirements were met.

Hospital confinement remained an option for sex offenders who were also assessed as being mentally disordered. The Lunacy Act 1890 and the Mental Deficiency Act 1913 provided the legislative framework for compulsory detention, and for those considered the most 'dangerous', there was Broadmoor 'criminal asylum' (opened in 1863), Rampton Hospital (built in 1910) and Moss Side Hospital (built in 1914, but only taking mentally disordered patients after 1933). These three hospitals – later designated 'special hospitals' – would be joined by a fourth, Park Lane Hospital in Lancashire (in 1974), and in Scotland by Carstairs State Hospital. Ultimately, Moss Side and Park Lane – physically adjacent to each other – would amalgamate and form Ashworth Hospital in 1990.

The Mental Health Act 1959 introduced some new sexual offences; it made it an offence for a male member of staff at a hospital to have sex with a woman under treatment for a mental disorder and a similar offence was introduced for a male guardian (s. 128). In the case of R v. Goodwin (unreported, 19 May 1994) a male nurse who developed a sexual relationship with a patient that continued after her discharge received two years in prison. The court held 'this was as gross, deliberate and wicked breach of trust as one might regret to see' (Hill and Fletcher-Rogers 1997: para. 11.14). The 1959 Act also amended the Sexual Offences Act 1956 by making it an offence for any man to have sex with a woman he knows is 'defective' or mentally impaired (s. 27).

Mental health legislation received a further overhaul in the 1980s. In England and Wales the new law was the Mental Health Act 1983, in Scotland the Mental Health (Scotland) Act 1984 and in Northern Ireland the Mental Health (Northern Ireland) Order 1986. Common to them all was a focus on the rights of hospital in-patients and improved training for those empowered to take away the right of freedom to live in the community. In England and Wales, the 1983 Act introduced a right of after-care for previously detained patients and new supervisory arrangements for those who had been detained on a Hospital Order with added restrictions (Home Office/DHSS 1987). Later, the after-care of former mental health patients would be strengthened by yet another new register – the 'supervision register' for those still 'at risk' (Department of Health 1994a) and, in 1995, amendments to the 1983 Act allowing for more 'supervised discharge' into the community; the 'supervision registers' were subsequently found to be not very useful and were wound up in 2001.

The Mental Health Act 1983 proved less than helpful in dealing with many sex offenders. As we have seen (Chapter 2) the Act specifically excluded 'sexual deviance' as a condition the Act should apply to (Mental Health Act 1983, s. 1(3)) and also required the detention of psychopaths only to take place when 'treatment is likely to alleviate or prevent a deterioration of his condition' (Mental Health Act 1983, s. 3(b)). This has allowed some psychiatrists to say that sex offending was not something they needed to be involved with, especially if there was no clear mental illness present. Ultimately this has led to attempts to change the mental health law so that psychiatrists could *not* walk away from the problem (see Chapter 2).

What psychiatric interventions did take place, were a mixture of medication and individual and group therapeutic work. Experiments with various forms of aversion therapy were falling into disuse by this time (see Chapter 2).

The post-war years saw the enlargement of the personal social services to be 'administered' locally by health and local authorities. Community mental health services employing mental welfare officers (MWOs) came under the health service and local authorities had charge of welfare departments for elderly and disabled people and children's departments for children and families. The war years had created a greater awareness of the conditions of city life, when thousands of child evacuees had been relocated to rural areas and fostering had become a way of life for the children and their host families. Ultimately, the Children Act 1948 created local authority children's departments in England, Wales and Scotland which were centrally accountable to the Home Office.

In 1971, children's departments were incorporated into the new social services departments along with the mental health departments and welfare departments. The rationale was to have a more integrated service, meeting all personal needs under one roof through the 'generic' social worker, who replaced the child care officer, welfare officer and mental welfare officer. The Social Work (Scotland) Act 1968, based on the Kilbrandon Report (1964), had made similar arrangements for north of the border, with the added embellishment of including the Probation Service into their social work departments.

In terms of law, the Children and Young Persons Act 1963 had defined the circumstances whereby a child might need 'care, protection or control', and those circumstances would include the presence in a child's household of someone convicted of a 'Schedule One offence' (see Chapter 6) , including sexual offences against a child. The 1963 Act was replaced by the Children and Young Persons Act 1969, with its 'grounds' for care including a child being in 'moral danger' (s. 1(2)(c)) or being harmed by a 'Schedule One offender' joining the household (s. 1(2)(bb)).

Summary

In this chapter, we have considered a selective outline of historical aspects of sexual offending and the social response to it. Certain themes can be seen to have a resonance with contemporary preoccupations. The keeping of registers on certain criminals and the requirement for ticket-of-leave offenders to report to the police have a clear link to our current sex offenders register (see Chapter 9); we have also noted early attempts at pre-employment screening by reference to conviction records and the attempts by the police to enhance the quality of their record keeping. Populist agitation against the sex offender also has a long history, and the sensationalising of such offenders by the press is also a well established phenomenon, as witnessed in the 'Ripper' murders of 1888. Current concerns to find a way to incarcerate the 'dangerous' person before he or she offends (see Chapters 6 and 9) also have earlier attempts at 'preventive detentions' to guide their deliberations.

Chapter 4

Policing sex offenders

The police are the initial 'gateway' for all criminals coming into the criminal justice system. The police receive reports of new crimes, investigate and detect who is responsible and, when satisfied, pass their work on to the Crown Prosecution Service for prosecution. For present purposes, police activities are considered on three levels – local, national and international. The police approach to sexual offending on all three levels is outlined, and the emerging importance of 'personal information' on offenders for purposes of policing is drawn out. The final part of the chapter examines the work of the Forensic Science Service and especially the creation of a National DNA Database to assist the police in the identifying of offenders.

Local policing

Reports and investigations

Initial crime reports of sexual offending are made to the local police for them to investigate and put together a case for possible prosecution in the courts. The way in which the police received these reports and acted upon them has, in the past, been criticised as clumsy and insensitive, and the number of reports never getting beyond the police has been a cause for concern. Critics started to talk about an unacceptable 'attrition' rate to describe the way in which the police failed to act – decided there was no case to answer or found other reasons to file cases rather than ensure they went forward for prosecution. In turn, the attrition rate was blamed for making many victims of sexual assault decide not to bother reporting it to the police in the first place.

The general feeling in the 1970s was that the police 'did not take reports of sexual assault as seriously as they should have done'. Investigating officers were often unsympathetic men who had little empathy with the 'stories' they were hearing; 'stories' they believed the women made up to get themselves out of various scrapes they should never have got into in the first place. The apocryphal police approach seemed to be 'listen to the story, then drive a coach and horses through it'. Some police surgeons actively tried to research the number of false rape allegations they came across because 'innocent men must be protected against baseless allegations' (MacLean 1979; see also Geis *et al.* 1978).

The end product of attitudes like this was the police decision not even to record a crime having taken place – the practice of 'no-criming'. If they did record it as a crime, it still often resulted in 'no further action' being taken. Either way, it led in turn to an under-reporting of sexual crimes once women realised what they had to face when they did report. Two national events contributed to a challenge to these attitudes.

The spotlight first fell on West Yorkshire police and their search for the serial killer the press called the 'Yorkshire Ripper'. From 1975 onwards, this unknown assailant had started to murder women at regular intervals, with the police seemingly inept and unable to detect him. The early victims were women acting as prostitutes in red-light areas, but in 1977, the chosen victim was Jayne MacDonald, described by the police as an 'innocent' teenager (Burn 1985: 181). The clear upgrading of the investigation after this date, with its blatant message that the murder of the earlier women did not matter as much, was not lost on the British public. After a massive police effort, the 'Ripper' – Peter Sutcliffe – was eventually caught in 1981, almost by accident, by the South Yorkshire Police (Bilton 2003).

The Thames Valley Police were the second police force to find the spotlight of the national media falling on them. Where the West Yorkshire Police were reluctantly in the glare of the lights, the Thames Valley Police had invited a television documentary crew in to film them at work. The series of programmes that resulted were shown in January 1982, and included insensitive police handling of a woman reporting a rape to them. The impact of the film was all the greater because the police obviously knew they were being filmed, but had not thought to change their approach or temper their attitudes of disbelieving the woman. The impression given was that this was a perfectly normal policing technique. The police have not helped themselves with stories of them using confiscated pornographic films for their own police station 'stag' parties (Cox *et al*. 1977: 168), or of male officers sexually assaulting female officers (Hilliard and Casey 1993).

Away from the media, more considered criticism was also coming from the women's movement that had emerged from the 1960s. A sophisticated analysis of male domination and oppression was being backed up by the stories told by women coming to the new network of refuges which were springing up throughout the 1970s (see Chapter 7). In academia, women researchers started to make inroads into a male-dominated criminology to throw light on the poor quality of the policing of sexual assault.

Research commissioned by the Home Office would later find that only 25 per cent of cases of rape reported to the police in 1985 resulted in a conviction. The key points of attrition were identified as the practice of 'no-criming', which helped the 'clear-up' rate because the police could not be accused of failing to clear up a crime that had not happened; the practice of 'no further action' and therefore not proceeding to prosecution; and the down-grading of charges to lesser offences by the time they got to court (Grace *et al*. 1992). Earlier research in Scotland had confirmed a dismal lack of sensitivity and similar levels of decision-making (Chambers and Millar 1983).

The research also clarified the different categories of rape which the police were not identifying and the break-up of the idea that rape was a monolithic form of crime. In practice the police now recognised:

- 'Stranger' rape, where the assailant was unknown to the victim.
- 'Acquaintance' rape, where the complainant and the suspect knew each other casually.
- 'Intimate' rape, where the persons concerned were in a relationship or even married.

Critics argued that this was an artificial categorisation and that the essential element of rape – the lack of consent – was the same whatever the circumstances.

The Home Office responded to the criticisms with two circulars giving advice to chief constables. The first, in 1983, called for an improvement in the investigation of rape allegations, including more sensitive inter-viewing and the need for early medical examinations to allow the victim to get washed and changed more quickly (Home Office 1983). The second, a few years later, addressed the wider crimes of violence towards women and recommended better training for officers, systems to keep the victim informed of the progress of the investigation and the need for separate examination suites for women away from police stations; no-criming was to be exceptional and only when a woman completely retracted a complaint (Home Office 1986a).

The problem with Home Office circulars was that they were just circulars, and were aimed at chief constables. They did not have the status of substantive law and their impact had to trickle down through a male-oriented organisation, which had other priorities to consider and was not always sympathetic to such crimes.

The Police and Criminal Evidence Act 1984 was substantive law (for England and Wales) and did carry provisions that the police could use in tackling violence against women. Section 17 of the Act empowered an officer to enter premises for purposes of saving life and limb, and to arrest for an arrestable offence such as assaults or wounding; however, there is some evidence that the police have not used s. 17 very much (Brown 1997: 36). Section 24 gave the powers for an arrestable offence, which are offences attracting a five-year sentence or more but also includes indecent assault on a woman, and s. 25 introduced the so-called 'protective arrest', where the officer thinks it necessary to prevent injury to another person or to protect a child or other vulnerable person.

The Police and Criminal Evidence Act also introduced new powers to compel a woman victim of violence or sexual assault to give evidence in court against her husband. The new s. 80 promised a way to reduce the number of women who chose to withdraw their complaints, leaving the prosecution high and dry. Later legislation enabled a woman's police statement to be used as evidence in court as an alternative to her attendance (Criminal Justice Act 1988, s. 23).

The police were given further circular advice in 1988 on how they should investigate sexual offences against children. The police had been participating members of local child protection arrangements since 1974, but the new advice came after the Cleveland affair of 1987 and called for better training, joint investigations with social workers where appropriate and, once again, for the provision of separate examination suites away from police stations (Home Office 1988; see also Chapter 7).

The effect of these circulars led some forces to form specialist teams of officers: Domestic Violence Units came into being for investigating offences against women, and Child Protection Units for offences against children. The actual names of the units might vary (e.g. Family Support Unit) and sometimes the two were joined together (e.g. in Northern Ireland, the RUC's CARE Units (Child Abuse and Rape Enquiry Unit)). Some units had uniformed officers, some had non-uniformed detectives or a mixture of both. When another Home Office circular appeared on domestic violence, it was able to note that 'some forces [had] dedicated domestic violence units with specially trained officers', and all chief constables were 'urged to consider setting up such Units where it is practicable and cost effective to do so' (Home Office 1990b: para. 10).

The 1990 domestic violence circular recommended that each force draw up a policy statement to help influence the attitudes and behaviour of officers who are called on to deal with cases of domestic violence. The policy statement was to emphasise the duty to protect victims and children, treat the crime seriously, use powers of arrest, be wary of trying for reconciliation and keep good records to assist policy evaluation (Home Office 1990b: para. 11; see also Scottish Office 1990).

Reports suggested that adult women victims of sexual assault and violence were happier with the new initiatives taken by the police (see, e.g., Adler 1991), but other research suggested there was still work to be done (e.g. Temkin 1999). Domestic Violence Units had improved the knowledge and skills of officers, but they still often felt marginalised by 'mainstream' policing. Separate examination suites and the move of some officers out of police stations had exacerbated this problem, but cultural attitudes of senior managers were also said to be part of the problem:

> We all do our own thing in this position. Nobody would have a clue if I was doing nothing. As it is I'm tearing my hair out ... There is no credibility in dealing with domestic violence as far as my colleagues are concerned ... the uniformed officers just don't want to get involved ... I talk at divisional meetings to inspector rank and below to raise awareness of domestic violence. I still get comments like 'didn't you used to be a policeman?' (Plotnikoff and Woolfson 1998: 11–12).

Yet further guidance in the form of a circular was issued to the police (Home Office 2000c).

The 2000 circular again outlined the action police should take in investigating domestic violence in terms of initial response, the use of bail and support for victims. The police had again to be reminded to come up with force policies on domestic violence and senior officers and managers again reminded to give a lead to this work and accord it some priority. Liaison with statutory and voluntary bodies was encouraged but the police were warned 'not to try and perform the roles of other agencies, in particular counselling roles'; their priority was stated to be protection of the victim and children, if applicable, and where a power of arrest exists, an alleged offender 'should normally be arrested' (ibid.: s. 4).

The 2003 white paper on domestic violence was optimistic that 'in recent years the police have been making strenuous efforts to improve their response to domestic violence' (Home Office 2003a: 25) and that most 'forces now have either specialist domestic violence units or domestic violence co-ordinators' (ibid.). The white paper still felt new powers were needed and these duly appeared in the Domestic Violence, Crime and Victims Bill published in December 2003 (for more details, see Chapter 7).

Returning specifically to sexual offending, research (Harris and Grace 1999) has shown that the reporting of rape increased threefold between 1985 and 1996, and a more receptive attitude on the part of the police had doubtless contributed to this increase. In terms of the categorisations of rape, the main increase was in 'acquaintance' and 'intimate' rape, with the figures for stranger rape staying roughly the same; some researchers have suggested male rapists may deliberately 'find out' details about their victims to get themselves actively into these categories to help any defence they may need (Gregory and Lees 1999: 100). If a man could be filmed on CCTV in a club or pub having amicable conversations with a woman, it could help his defence if that woman later became a victim of rape or sexual assault. Of more concern was the finding that conviction rates were not keeping up with this increase, and the attrition rate in terms of police decisions was still high (Harris and Grace 1999).

Child Protection Units (CPUs) dealing with child abuse suffered the same feelings of marginalisation by their colleagues in 'mainstream' policing. Officers within them might be fully committed and have raised their levels of skill and knowledge, but outside the CPU the allegations continued that it was the 'Andy Pandy Squad' and 'not real police work'. Researchers at the University of Manchester identified possible reasons:

- CPU work was seen as 'a cushy number' because staff worked a 'days and lates' system;
- CPUs were mostly staffed by women officers;
- Within CPUs women officers dealt with the victims, and male officers with the suspects; and
- Work with children was low status and 'unskilled' insofar as 'anyone can talk to children. Can't they?' (Hughes et al. 1996: 13).

CPUs could become isolated and demoralised. One unit worker expressed the lack of interest shown by the senior management, who never came near them: 'It shows in who visits you. We've never had a commander at the Unit, ever. But he visits other places' (ibid.: 16). One police child protection officer was awarded £135,000 in compensation for stress and breakdown caused by no proper support or supervision in her work in the mid-1990s for the Metropolitan Police ('Child protection officer wins depression payout', *Independent*, 27 October 2001).

The Manchester research summarised a common management view: 'They applauded the creation of ... Units as an important advance in the policing of child sexual abuse but most felt that more senior management now believed that "child protection is sorted" and the Units ... therefore, receive little attention "as long as a wheel doesn't come off" ' (Hughes *et al.* 1996: 11). CPUs have, none the less, continued to progress and develop, albeit with ups and downs. Comprehensive record systems of children and families have been developed and used to complement the mainstream systems of the local force. A Department of Health investigation heard complaints that the 'police [were] not always taking this work seriously ... sometimes appearing to sympathise with alleged perpetrators' (Department of Health 1994b: para. 3.25), and others have criticised the over-deployment of women police officers to CPUs, leading to the 'feminisation of policing' within child protection (Adams and Horrocks 1999). But, overall, they have become an institutionalised feature of current policing organisation, work closely with social workers, undertake evidence videoing (see Chapter 5) and are here to stay.

One innovation the police appear to have imposed on social workers is the practice of the 'dawn raid'. If children had to be compulsorily removed from a home because of alleged sexual abuse, an early morning visit might secure evidence that would otherwise be disposed of, and even reveal unacceptable sleeping patterns. Social workers – not, perhaps, known for their early start to the working day – went along with the practice despite misgivings ('Fury over dawn raid', *Social Work Today*, 13 September 1990).

A later ruling of Mr Justice Hollings in the Family Division warned against the practice: 'Early morning removals of children from their home, by police, even though in conjunction with social services, should only be effected when there are clear grounds for believing significant harm would otherwise be caused to the children or vital evidence is only obtainable by such means' (*Re A (Minors)* [1992] 1FLR 439). Later evaluations of police child protection work have noted continuing progress, but have still called for more consistent training and possibly a new core national curriculum for all police child abuse investigators (Davies *et al.* 1995). A report by HM Inspectorate of Constabulary, which pointed out the variation in provision between forces, has recommended that the Association of Chief Police Officers produce a standards-based service to ensure more consistency (HMIC 1999: para. 3.20).

Police Child Protection Units have also often found themselves excluded from investigations into sexual assault on women and children which takes place outside the home. Extra-familial abductions and assaults by strangers acting in public places continue to be the province of the CID or vice squad as though this is 'real' police work rather than child protection work. If anything, a national response is looked to rather than a local CPU one. The archetypal mobile sex offender striking anywhere in the country was the case of Robert Black, convicted in 1994 for a series of abductions and murders of young children in England and Scotland (Clark and Johnston 1994).

The deficiencies of the 'Ripper' inquiries in the 1970s included the realisation that the police, in large-scale investigations, had often been 'overloaded' with information and been unable to see the wood for the trees. An inquiry by HM Inspectors of Constabulary recommended better use of information technology in such investigations (Ackroyd *et al.* 1992: 150–6). The result was HOLMES (Home Office Large Major Enquiry System), a computerised system brought into play for large-scale police investigation involving serious crime (Maguire and Norris 1992: 57–9).

The HOLMES system – and its subsequent updated versions – has been particularly used by the police when investigating sexual crimes committed in institutions such as children's homes and residential schools. These investigations can involve many victims and many abusers ('networks' or 'rings') over a long period of time; many of the victims may now be adults and living miles away from the scene of the crime.

These complex cases of institutional abuse, sometimes involving organised criminal activities, can take up months of police time as officers go through old records of children and staff, links are made and victims and suspects tracked down. Investigations of this kind took place during the 1990s in Leicestershire, Castle Hill School, Shropshire, North Wales children's homes and Cheshire (see Oates 1998 for an account of the latter).

The Waterhouse Report into physical and sexual abuse in the children's homes of North Wales devoted three chapters (Chapters 50–52 and Appendix XII) to the way in which these police investigations were best carried out. The report emphasised the importance of police training to ensure 'appropriate sensitivity' in investigations and the need for 'close liaison between the police and other agencies, particularly social services departments' (Waterhouse Report 2000: para. 5.38). In view of the number of police investigations, it recommended: 'an inter-agency review of the procedures followed and personnel employed in these investigations ... with a view to issuing practical procedural guidance for the future' (ibid.: Recommendation 22). The report thought this guidance should look particularly at the safeguarding and preservation of records and files by both social services departments and the police where there have been earlier investigations, and at how police are to have access to social services' files. The guidance might also usefully look at the sharing of information generally for criminal investigation and child protection purposes (ibid.).

In 1995, the NSPCC had set up the first of its Regional Investigation Units – later renamed as Special Investigation Services – to help the police make sense of the world of residential child care and the circumstances in which this sort of sexual offending is taking place. The local authorities as the main employers in these investigations have to agree to the NSPCC workers coming in and having access to the records (Gallagher 1998).

These police investigations into serious allegations in children's homes going back many years have given cause for continuing concern. One criticism is that the retrospective police investigation – sometimes known as 'trawling' – was actually producing the allegations rather than collecting them: 'Police forces normally spend their time collecting evidence in relation to crimes whose reality no-one doubts. They embark on retrospective investigations, however, without knowing whether the crimes they are investigating have taken place at all' (Webster 1998: 22). Add to this the possibility of victims making false allegations because they believe there may be financial compensation on offer, and we have 'one of the most dangerous developments in methods of police investigations which has ever taken place' (ibid.: 33; see also Webster 1999). The Waterhouse Report, in fact, found little evidence to support the accusation that compensation was a motivating factor (2000: para. 57.31).

The investigations techniques used by the police received more media attention when the courts acquitted David Jones, the manager of a Premiership football club. Jones had been caught up in the police investigation on Merseyside known as Operation Care as he had once worked in a special school ('Former football manager cleared of child abuse charges', *Guardian*, 6 December 2000). One newspaper now revealed that the police were engaged in almost one hundred similar inquiries into past abuse in children's homes and schools ('Serial abuse inquiries "will top 100" ', *Independent*, 8 January 2001).

The concerns prompted the House of Commons Home Affairs Committee to conduct an inquiry into possible miscarriages of justice arising from these investigations. The committee's final report felt the police investigations *were* necessary and the process of 'trawling' was acceptable if there was an initial clear justification. They thought that the courts should give prior approval for any prosecutions to proceed if more than ten years had elapsed after a complainant had reached 21, and that audio or visual recording of statements from alleged victims should be made (House of Commons 2002; the Appendix to this report gave a list of all police institutional abuse investigations in England and Wales between January 1998 and May 2001).

The government's response was relatively muted. It accepted that this was an important area where care was needed, and rejected the word 'trawling' in favour of the term 'dip sampling' to describe these retrospective investigations. The idea of recording complainants was also turned down, as was the idea of having time limits on prosecutions that went too far back. In general the Home Office, while respecting the committee's views did 'not share its belief in the existence of large numbers of miscarriages of justice' (Home Office 2003b: para. 10). By this time the Home Office had also teamed up with the Department of Health to produce new guidance on these investigations (Home Office/ Department of Health 2002) and the Association of Chief Police Officers (ACPO) had produced its own new guidance for officers (ACPO 2002a).

In order to assist people who may have experienced miscarriages of justice in these trials of care workers a group of lawyers formed the Historic Abuse Appeals panel with funding from the Legal Services Commission. One of the panel's solicitors helped to have a verdict quashed on a man sentenced for offences of buggery allegedly committed when he had worked in a children's home some 20 years earlier. Some of the evidence against him had come from a youth who had not been at the home when the defendant had worked there; the man was released after two years of an eight-year sentence ('More cases in doubt as abuse verdict quashed', *Guardian*, 6 February 2004).

Arrest, detention and cautions

As a police criminal investigation proceeds, the actual holding of a suspect at a police station is governed by the time limits set down in the Police and Criminal Evidence Act 1984 (ss. 42–5). The custody officer at the police station ensures that the time limits are kept to, that evidence exists for charging and that the general welfare of the prisoner is seen to. The custody officer will also be instrumental in decisions to charge a suspect and bring him or her before a court, or to release him or her with or without a charge being made; if a charge has been made the release on police bail can have conditions attached to it.

Conditions of police bail of relevance to the suspected sexual offender might be a curfew to remain indoors after a specified time in the evening until a specified time in the morning; an exclusion zone to, for example, stay away from a witness's home or place of work; a requirement not to associate with named people; or a condition of regular reporting to the police station (Bail Act 1976, s. 3, as amended; Police and Criminal Evidence Act 1984, s. 47, as amended). Local authority social services departments are empowered at this point to offer assistance to help a man move out of accommodation where children are still living who have been his suspected victims (Children Act 1989, Sch. 2, para. 5) and, since 1996, courts have also had powers to add 'exclusion requirements' to an Interim Care Order or Emergency Protection Order granted to a local authority (Children Act 1989, s. 38A and s. 44A(2); see also Children (Scotland) Act 1995, s. 76).

Once a police investigation is completed, the 'case file' has to be prepared by them for submission to the Crown Prosecution Service (CPS) for furtherance of the prosecution. This work is normally carried out by the police Administrative Support Unit (ASU), who are responsible for liaison with the CPS and can consult them for advice on whether or not they have sufficient evidence or what is the 'best' charge. One thing the police should not be doing at this stage is taking 'no further action' because they have tried to 'second guess' whether the CPS will take it on to court and decided it is not going to be worth it. 'Gatekeeping' only adds to the police attrition rate and recommendations have been made that they should always pass it through if there is any 'case to answer' (Harris and Grace 1999: 24).

One alternative for the police is for them to issue their own caution as an alternative to a prosecution and necessity of going to court; the use of cautions for sexual offending has sometimes been queried ('Police forces allow rapists to go free with a caution', *The Sunday Times*, 18 February 1996).

The police caution has been an administrative device for the police to deal with the less serious offender who was, perhaps, a first-time offender and seemed unlikely to reoffend. It has been a formal affair delivered by a senior officer and could be brought up and cited in court if there was later reoffending. Sexual offenders have been the subject of police cautioning, but the Home Office guidance on how the police should caution offenders has warned against such practices: 'Cautions have been given for crimes as serious as attempted murder and rape: this undermines the credibility of this disposal. Cautions should *never* be used for the most serious indictable-only offences such as these' (Home Office 1994a: para. 5, emphasis in original). In 1999 New Labour replaced cautions for children and young people with its 'Final Warning Scheme' introduced by the Crime and Disorder Act 1998 ss. 65–6. This scheme allowed the police to administer 'reprimands' and 'final warnings' if the juvenile admitted the offence, the evidence for a prosecution existed and it was felt not to be in the public interest to prosecute. The Association of Chief Police Officers (ACPO) produced Gravity Scores to help officers make decisions on whether or not to use the 'final warning scheme' (Home Office/YJB 2002: Annex D).

Cautions, reprimands and final warnings can all result in an individual being placed on the sex offender register and, to that extent are seen as an appropriate way of dealing with some sex offenders (Sexual Offences Act 2003, s. 80(1)(d); see also Chapter 9). Two juveniles had their names removed from the register by a court when they argued that the police had not told them this would be a consequence of their 'final warning' ('Boys, 15, win fight to get names off sex offender list', *Daily Telegraph*, 30 November 2002). A special form of caution is given to adult women committing street offences (Home Office 1959).

National policing

British policing has always prided itself on being local policing. Local communities had their own forces in what became known as the Anglo-Saxon model of policing. If anything more were needed, local police forces could assist each other through the doctrine of 'mutual assistance'. Centralised policing was otherwise best left to other countries.

This position has been changing slowly. In 1974, a lot of small police forces disappeared by amalgamation into larger regional units and various national units have come into being. The Police National Computer (PNC), which came online in 1974, is the obvious example of a national unit, jointly financed by all 52 local forces to their common benefit. It is an apocryphal story that the PNC was not named the 'National Police Computer' deliberately to downplay the word 'national' by hiding it in the middle.

In 1992 the National Criminal Intelligence Service (NCIS) was formed and in 1997 the National Crime Squad (NCS). These initiatives were both intended to take on 'serious organised crime', and in February 2004 the government announced its intention to amalgamate the two into the new Serious Organised Crime Agency (SOCA) (Home Office 2004a).

The National Criminal Intelligence Service had a Serious Sex Offenders Unit (SSOU) from the outset; it was originally called the Paedophile Section but changed its name in 2000 after the Association of Chief Police Officers had produced its National Serious Sex Offender Intelligence framework.

The sort of information held by NCIS has been described as 'soft' information or intelligence, as opposed to 'hard' verifiable information such as criminal conviction histories. Soft information invariably includes speculative suspicions that cannot necessarily be verified, and does not necessarily relate to any current crime under investigation. Local forces hold similar soft information as intelligence.

This information is controlled and regulated by the Data Protection Act 1998 and the police's own Code of Practice (ACPO 2002b). The police are also bound by the provisions of a Council of Europe recommendation, signed by the British government in 1987, and including the requirement that information on people's sexual behaviour should not be held by the police unless connected to a particular inquiry:

> The [police] collection of data on individuals solely on the basis that they have a particular racial origin, particular religious convictions, sexual behaviour or political opinions ... which are not proscribed by law should be prohibited. The collection of data concerning these factors may only be carried out if absolutely necessary for the purposes of a particular enquiry (Council of Europe 1988: para. 2.4).

The British government, having signed up to this recommendation, then entered a 'derogation' which effectively gave it an exemption from having to abide by para. 2.4. When questioned about this in the House of Commons, the government was quite clear that in its view the paragraph 'Restricts police activities in collecting data on particular groups such as suspected paedophiles [and] could seriously inhibit the police in preventing and detecting crime' (HC Debs 15 October 1990, cols. 721–2). The wider question of police intelligence held on potential sex offenders – and indeed other would-be offenders – held at local and national level, came under the spotlight in the wake of the conviction in 2003 of Ian Huntley for the murder of two children in the Cambridgeshire village of Soham. The Bichard Inquiry took evidence from various quarters about the haphazard way information was kept – or not kept – on Huntley that might have given forewarning of his propensity to commit serious crime and recommended that a national intelligence-sharing system be created (Bichard Inquiry Report 2004).

Whatever the rights or wrongs of holding information on sex offenders or people's sexual behaviour when no particular crime is being investigated, the relationship between NCIS and local forces has not always been harmonious. When local forces have had to contain vigilante crowds, field national press inquiries and offer protection to unwanted child sex offenders, many have wondered where the NCIS Serious Sex Offenders Unit was. In their daily work, CPU officers have asked similar questions: 'NCIS is a waste of time. We need a proper national Intelligence system to assist in tracking paedophiles. The paedophile index? Where is it? Can someone Give me the 'phone number?' (Hughes *et al.* 1996: 31). The introduction of the sex offender 'register' in 1997 (see Chapter 9) answered some of these criticisms but, arguably, left the NCIS SSOU even further out on a limb, because local CPUs could have access to the register without any reference to NCIS. The HM Inspectorate of Constabulary found many forces now compiling their own local paedophile index which, in turn, 'minimised their incentive to update the NCIS database' (HMIC 1999: para. 4.15).

A final criticism of the NCIS Paedophile Section – as it then was – was made by HM Inspectorate of Constabulary, which found the database being held to be mainly on individual offenders. This presented something of a quandary because the NCIS terms of reference require it only to be dealing with 'serious organised crime', which involves two or more participants. On balance the Inspectorate decided to turn a blind eye (HMIC 1997: 20).

Another national database available to all forces is operated away from NCIS by the Derbyshire Constabulary. This is the system known as CATCHEM (Centralised Analytical Team Collating Homicide Expertise Management), which holds data on more than 3,000 child murders committed since 1960, whether solved or unsolved. New entries are made on a pro-forma document with over 200 questions on it, and the idea is to check the probability of the murder being part of a series of crimes (Gibbons 1997).

In 1996 NCIS had begun a review of all possible crimes connected to computers and the emergent Internet. In turn this review – known as Project Trawler – led to the creation of the police National High-tech Crimes Unit (NHTCU), which started operation in 2001. The aim was to track users of child pornography and those adult men who 'groomed' children in chatrooms with a view to possible meetings and sexual abuse. One of the outcomes was the ChildBase initiative to capture images of child pornography and to use the resulting database to find the actual children who were the victims of the crimes being committed in the images (Carr 2003; 'Secret hi-tech dragnet traps paedophiles', *Observer*, 13 July 2003).

International policing

Policing is usually by definition restricted to a given nation-state and police officers are not allowed to operate outside their authorised jurisdictions. In practice, they often have a need to work across national borders with their counterparts in other countries, but this work has to be largely restricted to the communication of personal data on individuals or groups wanted or suspected of crimes.

Increasingly, the dialogue between police forces has become the subject of international treaties and conventions to improve the efficiency and effectiveness of the communications, and the police have formed permanent transnational policing networks (TPNs) to formalise these communications. The two best known TPNs are Interpol (the International Criminal Police Organisation) and Europol (the European Police Office).

The origins of Interpol can be traced back to 1914 and a meeting in Monaco. The organisation has always been non-governmental and strictly by the police and for the police. In 1997, Interpol had a global membership of 177 countries, each with its own Interpol office – known as the National Central Bureau (NCB) – and a head office in Lyon, France.

In the past, Interpol has suffered from a poor image, but of late has transformed itself and now has: ... 'one of the most sophisticated automated search and image transmission systems in the world. It enables rapid reliable and secure exchange of information. NCB's will have access to an enormous store of data' (Benyon *et al.* 1993: 226). The UK's Interpol NCB is located at NCIS in the same building as the NCIS Serious Sex Offenders Unit. At international level, Interpol has a 'Standing Working Party on Offences against Minors', which has in turn produced a handbook of best practice in investigating crimes against children ('Concerns and division over tackling global child abuse', *International Police Review*, 1997: 24–5; Interpol 1997).

Europol has its political origins in the European Union and emerged from the 1991 Maastricht Treaty. As a TPN, it operates just between the EU member states and only deals with serious organised crime from its headquarters in The Hague; in contrast, Interpol will deal with any sort of crime. Europol is 'governed' by the Europol convention, which came into force on 1 October 1998 and includes within it a mandate to deal with organised trafficking in human beings defined as:

[The] subjection of a person to the real and illegal sway of other persons by using violence or menaces or by the abuse of authority or intrigue with a view to the exploitation of prostitution, forms of sexual exploitation and assault of minors or trade in abandoned children (Europol Convention 1995 (as amended), Annex to art. 2).

This mandate was added to the convention after the events of 1996 in Belgium when 200,000 people had demonstrated in the streets of Brussels on 20 October against the crimes of alleged child sex offender Marc Dutroux and the apparent ineffectiveness of the criminal justice system to stop his activities; in 2004 – some eight years on – Dutroux finally came to court to answer his accusers ('Dutroux is given life sentence for child murders', *Independent*, 23 June 2004).

Europol is also involved in work to combat trafficking in human beings, whereby women and children are coerced across international frontiers by organised criminals who force them into prostitution. The extent of such trafficking is hard to define accurately, but the International Organisation for Migration has estimated some 300,000 women a year are trafficked within and into Europe every year (IOM 1998; see also Kelly 2002). The European Union adopted its 'Brussels Declaration' in 2002 as a blueprint for future actions to prevent and prosecute trafficking. Within the UK laws against trafficking have been passed (initially in the Nationality, Immigration and Asylum Act 2002 but now included in the Sexual Offences Act 2003, ss. 57–60).

In London, Europol's UK office is also located at NCIS headquarters alongside the Interpol NCB and the Serious Sex Offenders Unit. Such proximity gives the UK a direct link into policing directed against sexual offending that has an international dimension to it; sexual offending that includes so-called 'sex tourism'.

'Sex tourism' was the term coined to describe the practice of men from developed industrialised countries, such as the USA, Japan and western Europe, travelling to less developed countries, such as Thailand, Sri Lanka and the Philippines, to use prostitutes – including child prostitutes. Sometimes these men were taking advantage of permissive legislation in these countries and sometimes the law was simply not enforced as it should have been. Non-governmental organisations such as ECPAT (End Child Prostitution, Pornography, Trafficking) and the Preda Foundation started to raise international awareness, culminating in the 1996 Stockholm World Congress against Commercial Sexual Exploitation of Children (Kane 1998; Alexander *et al.* 2000).

In the UK, a private member's bill promoted by Lord Hylton in 1995 sought to enable prosecution of men in this country for crimes against children committed abroad. The government appreciated the 'admirable aim' of the bill, but felt unable to support it because it failed to recognise the difficulties of British police investigating crime abroad and the inability of courts to compel foreign witnesses to appear before them. As a first step, the government preferred the approach of trying to prevent men going overseas for purposes of sex tourism, but did produce an extensive consultation paper to see what further options existed (Home Office 1996b).

In 1996, the government supported another private member's bill, which sought to allow the prosecution in Britain of people who conspired, or incited others, to commit sexual offences against children abroad. The Sexual Offences (Conspiracy and Incitement) Act 1996 was aimed at the organisers of travel arrangements for purposes of sex tourism; the Act was implemented from 1 October 1996.

Interpol had by this time already formed its own Standing Working Party on Offences against Minors (Interpol General-Secretariat 1995). Sex tourism was high on its agenda, and when London hosted one of the working party's regular meetings in November 1995, police officers from Sweden explained how they had successfully prosecuted a man in Sweden for sexual offences against children committed abroad (NCIS 1995; Home Office 1996b: Annex D).

When the Sex Offenders Act 1997 was implemented on 1 September 1997, most of the attention was on the introduction of the 'sex offenders register' in Part I of the Act (see Chapter 9). Part II of the Act, however, gave UK courts jurisdiction to prosecute those who travel abroad to commit sexual offences against children; the offence had to be a crime in both countries, and the Act applied only to British citizens or people resident in the UK, but the penalties for a crime would be the same as if the offence had been committed in the UK.

The police have developed their expertise to act under the 1997 law, and NCIS Serious Sex Offenders Unit officers have visited the Philippines to improve practical police co-operation (Drew 1997). In 1998 some of this work came to fruition in Operation Osprey, an inter-agency exercise led by the British Customs and Excise Service involving Belgium, Canada, Finland, Germany, Ireland, Luxembourg, the Netherlands and the USA. A reported ten arrests were made and a further 37 individuals became the subject of further investigation (Collins 1999). The first prosecution under the Act was against a man who had offended in France ('Camp site owner jailed for sex assaults on girls', *Independent*, 22 January 2000).

Further action against 'sex tourism' was instigated by changes to the sex offender register in 2001 which required registrants to tell the police when they were travelling abroad (Criminal Justice and Court Services Act 2000, Schedule 5, para. 4) and by the Foreign Travel Orders introduced by the Sexual Offences Act 2003 which effectively bans certain people from going abroad at all (see Chapter 9).

The Forensic Science Service

The UK's Forensic Science Service offers a support service to the police with a staff of over 1,200 scientists and their assistants at six regional laboratories. The service has traditionally analysed the contents of drugs and other evidence from scenes of crime, including the analysis of body fluids such as blood and semen.

One scientific development to help police investigations of sexual offending has been the use of DNA (deoxyribonucleic acid) to help identify and detect offenders. The technique had been pioneered by academics at the University of Leicester in the mid-1980s, but early attempts to apply the findings in practice were hampered by the need to get an optimum size of sample and a means of storage; police were also lacking any powers to compel suspects to give a suitable sample that could be then matched with samples found at a scene of crime or on a victim (Dovaston and Burton 1996).

The government moved to take these obstacles out of the way of the police. The Criminal Justice and Public Order Act 1994, Part IV made amendments to the Police and Criminal Evidence Act 1984 to give the police powers to take samples from suspects for DNA analysis in the course of investigations; if no proceedings followed, the samples were to be destroyed. The same amendment allowed the police to take DNA samples from offenders who had been convicted of a 'recordable offence' from 10 April 1995 onwards (a 'recordable offence' is an offence punishable with imprisonment or is otherwise specified in law, and 10 April 1995 was the day that the UK's National DNA Database opened for business). Similar police powers were introduced north of the border by the Criminal Procedure (Scotland) Act 1995.

The National DNA Database was based in Birmingham as part of the Forensic Science Service. All DNA samples were to be recorded on a computer for rapid search and retrieval. The database was set up in record-breaking time, which the Director of the Forensic Science Service described as: 'a tribute to the dedication, drive and expertise of the staff of Birmingham who have produced an operational service in five months' (Home Office 1995a). The 1996 Home Office consultation document on the 'Sentencing and Supervision of Sex Offenders' saw the

National DNA Database as a prime means of detecting sex offenders, and also of deterring them from committing crime in the first place. The document proposed building up the database by taking samples from convicted sex offenders currently in custody (Home Office 1996a: paras. 39–40).

The scientific accuracy of DNA tests had by now already been questioned (see, e.g., McLeod 1991; Brown 1993) and various rumblings were coming from the police about their dissatisfaction with the existing service they were getting from the national database (see, e.g., 'Police anger over database disorder', *The Times*, 10 September 1996), with some even wanting to break away and use a private company for DNA testing ('Police back rival DNA tests after Home Office delays', *Observer*, 14 April 1996). Despite these difficulties the consultation document proposals were accepted, and legislation duly followed to allow the taking of DNA samples from sex offenders in custody in the form of the Criminal Evidence (Amendment) Act 1997 and the Crime and Punishment (Scotland) Act 1997, s. 48 (see also Bagshaw 1997).

The taking of DNA samples in other circumstances remained a voluntary affair, and in particular where the police wanted to take samples from, perhaps, hundreds of men in a given area to help resolve a local sex crime; the samples were destroyed if not helpful to the inquiry (see, e.g., 'DNA checks for 200 in hunt for rapist', *Yorkshire Post*, 18 April 1998). The police have usually described this as 'eliminating' large numbers of men from their inquiry, with the men who choose not to 'volunteer' inevitably becoming the subject of a different and more intensive form of investigation.

Concerns about DNA samples started to emerge when it became apparent that the police were not being as rigorous as they should have been in destroying unwanted samples. A man suspected of a burglary in 1998 had given a DNA sample which should have been destroyed when he was acquitted of the charge. The sample was not destroyed but instead was used by the police to match him to an earlier crime of rape; the subsequent prosecution collapsed because of its reliance on an illegally held DNA sample. The Attorney General appealed against the decision all the way to the House of Lords which overturned the earlier judgements and allowed the conviction (*R* v. *B Attorney-General's Reference No. 3 of 1999*, *Times Law Report*, 15 December 2000; Pickover 2001).

Her Majesty's Inspectorate of Constabulary had been asked to look into the question of unlawfully held DNA samples and found 'many thousands of samples, perhaps as many as 50,000, may be being held on the database when they should have been taken off' (HMIC 2000: para.

2.23; 'DNA samples kept illegally', *Guardian*, 1 August 2000). The inspector wondered if 'perhaps the time has come to revisit the legislation' (HMIC 2000: para. 2.31). The Criminal Justice and Police Act 2001, ss. 82–3 duly legalised these illegalities as long as the retention of samples was only for purposes of the prevention or detection of crime; samples gathered in 'elimination' exercises could also be kept if the donor had given written consent.

The popularity of DNA testing has given it a momentum of its own. By January 1997, the National DNA database held more than 112,000 samples (HC Debs 20 February 1997, col. 1029), by 1999 this had risen to over 600,000 ('FSS clears DNA backlog', *Policing Today*, 5 (2) June 1999: 7), and reached two million in June 2003 ('Police DNA log now has 2m profiles', *Guardian*, 26 June 2003). In September 2000 the Prime Minister himself had said he wanted three million people to have their samples on the national database by 2004 ('3m face DNA tests in Blair crime initiative', *Guardian*, 1 September 2000). The Criminal Justice Act 2003, s. 10 enabled the police to take DNA samples from any arrested person.

The Council of the European Union wants all EU member states to develop their own National DNA Database within a standardised format to facilitate international exchange, and cites action against child sexual exploitation as a reason for doing this (Council of the European Union 1997). The Police Superintendents' Association of the UK has even suggested that we start talking about a National DNA Database for the entire population ('Police urge talks on DNA database for whole nation', *Guardian*, 6 May 1998).

Summary

Most policing activities in the UK, whether for action against sex offending or any other form of crime, take place at a local level. Criticisms of police attitudes towards the investigation of sexual crime (especially by women criminologists) have caused them to rethink their approach to this work over the last 20 years. Specialist units have been developed to improve the level of intervention required and to make the police more sensitive to the needs of women and child victims of sexual offending.

What has also become increasingly important to the policing of sex offenders – at local, national and international levels – is the obtaining, collating and analysis of 'personal information' on sex offenders. This increased importance of the database has been facilitated by the advances in information technology and the ability to retrieve or exchange data in 'real time', and by the specific advances in the use of DNA sampling technology in order to identify more easily the person to whom 'personal information' should be attached. These advances bring with them issues of civil liberties which will be returned to later.

Chapter 5

The search for justice – at court

When the police have completed their investigations and they believe they have a case to present to court, that case is passed to the Crown Prosecution Service (England and Wales), the Procurator Fiscal (Scotland) or the Director of Public Prosecutions (Northern Ireland). In turn, these prosecuting agencies make their own independent decisions, based on the evidence given to them, as to whether a prosecution is worth while in terms of a likely conviction or whether it is in the 'public interest' to prosecute.

Prosecuting

The Crown Prosecution Service came into being following the recommendation of the 1981 Royal Commission on Criminal Procedure that the investigation of crime should be separated from the prosecution of offenders; the aim was to end the system of police prosecutions that had been in place almost since the origins of police forces. The Prosecution of Offences Act 1985 created the Crown Prosecution Service (CPS), which started work in October 1986.

From the outset the new CPS had a rocky ride. Police resentment at the loss of their prosecuting role and the new demands the CPS was putting on them led to allegations of police obstruction. A 1992 Parliamentary Select Committee inquiry into what was going on aired some of the grievances and, by the mid-1990s, the CPS was more established as a part of the criminal justice system. Further reform was recommended by the Glidewell Report, which called for greater decentralisation, better liaison arrangements with the police and the ending of the division of work into magistrates' and Crown Court (Glidewell Report 1998).

Aside from organisational problems has been the CPS's seeming inability successfully to prosecute sex offenders. A critical report from two women's groups accused the CPS of regularly failing to prosecute rape crimes, and stated that the chances of justice for women and children who were raped or sexually assaulted were unacceptably low. The report also highlighted what it saw as the reluctance of the CPS to get involved in sex offending where there was a 'domestic' context or the alleged attacker was known to the women: 'Those who have been convicted of a crime they didn't commit are not the only victims of a "miscarriage of justice"; so are those who have suffered a crime and are denied justice' (WAR/LAW 1995). Others picked up on the fact that the first version of the Code for Crown Prosecutors had a clear statement that:

> sexual assaults upon children should always be regarded seriously, as should offences against adults, such as rape, which amount to gross personal violation. In such cases, where the Crown Prosecutor is satisfied as to the sufficiency of the evidence there will seldom be any doubt that prosecution will be in the public interest (CPS n.d.: para. 8(vi)(b)).

Yet in the revised (1994) edition, this statement had been deleted (CPS 1994). The CPS felt obliged to put out a further explanation that 'sexual assaults … are always serious offences and the service is committed to making sure that appropriate action is taken' (CPS 1996: para. 5.2).

At the heart of the criticism was the CPS practice of 'downgrading' charges in order to improve the chances of a successful prosecution, or the outright 'discontinuance' of proceedings because there was insufficient evidence, irregularities in its collection or it was not, somehow, in the public interest. It all added up to a continuation of the process of attrition started by the police.

Research examining possible reasons for discontinuance has found 'evidential difficulties' to be a prime reason for the CPS not taking a case to court. Evidential difficulties include:

- Victims who are vulnerable in terms of age or learning disabilities;
- The victim's previous sexual history;
- A prior relationship between victim and offender which can test the victim's willingness to give evidence – if the victim pulls out, the prosecution has no case;

- When the case turns on the issue of 'consent' it is often one person's word against another (Harris and Grace 1999: 26; see also ' "Lenient" sentence for rapist sparks outrage', *Independent,* 20 July 2001).

The CPS's instructing of barristers has been favourably commented upon by researchers, with perhaps only the need for more case conferences between them, and involving the police, to seek out any evidential weaknesses (Harris and Grace 1999: 36). The CPS maintains that it always tries to proceed to court and only 'discontinue' with 'very good reason' (ibid.: 25); court proceedings were more likely to take place when the victim was slightly older or very young (ibid.: 27).

A further study of the prosecution of sexual offenders was made in 2002 jointly by the Inspectorates of the CPS and the police. They found a possible CPS preoccupation to discontinue cases where a conviction may be difficult to secure and a need to be more proactive in seeking information and building a case. The idea of specialist prosecution teams for sexual offending was floated (HMCPSI/HMIC 2002). The CPS responded with its own consultation exercise on ways forward (CPS 2003).

One particular problem for the CPS and the police was the sex offender's access to witness statements or video recordings (see below) which made out the case against him. Any accused person is entitled to know what that case is, and the accused sex offender, therefore, has a right to see statements, videos, medical reports or photographs. The problem arose when the offender then chose to distribute this evidence amongst his friends as a form of pornography in its own right; an action that not only diminishes the seriousness of the offences, but also reasserts the defendant's position as being not so deviant after all.

In response to reports that this was happening (see, e.g., 'Rape statements used as porn', *Guardian,* 26 October 1989; 'Violated by prying prison eyes', *Independent,* 3 August 1990), the Home Office produced a consultation document suggesting a regime of supervised access to statements, photographs and videos that could not be removed (Home Office 1991). The Royal Commission on Criminal Justice recommended that instructing solicitors should take the lead in safeguarding the confidentiality of those disclosed documents (RCCJ 1993: 129), but reports that the Law Society was having to investigate its own members for hanging on to them were not encouraging ('Solicitor failed to return sex tape', *Daily Telegraph* 17 September 1996).

The Home Office's jointly produced guidance on the video-recording of children's statements had advised that defendants should be supervised when viewing them and sign an undertaking not to show them to other people (Home Office/Department of Health 1992: para. 4.12), but its 1996 consultation document went further and proposed making it a criminal offence to misuse victim statements (Home Office 1996a: paras. 78–86). Liberty responded by reminding the Home Office of the part non-disclosure had played in recent miscarriages of justice and cited the Prison Rules and the Criminal Justice Act 1988, s. 160, covering possession of indecent photographs, as possible alternative existing measures (Liberty 1996: paras. 60–5).

The Sexual Offences (Protected Material) Act received its Royal Assent on 21 March 1997, and in future, defendants could only view disclosed documents through their legal representatives and under supervised conditions; if they were not represented, supervision would be by the police or a prison governor; offenders against these conditions could be fined or imprisoned for a maximum of two years.

The court hearing

The conduct of court proceedings involving sexual offenders has been the subject of much debate. Women victims have felt more on trial than defendants, and the problem of an adult court hearing evidence from a child victim has been equally fraught. In the adversarial criminal justice system that we have, with the presumption that the accused is 'innocent until proved guilty', the onus is on the prosecution to prove the allegations made and on the defence to mount a reasonable opposition to the allegations.

Before we reach the point of conviction and sentence, however, the court will probably require an adjournment whilst the case against the accused is put together and, similarly, a defence is mounted. At this point, the court must make decisions about whether or not to remand on bail or remand in custody until the case is ready to proceed. The Bail Act 1976, s. 4 gave the defendant a 'presumption' of bail unless circum-stances dictate otherwise. Bail is not, however, available to a man charged with rape or attempted rape if he already has previous convictions for similar offences (Criminal Justice and Public Order Act 1994, s. 25). If he has no previous convictions but still faces the same charges, any court granting bail, where the prosecutor has raised objections, must state the reasons for giving bail in open court (Bail Act 1976, Sch.1, Part 1, para. 9A).

In non-rape cases, bail may be refused if the court is satisfied that there are substantial grounds for believing further offences would be committed, witnesses would be interfered with, the defendant was already on bail when the new allegations occurred or the offence is considered to be particularly serious.

If a remand on bail is granted over a remand in custody, conditions may be attached to that bail. As with police bail, this might include a condition of residence, a curfew, an exclusion zone which the defendant must not enter, a condition of non-association or the regular reporting to a specified police station (Bail Act 1976, s. 3, as amended). Research does exist from South Wales on how bail conditions were imposed, and the findings suggest it is a haphazard process that is sometimes used excessively; at worst it has been described as 'a pre-conviction punishment' (Hucklesby 1994).

In 1975, the case of *R* v. *Morgan* ([1975] 2 All ER 347) generated a wider debate on the definition of rape and the defence of the man believing he had consent; questions were also raised about the extent to which a woman's previous sexual behaviour could be admitted as a defence. A committee of inquiry was formed to look into these questions and recommended accordingly (Heilbron Committee 1975).

The Sexual Offences (Amendment) Act 1976 duly followed, with a clarification of the definition of rape and the meaning of consent; in future, juries were to consider whether there were reasonable grounds for a man to *believe* he had consent.

The Sexual Offences Act 2003 tried to clarify the law on rape even further. Section 1 of the Act now states that an offence is committed if the defendant does not *reasonably believe* that the complainant consents to the relevant sexual act. Whether a belief in consent is *reasonable* is to be determined having regard to all the circumstances, including any circumstances 'A' has taken to ascertain whether 'B' consents.

Section 2 of the 1976 Act prohibited any references to the woman's previous sexual conduct being used by a man in his defence; judges could still allow such references on application if they considered it might reveal previous similar conduct to the present proceedings.

The implementation of s. 2 in the courts has been criticised as still failing to protect a woman and making her feel that it is she who is actually on trial. Lawyers find ways round it and judges seem too ready to give exemptions (see, e.g., Adler 1987; Temkin 1993; Lees 1997). An unsuccessful attempt was made to strengthen s. 2 with amendments to the Criminal Proceedings and Investigations Bill; the opposition spokeswoman accused the government of 'indifference, and [refusing] to do anything about one of the most serious problems besetting women in the criminal justice system' (HC Debs 12 June 1996, col. 363). In Scotland, there was a change to the law in the Criminal Procedure (Scotland) Act 1995, ss. 274–5.

In time, the Youth Justice and Criminal Evidence Act 1999 did attempt to tighten up on the exemptions with its s. 41 that further restricted what evidence about an alleged victim's sexual behaviour could be considered relevant in a trial for sexual offences; such evidence would now only be admitted where it is relevant to the alleged offence.

Section 41 came into force in December 2000 and within weeks was being challenged in the House of Lords as being a breach of a defendant's right to a fair trial ('Curb on sex queries in rape trials challenged', *Guardian*, 6 February 2001). The Lords ruled that s. 41 would not be a breach of the European Convention on Human Rights, Article 6 (the right to 'a fair trial') and for the time being the section remains in place (*R v. A* [2001] UKHL 25, 3 All ER 1; see also Temkin 2002: 224–5).

The Sexual Offences (Amendment) Act 1976, s. 4 had introduced anonymity into rape proceedings for the first time for both complainant and defendant. The press could still report proceedings, but not identify any of the parties involved during the trial. The Sexual Offences (Amendment) Act 1992 extended these provisions on anonymity to sexual offences hearings other than rape. Reporting restrictions may be lifted by the judge if, for example, the accused wants publicity to encourage witnesses to come forward.

Some defendants in rape cases have been known to dismiss their defence lawyers and conduct their own defence. This move has been permissible in British law, but has been criticised in rape cases because it puts the alleged offender in a face-to-face confrontation with the victim for purposes of cross-examination. Much publicity was given to the defendant Ralston Edwards in 1996 when he cross-examined his victim for several days, causing her great distress and taking her through the ordeal a second time; Edwards reportedly wore the same clothes in court as he had worn during the attack ('Inquiry into rape victim's court ordeal', *Daily Telegraph,* 23 August 1996).

A subsequent Home Office Interdepartmental Working Group recommended a mandatory prohibition on unrepresented defendants personally cross-examining the complainant in cases of rape and serious sexual assault (Home Office 1998a: para. 9.39); such a prohibition already existed where the victim was a child (Criminal Justice Act 1988, s. 34A). The Youth Justice and Criminal Evidence Act 1999 in due course introduced measures that prohibited a defendant from personally cross-examining a witness who was the victim of an alleged sexual offence; powers were given to the court to appoint a legal representative to 'test the evidence' if the defendant refused to be represented.

The same Act also allowed an adult complainant in a sexual offence case to give evidence from behind a screen, or through a live TV link, or to have the public gallery cleared before giving evidence. Evidence could also be pre-recorded on a video tape. The Act gave a presumption in favour of all these 'special measures' in sexual offences should the victim ask for them.

On a non-statutory level, adult complainants could also be helped by the Witness Service; this is a service offered by Victim Support. It is a voluntary service to help vulnerable witnesses through the ordeal of appearing in the Crown Court and there are plans to extend the service to other courts. The Witness Service helps people before, during and after their attendance at court, explaining the layout of the court, going on 'familiarisation' visits and talking through the experience afterwards (see Home Office 1998a: Annex G).

Children's evidence

Sexual offending against children has required special provisions for children to give evidence. Child witnesses had first received protection when the 1987 Criminal Justice Bill brought in clauses to introduce 'live' video-links, allowing the child to speak to the court from a room removed from the court environs.

At the same time, the Home Office published a short briefing on the subject and invited comments on 'live' links and pre-recorded video tapes, whilst still holding that it is: 'an unfettered right to cross-examine by counsel of the defendant's choice [and this], is an indispensable part of our system of justice' (Home Office 1987: para. 27). The balance that had to be struck was between the needs of children in court as witnesses and the traditional safeguards afforded the accused by English criminal procedure. The resulting Criminal Justice Act 1988, s. 32 introduced live video links for children under 14 to give their evidence to court. The same Act (s. 34) also abolished the need for a judge to give a warning when a child's uncorroborated evidence had been heard; s. 34 did not extend to sexual offences, but the later Criminal Justice and Public Order Act 1994, ss. 32–3 did make that extension. The Government held back from introducing any pre-recorded tapes being used as evidence in court.

Chelmsford Crown Court achieved the distinction of being the first UK court to hear evidence on a live video-link from a 13-year-old victim in a rape case; the judge reportedly tried to put the girl at ease with the words 'What's it like being on the telly, not too bad?' ('Girl gives evidence by video link', *Independent* 10 January 1989).

Other experiments to improve the taking of evidence from children were more problematic. The use of 'anatomically correct' dolls in order that children could demonstrate what had happened to them were one device that had a short reign of fashion. The judiciary urged caution in their use when it was pointed out that children who had not been sexually abused might be just as willing to undress the dolls and show interest in their genitalia. In the same vein, social workers were warned not to refer to children's statements about sexual abuse as 'disclosures' because of its connotations of being 'factual' when the statements clearly might not be.

The arguments for and against pre-recorded testimony continued. The Children's Legal Centre was in favour ('CLC calls for legal reform to end trauma for child witnesses', *Childright,* October 1987) and the Cleveland Report considered the question, but made no recommendation other than to comment that 'not all the judiciary are in favour of video recording' 1988: para. 12.47). The chair of the Criminal Bar Association was clear that the defence lawyer's right to cross-examine a witness must be preserved, and challenged what he described as the 'dangerous climate of opinion that children virtually never lie about sexual abuse' ('Warning on child video evidence', *Guardian,* 2 October 1989).

Meanwhile, the Home Office had decided to convene an advisory group, to be chaired by Judge Thomas Pigot, to look more closely at the practical implications of allowing pre-recorded video statements. The resulting Pigot Report came down in favour of pre-recording and even the possibility of pre-recording a cross-examination (Pigot Report 1989). In Scotland, the Scottish Law Commission had recommended that trials be adjourned to enable a child's evidence to be obtained using a video-recorded deposition procedure; it preferred this idea to any live links.

The Criminal Justice Act 1991 allowed the use of pre-recorded video interviews of children in the Crown Court and Youth Courts of England and Wales, by amending the Criminal Justice Act 1988 with a new s. 32A; for sex offences, 'children' were defined as under 17 and live links were also extended from under-14s to those under 17. The Act did not implement the Pigot Report recommendation of pre-recorded cross-examination and, even with the present pre-recorded provisions, a child had to be available for follow-up cross-examination. Other new departures included allowing a child to give unsworn evidence and a faster 'transfer' system from magistrates' to Crown Court without lengthy committal proceedings.

The Home Office and the Department of Health jointly produced a Memorandum of Good Practice for police officers and social workers who would be conducting the video sessions. Advice was given on the need to go at the child's pace, and to avoid leading questions and other interventions that might render the tape inadmissible as evidence (Home Office/Department of Health 1992). In practice, the police, with their understanding of criminal evidence and the needs of the criminal courts, invariably took the lead over social workers when it came to videoing, and today the taking of recordings is a standard part of the investigation of sexual offences against children, even if many of them never get used in court (see, e.g., Davies *et al.* 1995). The Pigot Report recommendation that cross-examinations could be pre-recorded remained unimplemented, despite continuing proposals that it should be (see, e.g., CPSI 1998: Recommendation 45).

The NSPCC led a campaign in 1996 called 'Justice for Children', which sought to make it easier for children to give evidence in the intimidating atmosphere of the court, and followed this up with a video entitled 'A Case for Balance', which demonstrated examples of good practice when a child is a witness.

In due course New Labour picked up the baton and fulfilled its 1997 Manifesto promise to improve protection for victims in rape and sexual offence trials. The Inter-departmental Working Group that had examined procedures for rape victims (see above) had also looked at the position of children (Home Office 1998a) and this in turn led to new law in the form of the Youth Justice and Criminal Evidence Act 1999, and later to new guidance replacing the Memorandum of Good Practice on videoing children's evidence (Home Office, 2002a).

The Youth Justice and Criminal Evidence Act 1999 introduced 'special measures' for the child witness and, as for adults, these included the screening of witnesses, the giving of evidence through live links and the giving of evidence (including cross-examinations) on a pre-recorded video-tape. The Act made such 'special measures' automatically available for children (under 17), who were also deemed competent to give evidence as long as they understood the questions asked and could give answers capable of being understood.

Reports to court

Following a conviction, the courts may read a Pre-sentence Report (PSR) prepared by a probation officer or social worker before deciding on the appropriate sentence. In the 1960s, when the idea of reports to the criminal court started to take off, the reports were variously referred to as the Social Inquiry Report or simply Court Reports. The officers writing them had a relatively free hand in how they wrote them and what recommendations they made on possible sentences, but by 1990 the government was clear that we needed to take 'a fresh look at the purpose, content and format of these reports' (Home Office 1990a: para. 3.10).

When 'National Standards' were introduced in 1992, they gave advice on how to write PSRs. The focus was to be on the offence rather than the offender, and the views of victims were to be included in the report. The National Standards were revised in 1995, 2000 and again in 2002, when they stated that the report should 'assess the consequences of the offence, including what is known of the impact on any victim, either from the CPS papers or from a victim statement where available' (Home Office 2002c: B7). Another addition to the PSR, made by the revised National Standards, was the inclusion of a risk assessment. Every PSR is now expected to:

- Contain an assessment of the offender's likelihood of re-offending based on the current offence, attitude to it, and other relevant information;
- Contain an assessment of the offender's risk of causing serious harm to the public;
- Identify any risks of self harm (ibid.: B9).

The PSR requirements to look at the victims' views and to include a risk assessment clearly have direct relevance for PSRs on sex offenders.

Sentencing

Following a finding of guilt (a conviction) and the reading of any reports to the court, a sentence has to be decided upon. Before moving on to the principles of sentencing, we cannot pass by without at least a reference to the sexist comments of some of our judges presiding over cases of sexual assault. Sampson, for example, cites the almost caricature comments of Mr Justice Wild in 1982:

Women who say no do not always mean no. It is not just a question of saying no, it is a question of how she says it, how she shows it and makes it clear. If she doesn't want it she only has to keep her legs shut and she would not get it without force and there will be marks of force being used (1994: 57).

and in 1993, the requirement in Newport Crown Court that a 15-year-old assailant be given three years' supervision and pay £500 compensation to the victim 'to give her a good holiday' (*ibid.*: 46; see also Pattullo 1984 for a litany of similar pronouncements). Hopefully, such comments are slowly being consigned to history as enlightenment falls upon the judiciary. In any event, judges in the Crown Court must now complete a Serious Sexual Offences course and be authorised by the Lord Chief Justice before taking such cases; this is known as getting their 'sex ticket'.

In general terms, the principles of sentencing require a balance between the need for retribution and 'just deserts' against the need for reform and the reduction of future crimes. Unless the criminal law specifies certain sentences, the autonomy of the courts in passing sentences means that there is no such thing as a 'correct' sentence for a given offence, and the belief that the courts have got it 'wrong' yet again is the staple diet of our tabloid press. The principles of sentencing that we do have are based on the precedent of previous court judgements and especially those of the Courts of Appeal. Since 1980, the Court of Appeal has periodically produced what are called 'guideline' judgements, which go beyond the confines of the immediate case to guide other courts coming across similar cases.

A guideline judgement on the appropriate sentencing in cases of rape was made in the case of *Billam* in 1986. The judgement defined five types of rape, graded in order of seriousness, and laid down the initial sentence that could then be raised or lowered depending on aggravating or mitigating factors (*R v. Billam* (1986) 82 Cr App R.347):

1   The least serious was a rape in wholly exceptional circumstances and the sentence might be non-custodial.
2   A single rape with no aggravating factors should lead to five years' imprisonment.
3   A single rape with aggravating factors (e.g. two or more men acting together, a break-in to the victim's home, etc.) should lead to eight years' imprisonment.
4   Multiple rape should lead to 15 years' imprisonment.
5   Multiple rape with 'perverted' or 'psychopathic' tendencies should lead to life imprisonment.

The aggravating factors that might raise these sentences included additional violence, use of a weapon, careful planning or a very old or very young victim; the mental or physical effect on a victim could also be taken into account. Mitigating factors would include a guilty plea, which reduced the victim's need to be in court.

The *Billam* guidelines were followed closely in 1987 during the sentencing of offenders in what became known as the 'Ealing vicarage rape'. The sentences were immediately picked upon by the press as being too lenient, and later research has revealed that the courts thereafter (until 1991) chose to depart from the guidelines in favour of their own heavier sentences. For the researchers, 'the Billam judgement is not shaping sentencing practice in the way intended ... [and] raises the issue of the value of current guideline judgements' (Ranyard *et al*. 1994).

The Criminal Justice Act 1988 had introduced to British law the concept of an appeal being made against a sentence considered too lenient, and the first use of this section was against a custodial sentence of three years for a man who had pleaded guilty to three counts of incest on one daughter and one count of incest with another daughter. The sentence was duly increased to six years, but at the same time, Lord Lane, the Lord Chief Justice, now set out sentencing guidelines for similar crimes.

In summary the maximum penalties were:

- Incest by a man with a girl under 13 – life imprisonment.
- Incest by a man with a girl over 13 – seven years.
- Attempted incest by a man with a girl under 13 – two years.
- Attempted incest by a man with a girl over 13 – two years.
- Incest by a woman – seven years.
- Attempted incest by a woman – two years (*Attorney-General's Reference (No. 1 of 1989)* [1989] WLR).

The guidelines were not universally welcomed, as they suggested that differing ages meant that the offender might see this as an 'excuse' for his own behaviour. The founder of Childline, Esther Rantzen, said they implied 'the offender is a victim and can be seduced by a child. It detracts from the fact that it is a man's responsibility not to abuse children, whatever the age' (cited in 'Project to educate judges on handling child sex offenders', *Independent*, 25 September 1989).

Lord Lane responded later the same year with yet further guidelines, making the point that all incest cases varied and were often very complex; the sentencing judge was reminded that 'a rigid arithmetical approach' was not the best way to approach them. Aggravating factors might include threats and violence, psychological damage to the child and the frequency of offending; mitigating factors were a plea of guilty, otherwise good relationships or where the girl had had previous sexual experience (*Attorney-General's Reference (No. 4 of 1989)* (1989) 11 Cr App R (S) 517). Two years later, this guidance was extended to cover nonincestuous sexual offending (*Attorney-General's Reference (No. 4 of 1991)* (1992) 13 Cr App R (S) 182).

The Sentencing Advisory Panel established by the Crime and Disorder Act 1998 to offer advice to the courts produced its own guidance in May 2002 on the offence of rape (SAP 2002) and instigated a consultation exercise on aspects of sentencing all sexual offenders when the Sexual Offences Act 2003 became law (SAP 2004).

The government was approving of these guideline judgements but was now prepared to impose its will on the courts to ensure sentencing was based on the seriousness of the offence – the 'just deserts' approach took over from an earlier treatment-orientated approach which had become increasingly discredited. The 1990 white paper explained the new way forward:

> The recent guideline judgements, such as those on rape [and] incest … have provided much clearer guidance on how sentencing decisions should be reached … To achieve a more coherent and comprehensive consistency of approach in sentencing, a new framework is needed for the use of custodial, community and financial penalties (Home Office 1990a: para. 2.3).

Part of this new framework was to give the courts new powers to sentence according to seriousness of offence, and, in so doing, to sentence persistent violent and sexual offenders to longer custodial sentences. The target was 'a small number of offenders who became progressively more dangerous and who are a real risk to public safety' (ibid.: para. 3.13). The new sentencing provisions duly appeared in the Criminal Justice Act 1991.

The 1991 Act was clear that offences of violence or sexual offending could always result in a custodial sentence (s. 1(2)(b)) and that that sentence could be lengthened if necessary in order to protect the public from serious harm (s. 2(2)(b)); in the latter case the court had to explain in open court why it was of the opinion that s. 2(2)(b) applied (s. 2(3)). The Act also defined what it meant by sexual offences (s. 31(1)) (see Figure 1.1 in Chapter 1).

Before deciding on the length of a custodial sentence, the court had to consider a Pre-sentence Report (1991 Act, s. 3(1)). There was no require-ment in the Act that the court should consider medical reports, but the Court of Appeal has stated its opinion that 'if the danger is due to a mental or personality problem, the sentencing court should, in our view always call for a medical report before passing sentence under section 2(2)(b)' (*R v. Fawcett* (1995) 16 Cr App R (S) 55).

The just-deserts approach to sentencing takes little or no account of 'treatment' approaches; the whole idea has been to replace the 'treatment' approach which begged too many questions about 'what works?' The Criminal Justice Act 1991, however, coincided with the launch of the Prison Service 'sex offender treatment programmes'; the problem occurred when the programmes turned out to be longer than the sentences. The more serious sex offenders got treatment because of their longer sentences, but the less serious did not (Henham 1998).

In the light of mounting public disquiet about sex offending, and in keeping with the just-deserts approach, the government now moved forward with its most controversial proposals for sentencing. This was the idea for automatic life sentences for persistent violent or sexual offending, based on the American model of similar legislation, where it was known as 'three strikes and out' (a reference to the sport of baseball). For this country, the recommendation was that it be just 'two strikes and out' (Home Office 1996c).

One of the underlying premises of the proposal was the political policy slogan that 'prison works' and that public confidence in sentencing needed to be restored; treatment approaches had fallen into disrepute. The arguments against it were that longer sentences did not deter crime, prisons would become overcrowded, and sexual offenders who have already been convicted would now be more likely to kill their victims, either to avoid detection, or because they know they are going to get a life sentence whether or not they kill. Some believed the idea was inconsistent with the interests of justice and the judiciary, which was having its discretion to consider individual circumstances taken away.

The government view prevailed and the Crime (Sentences) Act received the Royal Assent on 21 March 1997. Section 2 of the Act requires a court to impose an automatic life sentence for a second serious violent or sexual offence, unless there are exceptional circumstances relating to either offence or offender which justify it not doing so. If a life sentence is not imposed, the court must state what the exceptional circumstances are in open court.

It was left to the incoming Labour government of 1997 to think about the 'two strikes and out' laws, which they eventually implemented. They also introduced the 'extended sentences' of the Crime and Disorder Act 1998 for sexual offenders (see Chapter 6) and the new sentence of 'imprisonment for public protection' in the Criminal Justice Act 2003. The 'imprisonment for public protection' could be for a first-time offender and would follow a statutory risk assessment (Criminal Justice Act 2003, s. 229); an offender – even a first-time offender – could be detained indefinitely.

Summary

Within the courts, the response to sexual offending has been another arena for male attitudes to predominate and, possibly, obstruct the course of justice. The Crown Prosecution Service and the judiciary have been criticised for their unhelpful attitudes and steps have been taken to try to improve matters.

The importance of information on the offence and the offender in the form of Pre-sentence Reports has been enhanced to help sentencers make their decision; part of these reports should now make an assessment of the risk that the offender might pose in the future. At the same time as these measures have sought to help sentencers, the politics of 'law and order' have resulted in heavier sentences being made 'automatic' for some sexual offending and thereby at the same time reducing any discretion the courts might have.

Chapter 6

The search for justice – punishment or treatment?

After a conviction and sentence have been made, the sex offender passes into the hands of those agencies of the penal system charged with dealing with him or her. These post-court services are the probation and social services and the custodial or prison elements of the criminal justice system. Together, they provide for community sentences, custodial sentences or a period of community supervision following a custodial sentence.

Community sentences

In theory, the whole range of community sentences including community punishment orders, attendance centre orders, curfew orders, supervision orders and community rehabilitation orders are available for sex offenders. Here we look at the two most significant orders – the community rehabilitation order (formerly the probation order) and the supervision order.

Offenders put 'on probation' in the 1970s and 1980s were supervised by probation officers very much according to the professional judgements of those officers. Probation officers received a social work education that gave them various forms of 'intervention' or 'treatment' which they could apply. The offender had had to consent to be 'on probation' and was expected to report to his or her probation officer as required and to receive the officer on home visits. Failure to comply might lead to a reappearance in court for 'breach' of probation.

At the end of the 1980s, this relatively laissez-faire approach came under attack. The government wanted probation orders to be community sentences of the court rather than – as they currently appeared – an alternative to sentence. It also wanted to promote probation as a form of 'punishment in the community' rather than just treatment, and for the probation service to work more collectively with other agencies in the community: 'one to one work with individual offenders will not usually be enough to turn [offenders] away from crime' (Home Office 1990a: para. 7.20).

The Criminal Justice Act 1991 introduced the probation order as a sentence of the court for the first time, and defined it as:

(a) securing the rehabilitation of the offender; or
(b) protecting the public from harm from him or preventing the commission by him of further offences (Powers of Criminal Courts Act 1973, s. 2(1), as amended by the Criminal Justice Act 1991).

Accompanying these legal changes was the introduction of 'National Standards for the Supervision of Offenders in the Community' to challenge individual approaches of different probation officers; the National Standards appeared in 1992, and have been subsequently updated (Home Office 2002c). In 1995, the government removed the necessity to receive a social work education to become a probation officer; for probation the age of professionalism was giving way to the age of managerialism (see Worrall 1997: esp. Part 2).

The Criminal Justice Act 1991 allowed a range of 'additional requirements' to be attached to probation orders, including requirements as to activities to be undertaken, activities to be refrained from, attendance at a probation centre, a specified residence, or treatment for drugs and alcohol dependency. These additional requirements could last for a maximum of 60 days, but this could be extended in the case of the sex offender (Criminal Justice Act 1991, Sch. 1, Part II, para. 4); offenders could also be required to attend for psychiatric treatment.

The sort of 'additional requirements' a sex offender might expect to see were as follows:

• Not to seek or undertake employment which would bring the offender into direct contact with young people under the age of 16 years.
• Not to receive visits at home from any child under the age of 16 years and not to visit the home of any child without prior permission from the supervising officer.

- Not to undertake any leisure pursuit or hobby which brings the offender into direct contact with any child.
- To reside where approved by the supervising officer.
- To attend group work sessions to confront sex offending, and not to have any contact with group members between sessions, etc. (see HMIP 1998a: para. 4.31).

In Scotland, the system is slightly different because the local authority social work departments carry out probation order supervision as part of their criminal justice social work services. Orders last between six months and three years and can include any 'requirement' which is 'conducive to securing the good conduct of the offender or for preventing a repetition of the offence or the commission of a further offence' (Criminal Procedure (Scotland) Act 1995, ss. 228–9).

The Criminal Justice and Court Services Act 2000 centralised the probation service by introducing the National Probation Service. It was this Act which also renamed probation orders as community rehabilitation orders.

Supervision orders are, broadly speaking, the same as the old probation orders – community rehabilitation orders – but for young offenders. In fact, they have in the past, arguably, been less structured than probation orders, requiring the supervisor only to 'advise, assist and befriend' the offender. Various additional requirements can be included in a supervision order (Children and Young Persons Act 1969, s.12, as amended) and the expectation that supervisors will abide by the National Standards have more recently increased the standing of the supervision order. Supervision orders have usually been the province of local authority social workers, and the probation service has taken on probation orders; the introduction of Youth Offending Teams in 1999 has led to a legal relaxation of any clear-cut demarcation in this respect (Crime and Disorder Act 1998, s. 71(5)).

The purpose of a community sentence, including both the community rehabilitation order and supervision orders has been defined by the Home Office as being to:

- provide a rigorous and effective punishment;
- reduce the likelihood of re-offending;
- rehabilitate the offender, where possible;
- enable reparation to be made to the community; and
- minimise risk of harm to the public (Home Office 2002c: C7).

Within that punitive framework supervision then seeks to:

- address and reduce offending behaviour;
- challenge the offender to accept responsibility for the crimes committed and their consequences;
- contribute to the protection of the public;
- motivate and assist the offender towards a greater sense of personal responsibility and discipline;
- aid re-integration as a law abiding member of the community; and
- be arranged so as not to prevent the offender from being readily available to seek or take up employment if unemployed, nor conflict with an offender's entitlement to benefit, nor disrupt the working hours of an employed person, or the education of an offender in full-time education and to take account of religious and cultural requirements (ibid.: C8).

Achieving compliance and ensuring enforcement of orders and any additional conditions have become progressively more central to super-visory work over the last decade; probation officers, in particular, have been encouraged to be tougher and to return offenders to courts more readily if in breach of orders (ibid.: D21ff), and the additional use of technology like 'lie detectors' has been put forward as an idea to help supervision of sex offenders ('Sex offenders may face lie detector tests', *Guardian,* 28 May 2004).

Supervisors can carry out individual one-to-one work with the offender or, increasingly, can become 'case managers' who involve others in different parts of the work. Specialist workers with sex offenders carry out both 'direct' and 'indirect' work as advisers to colleagues. Community-based treatment for sex offenders can be group-work carried out on an interdisciplinary basis by probation, social services and voluntary agencies (ACOP 1996). The Home Office has commissioned an independent evaluation of these community-based treatment programmes through its Sex Offender Treatment Evaluation Project (STEP) study. Reports have generally been favourable, but variation between programmes has been noted, as well as their strong and weak points:

> While offenders became more able, after treatment, to admit to having planned their sexual offences and have an improved appreciation of their offence antecedents, there was little evidence that they had developed skills to cope with 'risk' situations in the future (Beckett *et al.* 1994; see also Barker and Morgan 1993).

The use of hostels run by the probation service for housing offenders, including sex offenders, is seen as an extension of supervision arrangements rather than simply a form of housing. Staff there can monitor and make risk assessments which are constantly discussed with the probation officer. The problem has been, in recent times, the reluctance of hostels to take on sex offenders when they know it will cause public disquiet in their local community and ultimately could distract them from carrying out their work with other offenders (see, e.g., HMIP 1998a: paras. 4.67–4.73).

In 1997, public anxiety was heightened when the Home Office took the unusual step of releasing figures to show that a high number of people charged with serious crimes, including murder, were already under the supervision of the probation service. The figures were described as a 'damaging blow to the probation service' and as prompting 'fresh concern about the level of supervision carried out by officers' ('One in eight accused of murder is on probation', *The Times*, 2 July 1997). There has been subsequent speculation that this disclosure by the Home Office was deliberately engineered to embarrass the probation service and 'soften up' any resistance it might offer to the spreading use of electronic monitoring, or tagging, of offenders (Brownlee 1998: 122).

Whatever the truth of the matter, HM Inspectorate of Probation was able to report more positively the following year with the publication of a thematic report on the supervision of sex offenders. High levels of 'rigour' and 'vigilance' were noted with just a few gaps, such as the lack of provision for adolescent sex offenders and a lack of integration with prison treatment programmes, to take away from the overall good impression (HMIP 1998a). Home Office Minister Joyce Quinn said: 'This report is a testament to the dedication and professionalism of probation staff and sends a clear and reassuring message to the public that sex offenders are being supervised to an excellent standard in the community' (Home Office 1998b; see also Home Office 1999c). Not that the probation service could now relax, as the Home Office now made its push towards more 'effective supervision' using 'evidence based' practice (HMIP 1998b; Home Office 1998c). Probation services were invited to nominate successful projects, including projects working with sex offenders, as 'Pathfinder Projects'. These were to be evaluated and approved by a new Joint Prison and Probation Accreditation Panel and the results of the successful projects disseminated across the country (Home Office 1999d).

Another adjunct to supervision has emerged from technological innovations which allow for the electronic monitoring or tagging of offenders; from the start, sexual offenders were seen as candidates for tagging (see 'Rapists tagged for life', *Today*, 27 July 1989). When electronic monitoring originally became a possibility, there was talk of it being used in its own right as a stand-alone technique. Today, there is a consensus that it needs to be accompanied always by appropriate supervision arrangements (Whitfield 1997).

Experiments with the electronic tagging of offenders had been tried in 1989–90 and again in 1995. Systems generally worked on the basis of a person being subject to a curfew requiring him or her to be at home during certain hours of the day, and this requirement could be confirmed by a monitor permanently attached to the wrist or ankle (the Personal Identification Device (PID)) and equipment placed in the home (the Home Monitoring Unit (HMU)), which 'reported' to a local control centre. The first experiments had proved problematic, but later experiments, in Reading, Manchester and Norfolk, looked more promising (Mair and Mortimer 1996) and in late 1997, the government announced plans to extend the use of tagging to Suffolk, Middlesex, West Yorkshire and Cambridgeshire. The same announcement foresaw an extension to its use from straight supervision to those on bail, fine defaulters, juveniles and persistent petty offenders; the legal arrangements were put into the Criminal Justice Act 1991, s. 13 and the Crime and Punishment (Scotland) Act, s. 5 (Home Office 1997a).

Further developments for tagging might include using technology already in use for mobile phones to devise systems for tracking offenders across wider geographical areas, rather than just confirming their whereabouts at a given point ('500 paedophiles to be tracked by satellite tags', *Observer*, 21 September 2003). In the case of sex offenders, the piloting of so-called 'reverse-monitoring' systems might also offer new options. In the USA, reverse-monitoring has been tried in domestic violence cases, giving the potential victim – usually a woman – a device in her home that is triggered off by the approach of a person who is tagged. It is not too fanciful to imagine, for example, a school having such a device to give warning when a tagged sex offender comes within a certain range of it (see Whitfield 1997: 111–12).

Other uses of technology have been proposed, including the identifying of sex offenders by scanning the unique pattern on the iris of the eye (Home Office, 2002b: para. 23).

Custodial sentences

Sex offenders in prison have traditionally been given a rough ride. For many years they were offered no particular treatment programmes, were widely despised by other prisoners and received open hostility if their victim had been a child.

Invariably, the prison service has had to class them as 'vulnerable prisoners', while other prisoners class them as 'nonces':

> hostility towards 'nonces' from 'straight' prisoners is routine. It is usually expressed in straightforwardly vehement moral terms ... to emphasise a sense of frustration at having to share their living space with men whose crimes they consider monstrous. By tradition 'nonces' are expected to know their place and keep out of the way of 'straight cons' (Sparks *et al.* 1996: 179).

In more colourful language, Coggan and Walker have described how direct action may be taken against the 'nonce' with prison officer collusion:

> [the] sex offender runs considerable risk of being attacked with razor blades, hot fat or boiling water, invariably while prison officers are conveniently looking in another direction ... in many instances it is the prison officers themselves who have provoked the assaults by passing on to the attacking prisoners details of the offence for which a newly arrived prisoner was sentenced (1982: 119).

Faced with such a threatening environment, the sex offender, as a 'vulnerable prisoner', has often had to be 'removed from association' with other prisoners for his own protection; this used to be done under Prison Rule 43 which became Rule 45 under the revised Prison Rules introduced 1 April 1999 (S.I. 1999, No. 728).

No one has been very happy with this need to segregate certain offenders, and the Home Office has been pursuing a low-key 'integrationist' policy to try to keep them in normal locations, or to develop Vulnerable Prisoner Units (see Sparks *et al.* 1996: 205 and Chapter 6).

The propensity for the sex offender to turn in on himself in the face of constant harassment and bullying has also been noted. Suicides and self-inflicted injury have been a recurring factor of prison life. The prison service has tried to address the problem and has given guidance to officers on suicide risk indicators; one such indicator being 'a conviction for homicide, sexual offences or offences against a child' (HM Prison Service 1989: para. 8).

What many in the prison service wanted was some systematic treatment programmes for sex offenders. Some programmes did exist, but it was all a bit hit and miss. The Home Office actually claimed as many as 60 programmes existed at the end of the 1980s, but 'they have failed to mention that "treatment" in this respect might simply mean the provision of social skills training by a part time teacher for an hour, once each week' (Seven 1991). What was needed was a fully worked out strategy.

The prison service strategy for sex offenders, including their treatment, was unveiled in June 1991. The main features of the strategy were to:

- hold sex offenders in fewer prisons to enable consistency of approach, effective use of skills and resources in working with them and the promotion of a safe and supportive environment to counter the worst excesses of violence towards them;
- provide Sex Offender Treatment Programmes (SOTPs);
- give priority to treatment for those likely to represent the greatest risk to the community on their release; and
- assess which prisoners are most in need of treatment in terms of previous offending patterns.

The SOTPs were to be of two kinds, with a 'core programme' for most offenders and an 'extended programme' for the more serious offenders. Both programmes were to be built around group work based on cognitive-behavioural principles to reduce the risk of offending (HM Prison Service 1991; Guy 1992).

The prison service has put a lot of effort into its SOTPs to make them meaningful and practical. Teams of staff involving psychologists, probation officers, prison officers and others are carefully selected and trained, and the programmes are monitored for 'programme integrity' to ensure that they are delivered as designed.

Most work has taken place on the 'core programmes', which, in the light of experience, were revised in 1994 and are due for further revision at the time of writing. The core programmes were seen as a 'responsibility-building' strategy, which may not 'cure' sex offenders, but should develop their self-control and help them recognise situations where offending might take place. Men with a mental illness, insufficient intelligence or assessed as having 'severe personality disorders' were debarred from the programme (HM Prison Service 1996: 2).

The extended programmes were for those who had normally completed the core programme, but needed extra help for, for example, an inability to control anger or manage stress. The extended programmes were seen as part of a resource-building strategy.

Other programmes have been added since the strategy was first drawn up. The 'booster programme' was a follow-up to the core programme for prisoners coming into the last 12 months of their sentence and needing some revision of key treatment concepts and a rehearsal of their relapse prevention plan. An 'adapted core programme' has also been designed to help those prisoners with learning and communication difficulties (HM Prison Service 1998).

Evaluation of the prison service SOTPs offered to child sex offenders has found evidence of success. As the prison service itself had predicted, an outright 'cure' was never a realistic possibility but the SOTPs did make some progress:

- there was an increase in the level of admittance of sexual offending behaviour;
- offending attitudes were reduced and there was more awareness of the impact on victims;
- overall levels of social competence were increased;
- 67% of the sample evaluated were judged to have shown a treatment effect; and
- longer-term treatment programmes produced better results (Beech *et al.* 1998).

One controversial element of work with sex offenders in prisons was the use of the device known as the penile plethysmograph (PPG).

Staff assessing sex offenders, either in advance of a treatment programme or during a programme, have sometimes used a PPG. This device consists of a loop of rubber tubing containing a mercury column which is placed around the subject's penis. Instruments monitor the electrical resistance of the mercury as the subject's penis volume increases in response to stimuli he is shown. The PPG had been used by medical staff at Wormwood Scrubs Prison between 1970 and 1981, when questions were asked about the ethics of its use. The Prison Reform Trust has described it as 'a degrading breach of human rights' ('Doubts cast on "sex crime" tests in prisons', *Independent,* 24 August 1995; see also PRT 1995).

Post-custodial supervision

Arrangements for leaving prison have long included an element of 'early release', accompanied by a form of continued supervision. Earlier we noted the Victorian ticket-of-leave system and the Borstal innovation of licensed release. For most of the twentieth century prisoners were given 'remission' on their sentences and since 1967 'parole' arrangements allowed prisoners to be released 'early'. Not everyone has been happy with these arrangements and confusion has sometimes set in. The populist argument has been that prisoners are getting out 'too early' and that 'five years' or 'life' should mean what it says. These arguments become more forcibly expressed when a prisoner so released commits further offences.

The Criminal Justice Act 1991 tried to clarify the arrangements for England and Wales with its philosophy of a sentence being part custodial and part community based. The offender was not getting out early, but was still having a form of 'punishment' in the community by having his or her freedom curtailed by continued supervision. For either an Automatic Conditional Release (ACR) or a Discretionary Conditional Release (DCR) prisoner, the period of post-custody supervision could be extended if the original offence was a sexual offence (Criminal Justice Act 1991, s. 44). The decision would need to have been made by the judge in open court, perhaps on the advice of a probation officer through a Pre-sentence Report (Home Office 2002c: B.10; see also Home Office *et al.* 1995: para. 2.33; HMIP 1998a: paras. 4.14–4.17).

The Crime and Disorder Act 1998 amended s. 44 of the 1991 Act because of worries that sexual offenders were not getting sufficient periods of time under supervision after being released from custody; it introduced arrangements for 'extended supervision'. The 1998 Act gave courts the power to impose extended sentences (other than life sentences) on violent and sexual offenders, with the sentence being conceived as an aggregate of two elements – the 'custodial term' and the 'extension period' of supervision under licence. The maximum length of the extension period is ten years for sex offenders and five years for violent offenders and is, therefore, a significant development of post-release supervisory arrangements for prisoners considered 'high risk' (Crime and Disorder Act 1998, ss. 58–66 (England and Wales) and ss. 86–88 (Scotland); now Powers of Criminal Courts (Sentencing) Act 2000, s. 55). Discharge arrangements exist in Scotland to allow for the early release of short-term prisoners (under four years) with the possibility of a 'supervised release order' covering the last part of their sentence; the courts must stipulate the need for this order at the time of passing sentence. That such extended supervision might be necessary was reaffirmed by research suggesting reoffending could go on over a long period (Cann *et al.* 2004).

Life sentence prisoners are subject to a different release system. Life sentences are classified as either 'mandatory', 'discretionary' or 'automatic'. A mandatory sentence is fixed by law and gives the judge no discretion; it applies in cases of murder. Scotland has a similar mandatory life sentence for a second serious offence in the Crime and Punishment (Scotland) Act 1997, s. 1. A discretionary life sentence is usually given for serious violent or sexual offences, and automatic life sentences for a second serious violent or sexual offence (Crime (Sentences) Act 1997, s. 2).

All life prisoners may be liable for early release and follow-up licence or supervision in the community. Whatever the precise legal circumstances of a prisoner's release, it falls to the probation service – or in Scotland the social work department – actually to fulfil the supervision. All prisoners may also be liable to 'extra licence conditions' being added on to their supervision arrangements. The imposing of extra licence conditions is made after discussion between the supervising authorities and the prison governor or Parole Board.

The 1995 edition of the National Standards listed the sort of conditions that could be insisted on, and these included conditions of particular relevance to sex offenders:

- not to engage in any work or other organised activity involving a person under a given age, either on a professional or voluntary basis;
- not to reside in the same household as any child under a given age; or
- not to seek to approach or communicate with family members including children without permission of the supervising officer (Home Office *et al.* 1995: s. 7, Annex A).

Particular note was to be taken of child protection issues during these discussions (ibid.: paras. 7.20–7.21, 7.24). The 2002 edition of the National Standards is less specific on the conditions and the child protection issues.

The decision to add on extra licence conditions for sex offenders is made after an assessment of the prisoner's progress in custody and the likelihood of any continuing risk he may pose. The decision also takes into account the views of the offender's victim or victims.

In the late 1980s, pressure was starting to build that victims should know when an offender was due for release from prison, and should have their views taken into account regarding any post-custody conditions imposed on the offender. The aim was to remove any possibility of the victim accidentally bumping into the offender in the same street when they did not even know he had been released. In 1993, a 14-year-old boy had committed suicide in Mid-Glamorgan when he found out that his sexual assailant was coming out of prison ('Boy hanged himself over fear of sex offender's release', *The Times* 11 November 1993).

An unsuccessful attempt was made to amend the Criminal Justice and Public Order Act 1994 to make it a statutory requirement to notify victims of release dates (HC Debs, 28 March 1994, cols. 747–56). Instead, reformers had to content themselves with administrative guidance that this should be done.

Victims were to be contacted during the initial part of an offender's prison sentence and given general information about likely timescales of custody and release considerations. Nearer to the time of release, they were to be contacted again and invited to comment on any conditions of release which might be imposed. The victim had to accept that a prisoner was entitled to know the grounds on which release conditions are decided, but in exceptional circumstances the victims' concerns could be withheld (Home Office 1995b; see also Home Office 2002c: C3; ACOP/ Victim Support 1996).

Before a child sex offender leaves prison, a check is made on the home address he says he will be going to live at to ensure the safety of any children who may be living there. The system whereby this is done applies to anyone who has committed *any* offence against a child and not just sexual offences. In effect, the systems cover any offence against a child listed in Schedule 1 to the Children and Young Persons Act 1933, giving the offender the shorthand name of being a 'Schedule 1 offender'. A similar list in Scotland, started by the Children and Young Persons (Scotland) Act 1937, is now contained in Schedule 1 to the Criminal Procedure (Scotland) Act 1995, and for Northern Ireland in Schedule 1 to the Children and Young Persons Act (Northern Ireland) 1968 (see Figures 6.1–6.3). The Sexual Offences Act 2003 has required the extension of all of these lists to account for the new offences (see Figure 6.1).

The origins of these checks on home arrangements can be traced back to the 1960s, when a Home Office circular confirmed that the police would notify local authorities when a person was convicted of incest, a sexual offence from the list of 'Schedule 1 offences' or any offence involving cruelty or ill-treatment of a child, whenever it was believed a child at risk was still living in the household; the notification took place whether or not the sentence was a custodial one.

The circular also revealed that it had been the practice 'for many years' to notify local authorities when people convicted of incest offences were leaving prison; the circular now widened the categories of offenders and extended the provisions to those receiving non-custodial sentences (Home Office 1964: para. 6–7).

These systems were reviewed in 1975 after the death of another child at the hands of her parent. John Auckland from South Yorkshire had served time in Durham Prison after killing his 15-month-old daughter in

Common law offences

- The murder of a child or young person under 18.
- Common assault and battery.
- False imprisonment.
- Kidnapping.

Offences against the Person Act 1861

s.1 Murder of a child under 18.

s. 4 Conspiring or soliciting to commit murder.

s. 5 Manslaughter of a child or young person under 18.

s. 11 Administering poison or wounding with intent to murder a child under 15.

s. 23 Maliciously administering poison so as to endanger life or inflict grievous bodily harm on a child under 18.

s. 27 The abandonment or exposure of a child under 2 so as to endanger its life or health.

s. 56 Child stealing or receiving a stolen child.

Infant Life (Preservation) Act 1929

s. 1 Child destruction.

Children and Young Persons Act 1933

s. 1 Cruelty to (including assault, ill-treatment or neglect) a person under 16.

s. 3 Allowing a person under 16 to be in a brothel.

s. 4 Causing or allowing a person under 16 to be used for begging.

s. 11 Exposing a child under 7 to risk of burning.

s. 23 Allowing a person under 16 to take part in a dangerous performance.

Infanticide Act 1938

s. 1 Infanticide.

Suicide Act 1961

s. 2 Aiding, abetting, counselling or procuring the suicide of a person under 18.

Figure 6.1 Offences listed in Schedule 1 to the Children and Young Persons Act 1933 ('Schedule 1 offences') in England and Wales.

Sexual Offences Act 1956

s. 1   Rape (or attempted rape) of a girl aged under 18.

s. 2   Procurement (or attempted procurement) of a girl under 18 by threats.

s. 3   Procurement of a girl under 18 by false pretences.

s. 4   Administering drugs to a girl under 18 to obtain or facilitate intercourse.

s. 5   Intercourse (or attempted intercourse) with a girl under 13.

s. 6   Intercourse (or attempted intercourse) with a girl between 13 and 16.

s. 7   Intercourse (or attempted intercourse) with a mentally deficient girl under 18.

s. 10 Incest (or attempt to commit incest) by a man against a female, where the victim is under 18.

s. 11 Incest (or attempt to commit incest) by a woman, where the victim is under 18.

s. 12 Buggery (or attempt to commit buggery) with a person under 18.

s. 13 Indecency between men where one or both is under 18.

s. 14 Indecent assault on a girl under 18.

s. 15 Indecent assault on a male under 18.

s. 16 Assault with intent to commit buggery.

s. 19 Abduction of an unmarried girl under 18 from parent or guardian.

s. 20 Abduction of an unmarried girl under 16 from parent or guardian.

s. 22 Causing (or attempting to cause) prostitution of a girl under 18.

s. 23 Procuration (or attempted procuration) of a girl under 18.

s. 24 Detention of a girl under 18 in brothel or other premises.

s. 25 Permitting a girl under 13 to use premises for intercourse.

s. 26 Permitting a girl between 13 and 16 to use premises for intercourse.

s. 28 Causing or encouraging prostitution of, intercourse with, or indecent assault on, a girl under 16.

Protection of Children Act 1978

s. 1   Indecent Photographs of Children.

Criminal Justice Act 1988

s. 160 Possession of indecent photographs of children.

Figure 6.1 Continued

Child Abduction Act 1984

s. 1   Abduction of a child by a parent.

Sexual Offences Act 2003

Any offence against a child or young person under any of the following sections of the Sexual Offences Act 2003 (replaces offences under the Sexual Offences Act 1956):

s. 1   Rape.
s. 2   Assault by penetration.
s. 3   Sexual assault.
s. 4   Causing a person to engage in sexual activity without consent.
s. 5   Rape of a child under 13.
s. 6   Assault of a child under 13 by penetration.
s. 7   Sexual assault of a child under 13.
s. 8   Causing or inciting a child under 13 to engage in sexual activity.
s. 9   Sexual activity with a child.
s. 10   Causing or inciting a child to engage in sexual activity.
s. 11   Engaging in sexual activity in the presence of a child.
s. 12   Causing a child to watch a sexual act.
s. 13   Child sex offences committed by a child or young persons.
s. 14   Arranging or facilitating commission of a child sex offence.
s. 15   Meeting a child following sexual grooming, etc.
s. 16   Abuse of position of trust: sexual activity with a child.
s. 17   Abuse of position of trust; causing or inciting a child to engage in sexual activity.
s. 18   Abuse of position of trust: sexual activity in the presence of a child.
s. 19   Abuse of position of trust; causing a child to watch a sexual act.
s. 25   Sexual activity with a child family member.
s. 26   Inciting a child family member to engage in sexual activity.
s. 30   Sexual activity with a person with a mental disorder impeding choice.
s. 31   Causing or inciting a person, with a mental disorder impeding choice, to engage in sexual activity.
s. 32   Engaging in sexual activity in the presence of a person with a mental disorder impeding choice, to watch a sexual act.
s. 33   Causing a person, with a mental disorder impeding choice, to watch a sexual act.
s. 34   Inducement, threat or deception to procure sexual activity with a person with a mental disorder.
s. 35   Causing a person with a mental disorder to engage in or agree to engage in sexual activity by inducement, threat or deception.

Figure 6.1 Continued

Sexual Offences Act 2003 (continued)

s. 36   Engaging in sexual activity in the presence, procured by inducement, threat or deception, of a person with a mental disorder.

s. 37   Causing a person with a mental disorder to watch a sexual act by inducement, threat or deception.

s. 38   Care workers; sexual activity with a person with a mental disorder.

s. 39   Care workers; causing or inciting sexual activity.

s. 40   Care workers: sexual activity in the presence of a person with a mental disorder.

s. 41   Care workers: causing a person with a mental disorder to watch a sexual act.

s. 47   Paying for the sexual services of a child.

s. 48   Causing or inciting child prostitution or pornography.

s. 49   Controlling a child prostitute or a child involved in pornography.

s. 50   Arranging or facilitating child prostitution or pornography.

s. 52   Causing or inciting prostitution for gain.

s. 53   Controlling prostitution for gain.

s. 57   Trafficking into the UK for sexual exploitation.

s. 58   Trafficking within the UK for sexual exploitation.

s. 59   Trafficking out of the UK for sexual exploitation.

s. 61   Administering a substance with intent.

s. 62   Committing an offence with intent to commit a sexual offence (if intended offence is against a child).

s. 63   Trespass with intent to commit a sexual offence (if intended offence is against a child).

s. 66   Exposure.

s. 67   Voyeurism.

Attempt, conspiracy, incitement, aiding and abetting, counselling or procuring in relation to any of the above offences.

Other offences:

Any other offence involving bodily injury to a person under 18.

Figure 6.1 Continued

Criminal Law (Consolidation) (Scotland) Act 1995

s. 1   Incest.

s. 2   Intercourse with a step-child.

s. 3   Intercourse of a person in position of trust with a child under 16.

s. 5   Unlawful sexual intercourse (or attempted intercourse) with a girl under the age of 16 years.

s. 6   Indecent behaviour towards a girl aged between 12 years and 16 years.

s. 7(1)   Procuring unlawful sexual intercourse or for the purpose of prostitution.

s. 7(2)(3) Procuring by threats, etc.

s. 8   Abduction of a girl, or unlawful detention with the intent to have sexual intercourse.

s. 9   Permitting a girl under the age of (a) 13 and (b) 16 to use premises for sexual intercourse.

s. 10   Causing or encouraging the seduction or prostitution, etc., of a girl under the age of 16 years.

s. 12   Allowing a child (aged between 4 years and 5 years) to live in a brothel.

s. 13   Procuring or being party to the commission of a homosexual act in certain circumstances (i.e. person under 16).

Children and Young Persons (Scotland) Act 1937 (as amended by the Sexual Offences (Scotland) Act 1976

s. 12   Cruelty to a child or young person under the age of 16 years.

s. 15   Causing or allowing persons under 16 years of age to be used for begging.

s. 22   Exposing children under 7 years of age to risk of burning or scalding.

s. 33   Prohibiting of persons under 16 yeas of age taking part in performances endangering life or limb.

Any other offence involving bodily injury to a child under the age of 17 years.

Any offence involving the use of lewd, indecent or libidinous practices or behaviour towards a child under the age of 17 years.

Figure 6.2 Offences listed in Schedule 1 to the Criminal Procedure (Scotland) Act 1995 ('Schedule 1 offences') for Scotland.

Common law offences

- The murder or manslaughter of a child or young person.
- Infanticide.
- Aiding, abetting, counselling or procuring the suicide of a child or young person.

Offences against the Person Act 1861

s. 27   Abandoning a child. Exposing a child whereby life is endangered.

s. 55   Abduction of a girl under 16 years of age or if a child or young person is involved:

s. 42   Common assault or battery.

s. 43   Aggravated assault on females and boys under 14.

s. 52   Indecent assault on a female.

s. 61   Sodomy, which is intercourse by rectum.

s. 62   Attempted sodomy, assault with intent to commit same, or any indecent assault upon a male, which is attempting the intercourse described above and includes the indecent assault for that purpose.

Criminal Law Amendment Act 1885

s. 2(1)   Procuring – taking a female being a child or young person away against her will for the purpose of sexual intercourse with any person anywhere.

s. 2(2)   Procuring – taking a female being a child or young person away against her will for the purpose of making her a prostitute.

s. 2(3)   Procuring a child or young person to leave UK to become an inmate of a brothel.

s. 2(4)   Procuring a child or young person to leave place of abode to become an inmate of a brothel.

s. 3(1)   Procuring as described at above by threats or intimidation.

s. 3(2)   Procuring as described at above by deceit, false pretences, etc.

s. 3(3)   Procuring as described at above by using drugs.

s. 4   Sexual intercourse with a girl under 14 years.

s. 5   Sexual intercourse with a girl under 17 years.

s. 6(2)   Inducing a girl under 17 years to resort to premises for sexual activity.

s. 7   Abducting a girl under 17 years for the purposes of sexual intercourse.

Figure 6.3 Offences listed in Schedule 1 to the Children and Young Persons (NI) Act 1968 ('Schedule 1 offences') for Northern Ireland.

s. 8(1) & Unlawful detention for sexual purposes of any girl under 17
(2) years in any premises or in a brothel. Taking away victim's clothes or other property would amount to detention.

s. 11 A male committing an act of gross indecency in a public place with another male under 17 years or assisting in the commission of that act.

s. 20(4) Assault, ill-treatment of a person under 16 where the person convicted is interested in any sum of money payable in the event of the death of the person under 16.

Punishment of Incest Act 1908

s. 1 Male person having sexual intercourse with granddaughter, daughter, sister, half-sister or mother in respect of a child or young person.

s. 2 Female person of 1 years and over allowing a person of the relationship mentioned at (1) above to have intercourse with her, where the person is a child or young person.

s. 3 Attempts to commit any such offence.

s. 4 Upon conviction before any court of any male of an offence under this section to attempt to commit same against any female under 17 years the court has the power to divest the offender of all authority over such female.

Mental Health (NI) Order 1986

Art. 122 Having unlawful sexual intercourse with a girl or woman suffering from severe mental handicap.
Procuring a child or woman for the purpose of above.
Causing or encouraging prostitution of any girl or woman suffering from severe mental handicap.
Inducing or suffering a girl or woman to be on premises for the purposes of the above.
Making or causing to be taken a girl or woman out of possession of parent or other person having lawful care for the purposes of the above.

Art. 123 An officer on the staff of a hospital or nursing home or a guardian appointed under the Mental Health Order:

• having unlawful sexual intercourse with a girl or woman receiving treatment for a mental disorder, or

Figure 6.3 Continued

- committing a homosexual act with or in relation to a boy or man receiving treatment for a mental disorder.

Children and Young Person (NI) Act 1968

s. 20   Cruelty to a child or young person under 16 by a person that age or over.

s. 21   Causing or encouraging seduction or prostitution of a girl under 17 years by a person having custody or care of her.

s. 22   Acts of gross indecency with a child or young person or inciting a child or young person to commit acts of gross indecency.

s. 23   Allowing a child or young person of 4 years or more in a brothel.

s. 24   Causing or allowing persons under 16 years to be used for begging.

s. 29   Exposing children under 12 years to risk of burning.

Children (NI) Order 1995

Art. 147(2) in respect of a contravention of Article 141 of that Order:

Prohibition against persons under 16 years taking part in performances endangering life or limb.

Any attempt to commit against a child or young person an offence under:

Offences against the Person Act 1861 (ss. 61 or 62).
Criminal Law Amendment Act 1885.
Punishment of Incest Act 1908.
Mental Health (NI) Order 1986.
Articles 122 and 123.

Any offences under:

Child Abduction (NI) Order 1985.

Figure 6.3 Continued

1968. On his release, Auckland had gone on to kill a second daughter, only 9 weeks old, in 1974. One feature that bothered the committee of inquiry set up to examine what had happened was the lack of communication between the prison and community-based services, which could have alerted practitioners that a child was potentially at risk; the committee recommended: 'when a prisoner is discharged who has been serving a sentence of an offence against a child we would like to see more information passed to agencies outside the prison so that they may be aware of any potential risk and takes steps to guard against it' (DHSS 1975: para. 151). The new arrangements now entered into consisted of a triangular exchange of information between prison, probation service and social services department to identify any possible child protection questions arising from the address at which a prisoner says he is going to live on release; a parallel exchange of information was to go from the prison medical officers to the offender's GP. The new system was just for prisoners who had offended against children in the home but covered all offences and not just sexual offences (DHSS 1978); the Scottish Office issued similar guidance to cover its prisons and departments of social work (Scottish Office 1979) as did Northern Ireland's Department of Health and Social Services (1978).

These arrangements were revised again in 1994 for England and Wales. The centrality of the Schedule 1 list was made clear and the list duly reproduced in Annex A of the new guidance. The age of the victims was raised from 17 to 18, and there was a new emphasis on telling prisoners that they had been identified and classified as 'Schedule 1 offenders'. Notification systems to local authorities and the probation service were more or less unchanged, but the notification system to GPs seemed to have disappeared from consideration (HM Prison Service 1994).

One change from the 1978 circular was the widening of the class of offenders by dropping the requirement that the offence had to have been committed in the home. The new arrangements reflected the widening concerns of the time to cover all offences against children, irrespective of where those offences were committed. The prison service said this was simply to implement more fully the recommendations of the Auckland Report published 19 years earlier (ibid.: para. 2), but the 1991 inquiry report into the Staffordshire 'pindown' affair had recommended such widening (Levy and Kahan 1991: para. 16.33) and in many areas the change was just ratifying what was already happening in practice.

Similar arrangements exist in Scotland, where liaison is between the prison and the local authority social work department (Scottish Office 1994). A joint initiative in Glasgow between the City Council's Housing Department and Social Work Department has led to the placing of a housing caseworker in Barlinnie Prison to help prisoners on discharge to find suitable accommodation at the same time as minimising the risk to public safety. In Northern Ireland, the release arrangements for Schedule 1 offenders are now to be found in a 1996 circular (DHSS (NI) 1996a) which has been revised once and is currently being revised again for inclusion in their wider manual on the assessment and risk of sex offenders.

Despite the guidance and the National Standards, reports still singled out the supervision of sex offenders as a group who gave 'particular concern' (HMIP 1995: para. 5.4). From the public point of view it was the spectre of the sex offender under supervision who chose to reoffend that caused anxiety.

Further Home Office thinking on supervision came in the 1996 consultation document's suggestion for post-custody 'extended supervision' periods and even indefinite supervision for the rest of an offender's life (Home Office 1996a). Liberty wanted clear statutory provisions outlining when it might be imposed in order to avoid its arbitrary imposition; essentially, this should only be when it was necessary to protect the public from serious harm (Liberty 1996: paras 72–94). More fundamentally, NACRO asked why people needing lifetime supervision in order to protect the public had been given determinate sentences in the first place and not life sentences (NACRO 1996a: 4). The Crime and Disorder Act 1998 amended the Criminal Justice Act 1991, s. 44 to introduce extended supervision for as long as ten years (see above).

One further attempt to manage the release of prisoners back into the community in a structured way was the decision to use electronic monitoring to allow prisoners to complete their sentences in the community. Until now, electronic monitoring had been restricted to a condition of bail or as an enforcement of curfews (see above). The idea now was to use it on prisoners in custody in England and Wales to help them out of prison.

The use of electronic monitoring in this way was known as the Home Detention Curfew (HDC) scheme, and provisions for it had been included in the Crime and Disorder Act 1998, ss. 99–105. Three private companies provided the service covering the North, the South and the Midlands and Wales respectively. The scheme was launched on 28 January 1999, with all prisoners being first subject to a risk assessment and a home circumstances report by the probation service (HC Debs 18 January 1999, col. 353 WA).

Sex offenders required to register with the police could be eligible for HDC but only in 'exceptional circumstances'. Any such offenders were to be subjected to a 'rigorous enhanced risk assessment' and would only be released following authorisation by the Director General of the Prison Service (HC Debs, 25 February 1999, 72369 WA). This option was later completely closed off to 'registered' sex offenders who are now statutorily debarred from even being considered eligible for HDC (Criminal Justice and Court Services Act 2000, s. 65).

Indeterminate sentences

Some offenders leaving prison, with or without post-custody supervision, have been considered to be still dangerous and liable to reoffend. Policy-makers have started to look at the possibility of some form of 'indeterminate sentences' for those people, which would result in their release only when the risk they pose has been reduced and they are no longer considered dangerous.

When Graham Seddon, a 48-year-old convicted sex offender, was released from prison, he was found wandering the streets of Liverpool with a teddy bear, toys and colouring pencils and reportedly stalking children. Here was a seemingly dangerous person who fell outside the remit of the Mental Health Act because psychiatrists said he was not treatable (see also Chapter 2) and yet the police could not intervene because he had not actually committed an offence ('Shunned child-sex attacker cannot be held', *The Times,* 5 July 1997).

The spectre arose of the sex offender leaving prison at the end of his sentence just as dangerous as when he went in, and openly telling prison officers of his criminal intent towards children when he left. In the case of Seddon, the matter was raised in the Commons:

> Mr. O'Hara: [the sex offender] can be released into the community under mental health law and be beyond the reach of the forces of criminal law until he commits an offence – not any old offence, but a sexual offence against a child. In other words, until he ruins a child's life, ruins a family and blights a community (HC Debs, 7 July 1997, col. 748).

For the Home Office, Minister of State Alun Michael acknowledged the seriousness of the problem and said the government 'was looking closely at the scope for further action on mental health and the criminal law to safeguard the public from people with apparently untreatable psychopathic disorders, particularly in relation to sexual offences' with one of the options being 'the possibility of using indeterminate sentences' (ibid.: col. 749).

As we noted in Chapter 2, the problem with mental health legislation was that the Mental Health Act 1983 for England and Wales allowed for compulsory detention of patients only if they were 'treatable' and their mental disorder made the Act applicable. The Act applied to those with a 'psychopathic disorder' (Mental Health Act 1983, s. 1(2)), but whether the disorder was treatable was open to debate. The courts had looked at the question and laid down 'principles of treatability' for the psychopath, which included the prevention of deterioration, the stabilisation of the patient and the general provision of care under medical guidance, but the debate continued (*R* v. *Cannons Park Mental Health Review Tribunal, ex p. A* [1994] 3 WLR 630).

In Scotland, the provisions of the Mental Health (Scotland) Act 1984 were similarly worded and were tested by a man held in Carstairs secure hospital. Alexander Reid claimed that his detention should be stopped because he was receiving no treatment. This case went as far as the House of Lords, which again took the line that the word 'treatment' has a very wide definition and could include prevention of deterioration (*Reid* v. *Secretary for Scotland* (1998) *Independent*, 8 December); Reid was not released.

During the late 1990s it was also apparent that the terminology was undergoing something of a change and instead of 'psychopaths' some sex offenders were now termed as having 'severe personality disorders' (see also Chapter 2).

Tony Butler, Chief Constable of Gloucestershire and spokesperson on sex offending for the Association of Chief Police Officers, explained the problem:

> The assessment of these people is that they have a severe personality disorder which isn't treatable, therefore they don't fall within the terms of the Mental Health Act, therefore they can't be detained under current provisions in mental hospitals ... we need a new law (cited in 'Police seek new powers to hold freed paedophiles', *PA Report*, 3 June 1998).

'Personality disorders' and 'anti-social personality disorders' had been around for some time, but the addition of the word 'severe' now found favour, and not least when applied to sex offenders. The dilemma was that those with severe personality disorders might not be detained for mental health treatment and might not be arrested because they had committed no crime, although, given time, they almost certainly would commit a crime – including possibly a sexual crime. Although it meant anticipating crimes before they were committed and taking action against people who had not actually done anything, the search was on for a 'third way' to deal with people with severe personality disorders.

Various states in the USA had introduced 'civil commitment' laws to achieve this end. Sexual offenders, known as 'sexual predators', coming to the end of a prison sentence (imposed by a criminal court) but still assessed as potentially dangerous and continuing to pose a risk, could be referred to a civil court to be detained by civil commitment when their prison sentence had ended. Washington State had been amongst the first to pass such laws in 1990 (Greenlees 1991), but in 1997, when Kansas appealed to the Supreme Court for a test of the legitimacy of what they were doing, some 38 other states joined them in the appeal. The Supreme Court duly ruled in their favour in the case of *Kansas* v. *Hendricks* in a narrow decision ('Sex offenders in the US face being locked up for life', *Guardian*, 26 June 1997; see also Janus 2000).

In the UK, the debate was spurred on by the problematic release from prison of Robert Oliver and Sydney Cooke amidst popular protest that had deteriorated into mob violence, and by the conviction of Michael Stone in 1998 for the killing of Lyn Russell and her daughter Megan. It was claimed that Stone had sought psychiatric in-patient treatment days before he attacked his victims, but had been refused admission because he was 'untreatable'. The terminology now changed again and the word 'dangerous' was added to the phrase 'severe personality disorder'.

Home Secretary Jack Straw announced his proposal to legislate to introduce indeterminate sentences comparable to the Americans' civil commitment in February 1999. Straw explained that:

> There is ... a group of dangerous and severe personality disordered individuals from whom the public at present are not properly protected, and who are restrained effectively neither by the criminal law nor by the provisions of the Mental Health Acts. The propensity of such people to commit the most serious sexual and violent acts may be well known and well recorded ... The Government propose that there should be new legal powers for the indeterminate but reviewable detention of dangerous personality disordered individuals (HC Debs, 15 February 1999, cols. 601–2).

Straw said he would be producing a consultation document jointly with the Secretary of State for Health outlining the options for a new legal framework.

The statement of the Home Secretary was greeted with a wave of concern at the idea of locking up people indefinitely when they had not done anything, and simply on the evidence of medical experts (see, e.g., 'Psychopaths plan will hit "the innocent" ', *Independent* 16 February 1999; Donnelly 1999; Valios 1999). The social work journal *Community Care* warned that the proposals should not be dismissed out of hand, 'but his consultation had better be good' ('A protection racket', *Community Care*, editorial 18–24 February 1999).

Meanwhile, Scotland headed out on a similar path with the formation of its own committee, chaired by the Hon. Lord MacLean, to look into the sentencing and treatment of serious violent and sexual offenders, including those with personality disorders. The MacLean Committee was formed in March 1999 (see Scottish Office 1999).

The Home Office consultation paper duly appeared in July 1999, and set out two broad options. Option A built on existing arrangements by amending the Mental Health Act 1983, extending the use of discretionary life sentence and introducing new powers of compulsory supervision. Option B involved new laws on indeterminate detention in new facilities separate from mainstream prison and hospital facilities; a new specialist service would be needed to manage these offenders who by now had their own new acronym – DSPD or dangerous severely personality disordered people (Home Office 1999b).

The urgency of the debate took on a new dimension when an investigation was ordered into the release of Noel Ruddle from Carstairs secure hospital in Scotland. This time the courts had ruled that Ruddle could not be detained because he was not receiving effective treatment, although he had previously killed a person and was considered dangerous ('Inquiry ordered into release of rifle killer', *Guardian*, 3 August 1999). In February 2000, the Home Office announced the first pilot assessment procedures for dangerous and severely personality disordered prisoners would start at Whitemoor Prison (Home Office 2000d).

The attempts to change the Mental Health Act in order to allow for the detention of people with a severe personality disorder were explored in Chapter 2. At the time of writing the government has not achieved its end of introducing a new law that would be able to square the circle of removing 'dangerous' people from the streets who had neither committed an offence nor were mentally disordered as currently defined (McAlinden 2001; Laing 2002).

The Criminal Justice Act 2003 has introduced new measures to detain those assessed as posing a risk and being 'dangerous' but only *after* they have committed a specified sexual or violent offence. The specified offences are listed in Schedule 1 of the Act and the sentence imposed is known as 'imprisonment for public protection' (s. 225). The court must make the risk assessment and: 'take account of all such information as is available to it about the nature and circumstances of the offence ... any pattern of behaviour of which the offence forms part, and ... any information about the offender which is before it' (Criminal Justice Act 2003, s. 229). Any release from 'imprisonment for public protection' is only after review by the Parole Board (Schedule 18). The campaign group Liberty believe the measures are liable to breach the European Convention on Human Rights, Articles 5 and 6 (Liberty 2002); at the time of writing it is too early to tell.

Summary

The court has the choice of custodial or community sentences for sex offenders and the amount of 'personal information' available on the offender and any risk assessment based on that information will determine which form of sentence is appropriate; mandatory custodial sentences are now prescribed for the more serious sexual offender. The probation service is the agency responsible for ensuring that community sentences are completed and that any conditions attached are complied with; the same agency has responsibility for any post-custody period of supervision in the community and, again, for ensuring that any conditions are met. Within a custodial prison sentence, Sex Offender Treatment Programmes are well established and a degree of continuity is now required between the practitioners within the prison walls and those outside to ensure that positive work is carried out. The efficient exchange of 'personal information' on the offender is a critical part of ensuring compliance, preventing relapse and protecting the public. In May 2004 the prison and probation service were brought together as the National Offender Management Service (NOMS) to yet further improve liaison and information flows.

The continuing fear of the 'dangerous' person in the community has led politicians to look for new ways of containing such people, whether or not they have committed an offence, in order to protect the public. At present, proposals have been put forward for indeterminate sentences for those considered 'dangerous' and a form of such a sentence now exists through the Criminal Justice Act 2003; how this risk will be assessed will be critical. Hopes of changing the civil law through the Mental Health Act remain to be seen.

Chapter 7

Protection in the home

This chapter considers measures in place to protect children and young people from sexual and violent offences in their own home. It also looks at children and young people who get involved in prostitution and how policy changes are trying to get this activity viewed more as a child protection matter rather than a straight criminal matter. The protection of adults – and particularly women – from violent and sexual offending in the home is also considered.

Children and young people

Although the sexual assault of children by strangers has been in the forefront of the public imagination and recent research would support that contention (Gallagher *et al*. 2002), it has also increasingly become the conventional wisdom that children are far more at risk from members of their own household and extended family. The protection of children from physical, emotional, psychological and sexual abuse within their own homes has always posed problems for the state. In general terms, we believe that families and households should be free to bring up their children the way they want to without 'official' interference. If it becomes apparent that they are struggling to meet identified levels of 'reasonable care', the children may be designated 'children in need' and we can offer them 'family support', such as substitute day care for children or other support in cash or kind, on the basis that the children are still best cared for by their family. If the official concerns rise sufficiently, the state may intervene to protect the child by removing it from the household and providing it with alternative care in the way of a foster home or children's home. Whilst these different positions on intervention are easily set down and an awareness of children's rights brought into play, the actual implementation of child protection arrangements is invariably a complex arrangement.

The death of 7-year-old Maria Colwell at the hands of her stepfather, and the resulting public inquiry in 1974 to investigate why this had been allowed to happen, led in turn to the formalisation of child protection arrangements as we know them today. In England and Wales, Area Child Protection Committees (originally called Area Review Committees) were established, with a membership of senior officers from all the local agencies in a local authority area likely to have contact with children and thereby child protection matters. Written policies and procedures were to be produced to guide all the practitioners of those local agencies in what to do in individual cases, and child protection conferences (originally called case conferences) were to be convened when there was a need to discuss a particular child or family (DHSS 1974, 1976). These arrangements are still in place today, albeit with various additions and refurbishments (Department of Health 1999).

In Scotland, the Area Child Protection Committees were called simply Child Protection Committees, but in Northern Ireland they took the same name as in England and Wales; Northern Ireland has a second-tier committee called a Child Protection Panel.

In simple legal terms, the police investigate the criminal aspects of abuse and social workers take on the civil aspects of child care, with a duty to investigate and invoke procedures of child protection. Social workers act under the relevant laws for England and Wales (Children Act 1989), Scotland (Children (Scotland) Act 1995) and Northern Ireland (Children (Northern Ireland) Order 1995).

An innovative feature of the 1974 arrangements was the introduction of the local child protection register (originally named the 'at risk' or 'child abuse' register), containing the names of all children in the area where there were child protection issues. The decision to add a name to the register was to be made by a child protection conference; any local agency with concerns for a child could then check the register to see if he or she were already 'known' and what the 'key' or 'focal' agency was. The register was to be maintained by the social services department or the local branch of the NSPCC. In essence, the register is a mechanism to help identify the child where there are child protection concerns.

Child protection registers have been criticised in the past for being bureaucratic, costly and ineffective (Morris *et al.* 1980: 116–17) and for being potentially oppressive and even 'dangerous' (*R v. Norfolk CC, ex p.*

M [1989] 2 All ER 359). None the less, they have stood the test of time and remain key features of local child protection arrangements.

In keeping with the times, the original guidance on registers said nothing about sexual abuse as a category of abuse needing registration. The sexual abuse of children in the 1970s was still well hidden away, and social workers, along with everyone else, were culturally blind to its existence. Further guidance on registers issued by the DHSS in 1980 made a point of saying that sexual abuse was a category that did *not* need registering (DHSS 1980: para. 2).

This position changed slowly during the first half of the 1980s, as child sexual abuse was 'discovered' by those professionals who had previously overlooked it. Until that time, the sexual abuse of children would need to have been clear cut and obvious for actions to have been taken. Then, as it came on to the professional agenda, practitioners could start to recognise symptoms, listen more carefully to children and seek out sexual abuse. Early surveys also suggested that Area Review Committees were unprepared for child sex abuse and had few procedures in place to guide practitioners (Mrazek *et al.* 1983; see also Porter 1984). In America Professor David Finkelhor was influential in opening up the debate in that country (Finkelhor 1986).

In Leeds, two paediatricians drew attention to a medical test they thought revealed evidence – or at least suspicions – of a child having been sexually abused. This was the so-called Anal Dilatation Test, whereby the anal canal remained open on buttock separation rather than closing (Hobbs and Wynne 1986). The same two paediatricians also noted the increasing awareness of child sexual abuse, which they attributed to 'doctors and others' willingness to confront an old problem and intervene' (Hobbs and Wynne 1987).

In 1986 the BBC had broadcast its television programme *Childwatch*, presented by Esther Rantzen, to launch the organisation 'Childline'. Childline was a national freephone help-line for children to phone if they felt they were in trouble or danger. Appropriate referrals were passed on to the relevant social services departments (see Macleod 1996).

Parton has described the *Childwatch* programme, which had an estimated audience of 16.5 million, as 'a significant intervention into the issue of child abuse, particularly in relation to sexual abuse ... its timing in late 1986 served both to raise public awareness but also disturb many previously untouched sensitivities' (1991: 93). This slowly wakening awareness of child sexual abuse was to be given a massive push the following year with the breaking of what came to be known as the 'Cleveland affair'. In June 1987, local newspapers in the Middlesbrough area started reporting huge numbers of children being admitted to local hospitals diagnosed by doctors as having been sexually abused. By the end of the month, the story had gone national and questions were being asked in the House of Commons ('Hand over your children, Council orders parents of 200 youngsters', *Daily Mail*, 23 June 1987).

The paediatricians in Cleveland, using the Anal Dilatation Test described in Leeds, had found enormous numbers of children displaying the symptoms of sexual abuse. The local social workers had accepted the diagnosis, but the police had not. A major inquiry was mounted to try to unravel what had gone on, and child sexual abuse would never be hidden away again.

The Cleveland Report sensitised all child care practitioners to the possibility of sexual abuse. All agencies were asked to rethink their approach to the problem, work more closely with parents and make better efforts at meaningful inter-agency work. The report reasserted the primacy of the child with its oft-repeated dictum: 'there is a danger that in looking to the welfare of the children believed to be the victims of sexual abuse, the children themselves may be overlooked. The child is a person and not an object of concern' (Cleveland Report 1988: 245). A flurry of Whitehall circulars were sent to the police, schools and every-one working with children. The key phrase was that we were all 'working together' for the child (DHSS 1988; Home Office 1988; DHSS (NI) 1989; Scottish Office 1989a). Sexual abuse was a category of abuse that needed to be registered.

Work on the new Children Bill being put before Parliament was held up so that the Cleveland Report recommendations could be included where appropriate, and the new Children Act finally became law in 1989. Sexually abused children were now defined as children having suffered 'significant harm' or 'likely to suffer significant harm' (s. 31). New guidance replaced previous versions when the Act was implemented in 1991 (Home Office *et al.* 1991).

The new guidance also made reference to abuse of children by groups using 'bizarre or ritualised behaviour, sometimes associated with particular "belief" systems' (ibid.: para. 5.26.2). Everyone else referred to this as 'ritual' or 'satanic' abuse.

The essence of ritual or satanic abuse was that the child was sexually abused as part of some ceremony hinting at 'witchcraft', which was supposed to frighten the child into silence when it was over. The arguments over whether or not this sort of abuse actually did exist or was imagined continued for some years, most infamously in the Orkney Islands, where a number of children were removed from home on the basis of such allegations (Clyde Report 1992). The government com-missioned independent research to look at the phenomenon, but the research concluded that there was little evidence for it (La Fontaine 1994; see also La Fontaine 1998); the most recent edition of *Working Together to Safeguard Children* omits any reference at all to this kind of abuse (Department of Health 1999).

In other parts of the UK, changes in the law led to changes in the published guidance on child protection arrangements. In Northern Ireland, the Children (Northern Ireland) Order 1995 was followed by a new 'Protocol for Joint Investigation' (1996), produced by all the agencies that would make those investigations and in Scotland, the Children (Scotland) Act 1995 was accompanied by a series of books of regulations and guidance.

Today, the routine investigation of child sexual abuse goes on within social services departments as a normal part of their work. Most of this goes on unheralded and makes no headlines; an account of this work using research based on 40 case studies can be found in Corby (1998).

Following the report into the death of 8-year-old Victoria Climbié by her carers (Laming Report 2003) the government decided yet again to reorganise the child protection system and outlined its plans in the consultation paper *Every Child Matters* (Chief Secretary to the Treasury 2003). An attempt was now made to involve all agencies in child protection rather than just the police and social workers at 'the sharp end'. New Local Safeguarding Children Boards were proposed to replace the Area Child Protection Committees and new Directors of Children's Services would become accountable for both local authority education and children's social services. Information was to be collated on all children in a given area and that information would be more freely available to all the agencies coming into contact with children through so-called 'information hubs' (ibid.: paras. 4.1–4.12). Pilot Identification, Referral and Tracking (IRT) schemes were introduced and a new Children Bill published in early 2004, to carry these proposals forward.

Child prostitution

Child prostitution has been with us since Victorian times at least (Brown and Barrett 2002). In recent years, a campaign has gathered momentum to force a rethink on our approaches to young people below the age of consent who resort to prostitution. In essence, the argument has been that the selling of sexual services by these young people and any associated criminal behaviour by them should be reconstituted as a form of child abuse and even be decriminalised.

As far back as 1959, the Home Office had advised the police when cautioning prostitutes to ensure:

> That no opportunity should be neglected of putting a girl or young woman who is in danger of drifting into prostitution into touch with a social welfare agency which may be able to persuade her to take up regular employment or to go home to her parents (Home Office 1959: para. 5).

During the 1980s, a loosely co-ordinated campaign was started to improve the lot of child prostitutes. Non-governmental organisations have taken a lead in this campaign. The Children's Society 'Safe in the City' project in Manchester found schoolgirls, engaged in prostitution, whom they felt needed protection rather than punishment (Chamberlain 1993; Lee and O'Brien 1995). Barnardos set up its 'Streets and Lanes' project in Bradford in 1994 to work directly with these young girls on a multi-agency basis; they too argued for protection over punishment (Barnardos 1998). The argument was that any criminality going on here should be ascribed to the male purchasers of sexual services, who should be recategorised as child abusers. Lynne Ravenscroft, a magistrate, put the subject on the agenda of the Magistrates' Association to add weight to the campaign (Ravenscroft 1997).

What was coming to light were the dreadful social circumstances of the young girls and boys (rent-boys) that were turning them to prostitution: runaways from home; children leaving local authority care; children using drugs.

The campaign started to see results. The police launched two pilot schemes in Nottingham and Wolverhampton in mid-1997 to try to take a different approach and to take the 'victims' not 'criminals' line. In February 1998, the government accepted the ease with which young people could become 'trapped in an unhealthy and illegal lifestyle' which led to prostitution, and saw the case for moving the focus of attention to the abusing adult: 'Children who become involved in prostitution should be seen primarily as children in need of welfare services and in many instances protection under the Children Act' (Department of Health 1998a: para. 5.40). In the meantime, cases of child prostitution continued to come to light. A number of men in their 50s were arrested in Middlesbrough and Darlington to be questioned about organising prostitution rings ('Town rocked by child prostitution', *Northern Echo*, 15 April 1998) and in Scotland, reports were made of a growing 'market' for young boys in the Calton Hill area of Edinburgh and around the two main railways stations – Queen Street and Central –

in Glasgow ('Fears for under age rent boys', *Scotsman*, 1 February 1999).

At the end of 1998, the government introduced a set of draft guidelines on how the police and other agencies in England and Wales could change the focus of their work with child prostitutes. These were duly finalised in 2000 and became supplementary to the *Working Together to Safeguard Children* guidance. The government held back from actually decriminalising under-age prostitute activities, because it was thought that this would 'send out the wrong message', but they did favour a more child-centred approach, with multi-agency co-operation to develop expertise, consider individual cases and devise overall strategies. The offering of individual 'exit strategies' for those caught up in prostitution was considered the best way forward (Department of Health *et al.* 2000; see also Phoenix 2004). The Sexual Offences Act 2003, s. 47 does now make it an offence to pay for the sexual services of a child.

Child prostitution throws a spotlight on many of the questions raised in this book. The age of consent could be said to invalidate the 'consent' of everyone under 16 and yet we hold them criminally responsible for their behaviour because the age of criminal responsibility is 10 (8 in Scotland). We choose to see the person buying the sexual service as the criminal, and see him as a possible child abuser, yet we refuse to decriminalise the activities of the young person because it would send the 'wrong message' to the men ('pimps') who organise and control these young people. Are we really holding back from dealing with the male abuser as well, because of his 'normality' on the 'continuum' of male attitudes and behaviour?

Women and adults

The position of women victims of violence and sexual assault in the home has traditionally been held to be different from that of children. Interventions to assist were held back by beliefs that adults, unlike children, had a choice in where they lived and the capacity to seek help when they needed it. On top of that, the 'privacy' of the home was held up as a 'cordon sanitaire' to keep official intervention at bay. The women's movement of the early 1970s challenged this orthodoxy with its intellectual analysis of the subordinate position of women, their economic dependency and inability to leave a household as easily as the apologists would suggest. This analysis was backed up by listening to the experiences of women who had been subject to violence and sexual assault in the home. Some of these women now sought help from the newly formed 'safe houses' or 'refuges' for women wanting to leave violent husbands or partners.

Throughout this period, refuges were opened across the country. Run by women for women, they were co-ordinated nationally through the Women's Aid organisation. Today there are more than 300 Women's Aid groups throughout the UK, giving shelter to more than 70,000 women and children each year. Some refuges specialise in taking black and ethnic minority women. Priority is given to the acceptance of a woman's story without disbelief or questioning (Hague and Malos 1998).

Rape Crisis Centres are another victims' group, taking a feminist analysis and run by women for women. The centres offer counselling services, telephone help-lines and general support. They have a campaigning and educational side to dispel some of the myths of rape, such as the idea that it is only committed by strangers in public places. The campaigning also challenges the very use of the word 'victim': 'there is not a separate category of women called victims – just as there [is] no category of men who are not "rapists" – victim takes away our power and contributes to the idea that men can "prey" on women' (London Rape Crisis Centre 1984). The preferred terminology was 'survivor'. The campaigning work of the Rape Crisis Centres was not always appreciated, especially in its early days. A survey of police surgeons found 36 per cent of the respondents thought they were a 'poor idea' and one doctor thought: 'The predominant role of a Rape Crisis Centre should be supportive. Unfortunately they are frequently used as feminist political tools using rape and rape victims in the general cause of women's lib rather than vice versa' (Geis et al. 1978). This antagonism to a contentious and challenging approach has been held to be responsible for Rape Crisis Centres not getting mainstream government support, unlike the more 'respectable' Victim Support organisation (Williams 1999: 94). None the less, Rape Crisis has also stood the test of time and is now co-ordinated through a central Rape Crisis Federation based in Nottingham.

In the early 1970s, the campaigning work and 'raising of consciousness' carried out by the women's movement were drawn into the deliberations of the House of Commons Select Committee on Violence in the Family, and recommendations on new laws were examined.

Civil legislation followed, in the form of the Domestic Violence and Matrimonial Proceedings Act 1976 and relevant parts of the Domestic Proceedings and Magistrates' Courts Act 1978. Women could now apply for injunctions against a man molesting or attacking them even if he continued to live with them in the same house. Men ignoring the injunctions were in contempt of court, but sometimes powers of arrest were also added to them. The Housing (Homeless Persons) Act 1977 allowed women leaving violent men to be designated as homeless and in 'priority need' of alternative emergency accommodation.

The laws were a great step forward, although implementation was not always as useful as it might have been (see, e.g., Atkins and Hoggett 1984). In 1988 (Scotland) and 1992 (England and Wales), the common law recognised for the first time that rape could take place within marriage and a number of women became causes célèbres when they had killed violent men after years of domestic violence. Arguments started to be made that these women could not use the defence of 'provocation' as easily as men could because of the wording of the law (see, e.g., HC Debs, 23 January 1992, cols. 477–8).

After a Law Commission (1992) report on the subject and another Select Committee examination, the Family Law Act 1996, Part IV overhauled the civil law on domestic violence for England and Wales. The new Act made it easier to obtain 'occupation orders' and 'non-molestation orders' to protect the 'health, safety and well-being' of applicants, and made it easier to have a power of arrest attached to breach of these orders (Department of Health 1997).

The Family Law Act also contained provisions to protect children by amending the Children Act 1989. In future, the courts would have a discretionary power to add an 'exclusion requirement' to any emergency protection orders or interim care orders they were making on children. The 'exclusion requirement' meant the suspected adult abuser could be ordered to leave a household, or stay away from a household or even to stay outside a defined area in which a house is situated (Children Act 1989, ss. 38A and 44A, as amended by Family Law Act 1996, s. 52 and Sch. 6). Until now the existing Children Act powers (in Sch. 2, para. 5) had been discretionary only for the assailant. These new public, rather than private, powers replicated powers provided for in Scotland with the 'exclusion orders' available under the Children (Scotland) Act 1995, s. 76.

Although the Family Law Act improved the lot of those in relationships, the media had discovered at this time a new phenomenon that affected those not in relationships. The 'stalker' had become a new 'hate figure' who needed to be dealt with. In essence, this was the label attached to people – usually men, but not always – who seemed to be compulsively obsessed by a particular person who in turn became the target of letters, phone calls, personal calls and all manner of other interventions, despite it being made quite clear that these were all unwelcome. Of themselves, these acts were not necessarily hostile or violent, although their cumulative effect was harmful; new laws were going to be needed.

The government responded with a consultation paper (Home Office/ Lord Chancellor's Department 1996) and followed this up with the Protection from Harassment Act 1997. The Act provided for both civil and criminal remedies, and came into force on 16 June 1997. The civil remedy introduced new restraining injunctions – restraining orders – and two new criminal offences of causing harassment and the more serious charge of causing fear of violence.

Legal measures apart, the government did appear to be directing more attention to violence against women, with activities such as the Home Office's 'Break the Chain' campaign and the consultation papers produced in all parts of the UK by the respective government offices (Scottish Office 1998a; NIO 1999; Cabinet Office/Home Office 1999).

On the legal front the Housing Act 1996 Part VII now incorporated the provisions of the 1977 Housing (Homeless Persons) Act that included rights to accommodation for victims of domestic violence and the 1996 Act was further amended by the Homelessness Act 2002 to include victims of *any* violence – not just domestic violence. The Adoption and Children Act 2002 made further amendments to the Children Act 1989, s. 31 to widen the definition of 'significant harm' to children to include children who had witnessed the ill-treatment of another person; invariably this would be through domestic violence.

In 2003 a new white paper, *Safety and Justice*, tabled proposals again directly to take on domestic violence, citing in its Foreword the statistic that two women on average die every week as a result of it. The proposals were built around three themes:

- Prevention – including better education, information, etc.
- Protection and justice – extending the law to include more easily available non-molestation orders, more powers of arrest and more restraining orders.
- Support – including easier access to housing, welfare benefits and counselling for victims and children (Home Office 2003a).

Most of these proposals were duly included in the Domestic Violence, Crime and Victims Bill published in 2003.

Summary

Over the last thirty years there has been a growing awareness that victims of sexual offending are more than likely to know their abuser and even to share the same household as that abuser. The privacy of the home has been used to excuse the abuse and exclude formal investigation and protective interventions. Such exclusion is slowly being broken down and abuse within the home is recognised and dealt with. In this chapter we have looked at child abuse, including child sexual abuse and domestic violence which is gender based in so far as most perpetrators are men, and which also contains elements of sexual coercion.

Chapter 8

Protection in 'care' settings

In a general sense all the activities of the criminal justice system (Chapters 4 and 5) and those civil measures we cover in the rest of this book contribute to the greater protection of the public. In this chapter we consider those measures specifically formulated to protect children and vulnerable adults who need care in social care settings, schools, youth clubs, leisure centres and day centres. The sexual exploitation of children, in particular, in these settings has been a source of concern for many years, giving rise to one popular theory that these workplaces – schools, children's homes, etc. – act as a 'honey pot' attracting would-be offenders to them because it gives them access to children.

The institutional settings

Schools

The worst excesses of violence and oppressive teaching have a special place in British literature, from *Tom Brown's School Days* to the Dickensian creations of Wackford Squeers and Mr Gradgrind. The school is seen as a potential site for the authority of the teacher to be used against the vulnerability of the pupil, and for that imbalance to lead on to possible sexual exploitation. Today, teachers are periodically found guilty of sexual offences against children (see, e.g., 'Teacher jailed for decade of sexual abuse', *Daily Telegraph*, 23 June 1998; 'Ex-teacher jailed for abuse after pupils traced on Friends Reunited', *Guardian*, 18 June 2003).

Teachers, however, often thought it had become too easy for children to make allegations of sexual abuse, and that teachers were vulnerable to malicious accusations against which they were unable to defend themselves; any child or young person wanting to 'have a go' at a teacher had only to report inappropriate behaviour, which led to suspension and investigation (see HC Debs, 16 January 1992, cols. 1207–16); careers were said to be ruined ('False abuse charges "ruin careers of 350 teachers each year" ', *Daily Telegraph*, 10 April 1999).

The complexity of this area was illustrated in the summer of 1998, when it was discovered that the Health Education Authority was drawing up guidelines to protect children from strong sunlight, which might cause skin cancer. On behalf of teachers, the Local Government Association jumped in to say the guidelines should not ask teachers to apply sun-tan creams to pupils for fear of being accused of child abuse: 'School teachers are very vulnerable to accusations of physical and/or sexual abuse. Their reluctance is well-founded ... we would counsel strongly against any suggestion that teachers, with or without parental consent, should apply sunscreen products to children in their care' (LGA 1998). According to the National Association of Schoolmasters and Union of Women Teachers (NASUWT) only 69 of the 1,782 allegations of abuse made by children against their members in the past ten years have led to convictions ('Teachers call for right to sue fake accusers', *Guardian*, 15 April 2004).

The British private boarding school has long held a special place in the popular imagination as a location for the sexual abuse of children. Abuse by teaching staff and other pupils has allegedly been 'covered up', dealt with internally and otherwise 'denied', or else seen as part and parcel of normal life in boarding schools (see, e.g., 'Sex abuse "at 75% of boarding schools" ', *Independent*, 9 December 1989). The journalist Paul Foot has recalled the 'sadism' of his former housemaster, Anthony Chevenix-Trench, at Shrewsbury School in the 1950s, where "Trench was assaulting boys in his charge for one reason only: his own sexual gratification"(Foot 1996).

Foot recalls how Trench moved on to be headmaster at Eton, where his practices continued until he was finally removed from office: 'Throughout the long process of dismissal there was hardly a public whisper about the conduct that had occasioned it. He applied [successfully] for the head-mastership of Fettes' (ibid.). In the summer of 1990, another headmaster, a mathematics teacher and an English teacher were all imprisoned for sexually assaulting pupils at Crookham Court School in Berkshire ('A shocking abuse of trust', *Independent on Sunday*, 15 July 1990). According to some observers, it was these convictions and the investigation proceeding them that had led to the inclusion of s. 87 in the Children Act 1989 ('An inspector calls', *Guardian*, 31 May 1994).

Section 87 gave local authorities the duty to inspect the residential care provisions of private boarding schools. Starting in 1991, regular inspections are now made to ensure the welfare of the children in any school with more than 50 boarders; the educational side of the school remained the responsibility of HM Inspectorate of Schools. As if to emphasise the importance of this work, an experimental telephone helpline for boarding-school children reported receiving over 10,000 calls ('Boarding school abuse help-line gets 10,000 calls', *Observer*, 29 September 1991). The Department of Health published guidance on how the new inspections should work (Department of Health 1991a).

New laws introduced in 2000 further protected children in schools – and other care settings – by prohibiting sexual activity between staff and young people under 18 – even if the latter were over 16. Such activity in future, would be interpreted as committing an offence of 'abuse of trust' (Sexual Offences (Amendment) Act 2000, s. 3; now in the Sexual Offences Act 2003, ss. 16–24).

Sports clubs and voluntary organisations

Sports clubs have also been identified as places where the sexual exploitation of children may take place. The ambition of young sports-men and women to achieve at the highest levels, together with the authority of the sports coach, has led to situations of 'grooming' and 'entrapment'. The closeness of the young athlete's bond with the adult figure has led some to describe any sexual abuse taking place as 'virtual incest' (Brackenridge 1997).

A great deal of work in this area has been carried out by Professor Celia Brackenridge at the Leisure and Sport Research Centre at Cheltenham and Gloucester College of Higher Education. Professor Brackenridge has outlined the way in which an initial analysis of sex discrimination in organised sport has led to an understanding of sexual abuse.

The opening of the subject, however, has not been easy and sporting authorities have been, at best, slow to respond (but see, e.g., NCF/NSPCC 1995) and at worst have denied there has been a problem:

[It] has been indeed a struggle to get the subject out of the ghetto: it is ironic, for example, that during a period when moral panics about 'stranger danger' and sexual abuse have escalated in society at large, many sport and leisure organisations have failed to acknowledge or confront sexual exploitation (Brackenridge 1998).

Despite revelations at the highest levels, including the 17-year prison sentence passed on a former Olympics swimming coach for convictions of rape and indecent assaults ('Swimming chiefs face legal action', *Daily Telegraph*, 29 September 1995), sports organisations have been criticised for playing down the problem. Arguments summoned against sexual abuse taking place include the idea that overall more people benefit from sport; the problem is exaggerated or 'couldn't happen here'; people who allege it are 'trouble-makers'; and, even if it does take place, it's not the responsibility of the sports authorities (Brackenridge 1998).

The Football Association is one authority that has included a statement of commitment to child protection in its policies for the development of young players (FA 1997: Appendix G), and Bristol Rovers was the first professional club to launch its 'Child Safe' programme in early 1999 ('FA hunts out the football sex abusers', *Independent*, 15 February 1999).

The voluntary sector as a whole has had an ambivalent relationship with child protection matters. Voluntary organisations which employ staff to work directly with children are rigorous in their selection and screening of staff. Organisations that literally rely on unpaid volunteers fear such rigour might put people off volunteering, as did the idea of imposing fees for criminal record checks (see below).

In Northern Ireland, it is worth noting that the voluntary sector has been particularly proactive in addressing the problems posed by sex offenders directly. Following criticism when a convicted sex offender managed to get work in the voluntary sector which gave him access to children (DHSS (NI) 1993), the Voluntary Sector Working Group on Sex Offenders was formed. The group has been active since its formation, holding conferences and specialist working parties looking at accommodation, employment, confidentiality and other issues (VSWGSO 1997a, 1997b).

The church

One particular 'workplace' where child abuse was not anticipated was the church. Unfortunately, a series of scandals has shown that even here children have not been safe.

In the Republic of Ireland, the revelation that 'celibate' priests were abusing children or fathering children was reported to have undermined the very authority of the church:

> large numbers of Catholics in Ireland, many disillusioned by scandals within the church, have abandoned regular practice of their faith ... an MRBI poll showed ... more than 90% of Catholics

believe controversies involving convicted paedophile priest Fr. Brendan Smyth who has since died, and Bishop Eamon Casey, have damaged the authority of the church ('Scandals undermine Irish Church authority – survey' Reuters, 4 February 1998).

Bishop Casey had moved to South America following allegations that he had fathered a child (see also ICBA 1996; O'Mahony 1996: esp. chap. 6).

In the UK, a Catholic priest was sentenced to five years' imprisonment by Preston Crown Court in September 1997 and another priest received an eight-year sentence at Cardiff Crown Court in December 1998; both had been convicted of sexual offences against children. A Church of England priest from Essex was imprisoned by a Bucharest court in July 1998 for having sex with under-age boys whilst in Romania, and the school chaplain from the private Tonbridge School in Kent was arrested and charged in Germany for importing pornographic videos in May 1998.

In the USA the same phenomena took place as Catholic priests were accused of sexual abuse across the country, and millions of dollars had to be paid out in compensation (*The Boston Globe* 2002).

What bothered some observers was the apparent ability of the churches to cover up the activities of their employees by moving them to different geographic locations to put off complaints and disrupt investigations. Whether these allegations were true or not remains debatable. The Church of England has produced its own guidance on child protection within church organisations, with particular reference to appointing workers with children (CCPAS 1998).

Children's homes

Residential care for children unable to live with their families takes many forms but, in essence, they are all children's homes. Most children's homes are run by local authorities through their social services departments, social work departments or Health and Social Services Boards; some children's homes are independent or in the voluntary sector. Children's homes have been accused of providing a haven for the abuse of children.

Reports of sexual crimes against children in residential care came to light from time to time in the 1970s, but were mostly dealt with on an individual basis. It was not seen as the major problem it was to become (see Ferris 1977 for an interesting account of local authority attitudes to the employment of homosexual people in social services departments at this time).

The slow realisation during the 1980s that children's homes could be prime sites for sexual offending has been described by the former Chief Inspector of Social Services at that time:

> The subject of sex abuse of children in institutions did not really become an issue until the early 1980s ... and there were tremendous pressures, I think, on everybody in the system at that time, to deny that those of us working in the system and accepted by the community as being devoted to the interests of children were in fact exploiting them and abusing them (House of Commons 1998: para. 799).

In Belfast, there were continuing stories emerging about the Kincora children's home and the long-term abuse of its residents. The Dublin-based *Irish Independent* had first published stories in January 1980 about Kincora being the centre of a homosexual vice-ring, but the true extent of the activities there and the alleged 'cover-ups' continued to mystify for many years (see, e.g., Rafferty 1986).

A 1984 parliamentary review of all forms of care for children, including residential care, made no mention of sexual abuse as a problem area. A passing reference was made to the 'trouble [*sic*] at the Kincora Boys Hostel' and the need for better complaints systems, and the imbalance between care staff as figures of authority and vulnerable children was noted: 'The risk of abuse of power by social workers and other adults concerned with children in care is ... sufficiently serious for there to be a need for some means by which a child can contact, without fear of reprisal, their local authority parent' (House of Commons 1984: para. 364; see also paras. 360–5). The pre-employment screening of staff going to work in children's homes in England and Wales started in 1986 (see below), but cases of abusing staff continued to crop up, most prominently in the case of Frank Beck. Beck was sentenced to life imprisonment for a series of offences against children in his care in Leicestershire ('Head of Children's Homes jailed for life, five times', *Independent*, 30 November 1991).

In the mean time, the Children Act 1989, with its greater emphasis on listening to children, had been passed and its accompanying guidance outlined what should be done if staff in a children's home suspected that one of their number was abusing children (Department of Health 1991b: paras. 1.34–1.37 and 1.179–1.192; the advice was updated in a later guidance – Department of Health 1999: paras. 6.2–6.30).

What everyone agreed was that the child sex offender was effectively 'invisible' once he had gained work with children in residential care.

Many were also very good at that work:

> paedophiles tend to work very secretively, planning to gain the confidence of children and those responsible for their care over a long period. They groom and seduce the children into sexual activities gradually by means of involvement in other activities which themselves may be acceptable and even commendable and they win the confidence of colleagues by taking on extra duties and responsibilities (SFCRC 1997: 88).

The Waterhouse Report, appearing in February 2000 after three and a half years of deliberation, was an exhaustive account of child physical and sexual abuse in the former local authority areas of Gwynedd and Clwyd in North Wales; the full report was over 900 pages long, and tracked events back to 1974 in all forms of residential child care and fostering, provided by the councils concerned, the private sector and the health services. The report found evidence of 'widespread sexual abuse of boys … in children's residential establishments in Clwyd' (Waterhouse Report 2000: para. 53–10) and singled out two institutions for particular attention: the local authority community home Bryn Estyn near Wrexham, and the private homes run by the Bryn Alyn Community, also in the Wrexham area. The report made no less than 72 recommendations on recruitment, selection, screening, management, inspection and other matters, including the specific role of the Welsh Office.

Many of the sexual offenders who had been active in North Wales had been apprehended and convicted by the time of the Waterhouse Report, but of equal concern to the inquiry was the length of time it had taken for the offending to be brought to light. At Bryn Estyn, the report found two senior members of staff engaged in sexual abuse of many of the young residents without detection. The Deputy Principal, Peter Howarth, who was eventually convicted and subsequently died in prison, abused children in his flat, which was part of the residential complex:

> Invitations to these sessions were by a 'flat list' compiled by Howarth or made up on his instructions and boys who went to the flat were required to wear pyjamas without underpants. Attendance was part of the agreed programme of activities available to boys in the evening. The sessions would begin at about 8.30 p.m. and end at 11.00 p.m. to 11.30 p.m (ibid.: para. 8.05).

The report said it was satisfied that all senior and junior members of staff knew about the 'flat list' but chose not to do anything (ibid.: paras.

8.10–8.12), and criticised what it called the 'cult of silence' that reigned (*ibid.*: paras. 11.01 and 29.22; overall see paras. 29.01–29.33). Many of the report's recommendations were to try to open up the closed world of the residential care system that allowed such offending. The key to 'identification' was to recognise potential offenders at the point of entry to work with children and make sure they did not get past that first point of entry. Screening mechanisms were needed to allow only suitable people into employment with children.

The pre-employment screening of child care workers

In order to prevent sex offenders getting work with children where they might abuse those children, mechanisms have been put into place to screen them out. In broad terms these mechanisms divide into two blocks – the 'discretionary' and the 'mandatory'. The 'discretionary' block is made up of information made available to employers to help them make a selection decision on a potential new member of staff; this information is primarily criminal conviction records, police intelligence and information from other government-held databases. The 'mandatory block' is a non-discretionary legal ban on certain people working with children; the individual and the employer both commit an offence if employment with children takes place.

The 'discretionary block'

The police check (1986–2002)

Applicants for any employment undergo a recruitment and selection procedure, but if that employment is for work with children they also undergo an additional screening process. Since the 1980s, applicants for work as teachers, social workers, probation officers, youth workers, children's homes workers, or any other public employment giving them 'substantial access to children' have been subject to pre-employment screening by means of a 'police check'; in effect a check made against any possible criminal record they may have. On receipt of a conviction record the employer has the discretion whether or not to employ.

As far back as the 1950s, arrangements had been made to allow police to notify the education authorities if they had arrested a teacher committing any offences that might put children at risk (Home Office 1954), but the new arrangements entered into in the 1980s were to ensure that people unsuitable for work with children never got that work in the first place. The model for this pre-employment screening already existed, in terms of vetting would-be childminders and people wishing to foster or adopt children, but the new scale of screening was wider than anything seen before.

First into the field was Northern Ireland. The impetus for action came from the long-running allegations of sexual abuse emerging from the Kincora children's home in Belfast. Various forms of inquiry tried to ascertain exactly what had gone on at Kincora, and one report suggested the introduction of effective pre-employment screening (Sheridan Report 1982).

The Northern Ireland Department of Health and Social Services instituted its Pre-employment Consultancy Service (PECS) in October 1983. Designated employers could now request background information from PECS on all short-listed candidates for a child care job. That information included all *relevant* offences – obtained by PECS from the Royal Ulster Constabulary and with the relevance decided on by PECS officials – and other information from the Department of Health and Social Security's Consultancy Service in London (see below). The system at this time did not include the vetting of teachers.

When England and Wales introduced its system of pre-employment screening in 1986 (see below), Northern Ireland reviewed its own PECS arrangements. Changes were made to ensure that checks only took place on a successful candidate and not whole shortlists, and that the full record was disclosed rather than a selected version (NI Working Party 1988). PECS was also supplemented by a separate system for vetting teachers; records were disclosed by the RUC directly to employing authorities (DENI 1990).

By 1990, the PECS arrangements screened applicants for the Northern Ireland Health and Social Services Boards and Trusts, the National Board for Nursing, Midwifery and Health Visiting, the probation service, the 26 district councils and 57 voluntary organisations. In all, some 400 checks were being made each month (DHSS (NI) 1995: para. 2.11). In 1996, the DHSS issued revised guidelines on how the system should work (DHSS (NI) 1996b) and separate guidance to the voluntary sector on how they should be protecting children (DHSS (NI) 1996c).

Police checks on child care workers in England and Wales started in 1986. The impetus for these checks is attributed to the murder of 4-year-old Marie Payne by Colin Evans in 1984. It emerged that Evans had a record of previous offences against children, but that had not stopped him obtaining voluntary work in the course of which he was able to associate with young children. Evans had not met Marie through his work, but concern was aroused (see 'List of errors that ended in child's death', *Guardian*, 18 December 1984) and the Home Secretary announced the forming of a working party with a brief to:

devise a system under which information about the unsuitability by reason of criminal background of people seeking positions where they will have substantial opportunities for access to children can be communicated to those bodies which are responsible for employing such people, whether in a paid or voluntary capacity (HC Debs, 27 March 1985, cols. 244–5 WA).

The working party's report (Home Office/DHSS 1985) formed the basis for pre-employment screening in England and Wales.

Screening was to be a non-statutory arrangement, laid down in government circulars outlining how local authorities as employers would have Senior Nominated Officers who would liase with their local police forces and establish a channel of communication for requests going one way and criminal record information going the other; requests were supported by the written consent of the applicant concerned. The full criminal record was disclosed and the employing authority would make its appointment decision based on this information. Adjustments were made to build 'exemptions' into the Rehabilitation of Offenders Act 1974 and the Rehabilitation of Offenders (NI) Order 1978 so that past convictions could never be considered 'spent' when applying for work with children (Home Office 1986b; see also Home Office 1986c).

The police were also asked to disclose other information which might give 'cause for serious concern' that a person was unsuitable to work with children. This other non-conviction information would be made up of police intelligence or other information such as acquittals on technicalities. It was often called 'soft' information and it constituted a very grey area. Any police disclosure of it as part of a pre-employment police check had to be authorised by a senior officer.

In 1990 a House of Commons Select Committee recommended that the practice of disclosing 'soft' information to employers should stop on grounds of civil liberties (House of Commons 1990: para. 41); the government of the day did not agree and thought 'a check of recordable offences only, would be insufficient' (Home Office 1990c: para. 12). Subsequent reports maintained this line (see, e.g., Warner Report 1992: para. 5.9; Home Office 1996d: para. 30; Utting Report 1997: para. 15.7).

The disclosure of 'soft' information became headline news at the end of 2003 when Ian Huntley was convicted of the murders of two children in the village of Soham in Cambridgeshire. At the end of Huntley's trial it was revealed that police held intelligence on him regarding nine earlier suspected sex crimes but none of this had been disclosed to employers when he got a caretaker's job at the college where he had access to children and young people ('Vetting failures let caretaker slip through net', *Guardian*, 18 December 2003). The Bichard Inquiry was established to see how this had been allowed to happen, including 'the effectiveness of the relevant intelligence-based record keeping, the vetting practices in the forces since 1995 and information sharing with other agencies' (Home Office 2003c; Bichard Inquiry Report 2004).

Meanwhile – returning to the 1980s – the new system of police checks slowly got into its stride. Minor adjustments were made to the system in 1988 and again in 1993, with the latter circular being the basis for checks throughout the 1990s (Home Office 1993a). As awareness of child sexual abuse rose, so too did the numbers subject to vetting; in 1985, it had been anticipated that some 100,000 people would be checked each year but in 1993, the actual number was 665,000 per year (Home Office 1993b: para. 23).

In 1989, three pilot schemes were started to try to extend pre-employment screening beyond its local authority and public sector standing to the voluntary sector. The pilot schemes were of only middling success (Unell 1992) but did result in a system modelled on the Northern Ireland PECS arrangements, whereby national voluntary organisations went through the Voluntary Organisations Consultancy Service (VOCS), who obtained police records and Consultancy Service records (see below) for them (Home Office 1994b; see also Home Office 1994c).

Scotland followed the 1985 Home Office/DHSS working party guidelines to start its checking system in 1989 (Scottish Office 1989b); some vetting already existed in residential establishments and schools (SWSG 1985). Instead of liaising with their local police forces, Scottish authorities contacted the Scottish Criminal Record Office (SCRO) in Glasgow, where their requests were handled by the SCRO's User Support Bureau.

From the initial brief given to the 1985 Home Office/DHSS Working Party to 'devise a system', pre-employment screening has been largely a bureaucratic exercise of information (criminal records) exchange and decision-making. The civil liberties questions of privacy and re-habilitation rights have been raised (see, e.g., NCCL 1988) and the inclusion of posts outside the 'access to children' criteria, the taking into account of non-relevant offences and the relatively powerless position of the job applicant in terms of effective redress have been examined (Hebenton and Thomas 1993: esp. chap. 6). The journal *Social Work Today* said these questions 'ought to be generating a fierce debate' but feared they were not ('Disclosing criminal convictions', editorial, 11 February 1988), and Essex Police declared its dissatisfaction with local authorities 'abusing' the Home Office circulars (cited in AMA 1995: 19).

Organisations representing the interests of ex-offenders produced guidance of 'damage limitation' to help ex-offenders into work (Apex Trust 1990; NACRO 1996b).

Researchers produced evidence to show the variation in decision-making based on criminal record disclosure, including the continuing possibility of sex offenders getting through (Smith 1998, 1999), and even a government-appointed task force reported that it was unhappy with the 'varying interpretations' and 'geographical inconsistencies' of checking arrangements (Better Regulation Task Force 1999: para. 4.3.4).

None of it made any difference. The conventional wisdom prevailed that criminal record checks were essential and should be an integral part of selection procedures, that information technology would improve things and the only real question was how we could possibly have managed without them before the 1980s.

Other databases
Apart from police-held information, employers had two other sources of information they could access to screen would-be employees.

The Consultancy Service was an index held by the Department of Health and made up of names sent into them by employers where, for example:

- a member of staff had been prosecuted for an offence against a child;
- a member of staff had been dismissed or resigned after a child's welfare had been put at risk;
- a member of staff had been disciplined and re-deployed away from work with children; and
- there were any other circumstances where a child had been put at risk.

It was originally up to employers to decide when to submit information to the index, unless it was an employee in a children's home, when it became a legal duty to submit (Children's Homes Regulations 1991, S.1. No. 1506, reg. 19(2)(b) and later the Children's Homes Regulations 2001 SI 3967, regs. 10 and 26); this position changed again when the Protection of Children Act 1999 was implemented and it became a duty to submit on all staff (see below). In 1996 there were a reported 7,000 names on the index and some 53,000 checks made annually (HC Debs, 28 October 1996, WA 779; Home Office 1993a: Annex C).

'List 99' was the second source of information open to employers to consult. It was much like the Consultancy Service, but applied to teachers and was held by the Department for Education and Employment. The Secretary of State had powers to 'direct' that certain people were 'unsuitable' and should have their names added to the list (Education (Teachers) Regulations 1993, S.1, No. 543), although this power applied only to England and Wales; the list itself covers the whole of the UK.

A need for change?

Meanwhile, periodic reports of individuals sexually abusing children in their care still made the headlines. The most notorious was the case of Frank Beck, who had abused children for over 13 years in the Leicestershire area (D'Arcy and Gosling 1998). The Beck affair led directly to two reports on improving residential care for children (Department of Health 1991c; Warner Report 1992) and the establishment of a Central Support force for Children's Residential Care; the Support Force produced further guidance on recruitment and selection of residential care staff (SFCRC 1997). The Warner Report focused on the recruitment and selection of staff for children's homes and the need to ensure that police checks were part of an integrated and effective system of selection; those responsible for selection started referring to new staff having been 'Warner interviewed' or 'Warnered'.

Despite all this activity, concerns continued to be raised and not just within children's homes. In Belfast, a sex offender had gained access to children through voluntary organisations (DHSS (NI) 1993) and in Newcastle, a man committed sexual offences in a nursery school against a number of children (Hunt Report 1994). In Scotland, the inquiry report into the Dunblane Primary School shootings went on to look at how Thomas Hamilton, the man responsible, had been able to find work in youth clubs that he himself had set up. Hamilton was not a convicted sex offender, but his behaviour towards children had been the subject of persistent complaints and concerns (Cullen Report 1996: chap. 11).

In the entrepreneurial spirit of the times, a private company called 'Faircheck' was established in London to see if the independent sector could lead the way in good practice in pre-employment screening. Launched on 9 May 1995, Faircheck offered a package of background checks, personality tests and interviews, primarily to local authorities and others looking for workers with children, elderly people or any other vulnerable group. The cost of the package was reported to be £950 per check, which seems to have been too high for some authorities and in less than a year the company went out of business ('Faircheck private vetting agency folds', *Community Care*, 15–21 February 1996).

In 1993 the Home Office started a review of the use of police records for pre-employment screening. With seven years' experience of operating the new systems it was clear that the number of checks was rising dramatically and the burden on the police was considerable. As the whole exercise was guided only by Home Office circulars and vetting took place in countless offices across the country, it seemed no one effectively had control of it (Home Office 1993b).

During the review period a number of reports started appearing in the press that said the government wanted to start charging for police checks; up to now they had been free. These press reports looked suspiciously like judicious leaks to sound out what the public thought of this idea (see, e.g., 'Bosses to buy crime files on job-hunters', *Daily Express*, 19 December 1994; 'Ministers plan police record sales agency', *Guardian*, 16 January 1995; 'Tories secret plan to sell off police records', *The Sunday Times*, 5 February 1995).

In 1996 a white paper was published suggesting an overhaul of all criminal record checks for employment screening, whether or not children were involved. *On the Record* proposed a new Criminal Records Agency to take this work away from the police and in future to have employers pay for each check; if the earlier press reports had been a 'sounding out' exercise the response had been muted to say the least. Conviction disclosures were to be on three levels:

1   an 'enhanced' criminal record check for child care workers, including non-conviction information;
2   a 'full' check for those with some contact with children; and
3   a Criminal Conviction Certificate for any employment and which individual applicants would apply for and pay for (see Home Office 1996d).

A similar consultation paper was published for Scotland, making similar proposals (Scottish Office 1996). Both consultation papers provided model codes of practice which they thought should be agreed to by employers having access to records, with the withdrawal of access being the sanction to ensure compliance.

The Criminal Record Bureau (2002 to the present)
The Police Act 1997, Part V received its Royal Assent on 21 March 1997 and gave the statutory underpinning for these new 'three-tier' arrangements. The Act made no reference to the creation of a Criminal Record Agency, but the new government coming in that year, after taking a careful look at the law, confirmed that it would go ahead and renamed the agency as the Criminal Records Bureau. The Bureau was to be based on Merseyside as a private–public partnership enterprise, would have direct access to the Police National Computer and was expected to start

operations in July 2001 (Home Office 1999e); the private company Capita had won the contract to create the new agency. Scotland was to have the same system but based on the Scottish Criminal Record Office in Glasgow rather than the Bureau (Scottish Office 1998b). Voluntary sector organisations immediately started campaigning against the cost element which had been introduced and which they foresaw as putting many volunteers off (see, e.g., HC Debs, 5 July 1999: cols. 432–5 WA); this campaign was eventually successful and the government agreed to make checks free for the voluntary sector (DfEE 2001).

Enhanced disclosure was very similar to the old police check on child care workers started in 1986. Instead of going to local forces, employers simply went to the CRB. The CRB had PNC terminals to read off conviction records and approached local forces for any other relevant information or intelligence; this information was now renamed as 'Approved' or 'Additional' information depending on whether the job applicant was informed of its existence ('Approved') or denied knowledge of its existence because it might hamper ongoing police investigations ('Additional').

The difficulties for the police in deciding whether or not to release 'Additional' and 'Approved' information were deep-seated. When it was not released in the case of Ian Huntley who went on to murder two children in Soham, there was an outcry and an inquiry (Bichard Inquiry Report 2004). At more or less the same time, much less attention was paid to a High Court decision that the West Midlands Police had been wrong to release information on a man investigated for 'indecent exposure' allegations; the man was neither charged or prosecuted but the disclosures effectively ended his social work career ('Police "wrong" to pass on allegation', *Community Care*, 29 January–4 February 2004: 6; *X v. Chief Constable of West Midlands Police* [2004] EWHC Admin. 61).

Enhanced disclosure also required the CRB to access the old 'Consultancy Service' and 'List 99' which had now been put on a statutory footing by the Protection of Children Act 1999. Inclusion on these lists also meant you were effectively barred from working with children. The 1999 Act renamed the lists as the Protection of Children Act List or POCA List and the Department of Education and Employment List (still usually referred to as 'List 99'). Regulations now place a duty on educational employers always to submit information to the Secretary of State on people considered unsuitable to work in teaching and always to ensure a check has been made against 'List 99' (Education (Restriction of Employment) Regulations 2000 SI 2419 Reg. 11; see also DfES 2002). The CRB in effect became the 'one-stop shop' for employers.

Employers were now required by law to input information on employees considered unsuitable to work with children regardless of any criminal proceedings having been instituted. The Secretary of State made the final decision on inclusion and individuals had the right of appeal to the new Protection of Children Act Tribunal (later renamed as the Care Standards Tribunal; see the Protection of Children and Vulnerable Adults and Care Standards Tribunal Regulations 2002 SI 816), given the new ban that now existed once you were on the lists (Department of Health 2000b). The old Consultancy Service had its 7,000 names weeded down to just 1,000 under the new arrangements for the POCA list which does beg questions about the sort of information previously held on that now 'discarded' 6,000.

The Care Standards Act 2000 created a similar list of individuals unsuitable to work with vulnerable adults – the Protection of Vulnerable Adults or POVA List which came on line on 7 June 2004 (Department of Health 2003). Listed individuals could also appeal to the Care Standards Tribunal. It was possible to be included on both the lists for children and adults and given the difficulties of deciding if you went on both or just one the possibilities of combining the various lists was a matter for continuing debate.

Even before the Criminal Record Bureau (CRB) started its work, questions had been raised about its ability to cope with the demands that would be put on it and the quality of the data it would be disclosing; evidence had emerged of a high level of inaccuracy within the criminal record database (Thomas 2001b). The Home Affairs Select Committee made an inquiry into what was going on and called for improvements in the data quality and suggested a delayed start in order to get everything right. The committee was particularly concerned to find that the CRB was unable to publish detailed financial estimates of its work, despite having been established for four years (House of Commons 2001: para. 48)! The government listened to the committee but was primarily concerned to proceed as fast as possible (Home Office 2001a).

The three tiers of disclosure were now called:

1   Enhanced Disclosure;
2   Standard Disclosure; and
3   Basic Disclosure.

Employers had to register – and become Registered Bodies – to receive the first two forms of disclosure at a fee of £300 and thereafter pay £12 for every check carried out (Home Office 2001b); the CRB also published its promised Code of Practice (for further general details, see Thomas 2002).

In March 2002 – a year behind schedule – the CRB made a delayed start on issuing enhanced disclosures. Standard and basic disclosures were put on hold. By August the whole system was teetering on the verge of breakdown as the CRB was overwhelmed by demand. Some schools were unable to start the new academic year because new teachers were unchecked and the backlog seemed to grow by the day.

The government responded by sending in an Independent Review Team (IRT) to sort out the CRB with short-term support and advice on necessary changes for the long term. The IRT's report appeared in February 2003 with a total of ten recommendations on making the CRB more efficient. A series of consultation exercises were started to explore the recommendations, which included possible fingerprinting of some applicants for work with children. Meanwhile, amidst much expressed angst about 'bedding down' and 'teething problems' the CRB was allowed quietly to increase its fees from £12 to £29 per enhanced check (Home Office 2003d) and increase it again to £33 from April 2004 (Home Office 2003e). Having been a free service, the commodification of criminal records was becoming a lucrative business.

The CRB and Capita were heavily criticised for their ineptitude (see, e.g., 'Capita punishment', *Observer*, 8 September 2002) and the failure was said to have 'a weary sad inevitability about it' ('Sad inevitability of criminal records failure', *Computer Weekly*, 6 March 2003): 'following the report on the CRB, the government is now paying Capita more money to do less ... it seems that in this case Capita has been rewarded for its failures' (ibid.). A later report from the National Audit Office was less critical, believing the CRB to have achieved a 'more comprehensive and consistent [system] than that which existed before it was set up' (NAO 2004a, 2004b).

Whatever the pros and cons of the new centralised CRB system were, it remained a fact that employers in receipt of disclosures from the CRB had still to make a decision on the basis of the information received. It was the belief that this exercise of discretion by employers was still not a sufficient safeguard that led on to the search for a complementary 'mandatory block'.

'The mandatory block'

The Home Office's 1996 consultation document on the *Sentencing and Supervision of Sex Offenders* had proposed making it a criminal offence for a convicted sex offender to apply for work with children, or even to accept the offer of such work (Home Office 1996a: paras. 64–77). This proposal was refined in yet another consultation paper, which tried to define more accurately concepts that included 'seeking work' and 'accepting an offer of work' involving contact with children (Home Office/Scottish Office 1997); civil liberty groups pointed out the inherent problems, such as someone obtaining work with no access to children but later being redeployed by an employer (Liberty 1997b).

In general terms the civil liberty lobby and campaign groups for offenders and ex-offenders were critical of the new proposals but child care organisations were happier with them. The government now formed an Interdepartmental Working Group to take the proposals forward. The group published two reports covering a number of questions including that of a legal ban on working with children (Home Office 1999f 1999g); key recommendations were:

1 to identify and ban unsuitable people from working with children;
2 to create a new criminal offence which the 'unsuitable person' would commit if they worked with children; and
3 to provide a new definition of 'working with children'.

It also affirmed the need for the CRB to become a one-stop shop (see above) and for 'Similar schemes to be put in place for Scotland and Northern Ireland with access to all information on those banned in each country to be available in all three and with reciprocal bans in place' (ibid.). Implementing these further recommendations was going to require new primary legislation. In the mean time, without any recourse to legislation, an agreement was entered into between the Home Office, the probation service and the employment service to ensure that information about sex offenders and other potentially dangerous offenders was passed to the employment service, so that these offenders were not directed towards work with children or work that would give them opportunities to reoffend, whether against children or adults (Home Office 1999h).

The Criminal Justice and Court Services Act 2000 eventually gave the courts powers legally to ban individuals from working with children. Part II of the Act enables courts when sentencing to add on a disqualification order if the offence is an 'offence against a child' and the sentence is one of 12 months or more in custody, or a hospital or guardianship order is made within the meaning of the Mental Health Act 1983. An 'offence against a child' is defined in Schedule 4 of the Act; disqualification orders may be made against both adult and juvenile offenders. The Criminal Justice Act 2003, s. 229, Schedule 30 made it even easier to make a disqualification order by removing the 12 months' custody requirement.

An offence is committed if someone subject to a disqualification order subsequently applies for or gains work with children, and an offence is also committed by an individual who allows someone, subject to an order, to work with children. Disqualification orders can be appealed against after ten years (five for a juvenile) to the Care Standards Tribunal.

Summary

Educational, care and leisure settings have all been sites of sexual abuse against children. Adults working in schools, children's homes, day nurseries and other statutory settings have been convicted of offences against children. The same has happened in voluntary settings, sports clubs and even the church. This chapter has outlined the measures now in place to exclude known sexual offenders and other individuals deemed unsuitable to work with children. In particular it has looked at the rise of criminal record disclosures as a means of pre-employment screening and the advent of the Criminal Records Bureau which started work in 2002; it has also considered the use of disqualification orders to place a legal ban on certain people being allowed to work with children.

Chapter 9

Protection in the community

In this chapter we explore the growing use of the civil law to contain and incapacitate the sex offender. These measures complement the investigation and punishment of the sex offender by the criminal law and do so in order greater to protect the public and improve public safety. In the UK a number of civil measures have been 'constructed' in the last eight years in the interests of public protection, including the sex offender 'register', sex offender orders, restraining orders, notification orders, sexual offences prevention orders (combining the sex offender order and restraining order), foreign travel orders and risk of sexual harm orders. We have also seen attempts – as yet un-successful – to change the law on mental health to bring sex offenders with a 'dangerous, severe personality disorder' into its ambit (see Chapters 2 and 6).

The sex offender 'register'

Origins of a policy

The idea of a register of sex offenders or paedophiles had been circulating in social work and police circles for some time, before the 1996 Home Office consultation document on the *Sentencing and Supervision of Sex Offenders* proposed that convicted sex offenders should be required to notify the police every time they change address. In effect, a register of all convicted sex offenders would be compiled and kept up to date by the offenders themselves (Home Office 1996a: paras. 41–62).

The introduction of specialist police 'Child Protection Units' and joint arrangements for videoing children's testimony had drawn the police yet further into this area of work. The creation of the Paedophile Section (later renamed as the Serious Sex Offenders Unit) at the National Criminal Intelligence Service had confirmed a national dimension to this work, but the police were still self-critical about their inability to collate and use intelligence on child sexual abuse and sex offenders as effectively as they would wish (Hughes *et al.* 1996).

Meanwhile, the American experience of sex offender registers was beginning to filter across the Atlantic to both police and child care practitioners. The general public also picked up on it and its associated ideas of letting the community know where these offenders lived. The father of Sophie Hook, a 7-year-old sexually abused and killed in North Wales, voiced his support for the idea of a register when it emerged that the police had kept a 'close eye' on the man who had attacked his daughter for a number of years before the abduction and murder ('Murdered girl's father supports register plans', *Independent*, 20 July 1996).

Within police circles, it was the Police Superintendents' Association which was the most vocal in calling for a UK sex offender register, and after two unsuccessful private members' bills had been introduced to the House of Commons, the government proposed a register in its 1996 consultation document.

The idea of registration itself was tentatively premised on three arguments:

- it would help police identify suspects after a crime;
- it *could* help prevent crimes; and
- it *might* act as a deterrent (Home Office 1996a: para. 43, emphasis added).

The consultation period ran from June to August 1996, and the Home Office received some 238 formal responses, with 87 per cent of respondents favouring the idea of the 'register' (HC Debs, 25 October 1996, WA 965). In political terms the opposition party of the day was in almost total agreement (Labour Party 1996); Alun Michael for the opposition gave 'an assurance that we will work with Government to get [this bill] through as quickly as possible' (HC Debs, 27 January 1997, col. 33).

The registration proposals included the requirement that the offender should notify the police of any change of address within 21 days of the change; special arrangements would exist for those of 'no fixed abode'.

The requirement to notify would continue, depending on the severity of the original sentence. Any custodial sentence of more than 30 months meant a lifetime's requirement to notify changes to the police. Lesser sentences would result in time periods equivalent to the provisions of the Rehabilitation of Offenders Act 1974, which allows convictions to be 'spent' in designated circumstances after a given length of time, and all these time periods would be halved for juvenile offenders.

Details registered with the police were to be stored on the Police National Computer (PNC) and it was signalled that other agencies engaged in child protection activities might have access to it. Although unnamed, the assumption was that this meant the probation service, social services departments and other agencies such as the National Society for the Prevention of Cruelty to Children (NSPCC).

The consultation document was silent on the role of the police in using the information they received and on how they might disseminate it. It said nothing on the role of the police in actively enforcing the registration requirements and said only that defaulters should be fined up to £1,000 or imprisoned for a month.

The Sex Offenders Bill published 18 December 1996 pretty well reflected the proposals in the consultation document, and there was a broad consensus in the press on the need for the bill. Having created the 'monsters' and the 'sex fiends' the press could not really 'disinvent' their creations and a register seemed a good way of tracking them. Only Matthew Parris in *The Times* was willing to criticise the bill, which he dismissed as meaningless: 'there is no reason for this Bill. No reason at all. It is simply a piece of electioneering' (Parris 1997); a general election was just four months away.

On some matters the bill revealed some interesting departures from the consultation document. The document, for example, had never mentioned offenders who had received a police caution as being in need of going on the register; the bill now included such offenders and made them liable to register. The time period for registering changes in the consultation document was 21 days; in the bill it came down to 14 days.

As we saw in Chapter 4, part of the rationale for a caution was that the offence was minor, 'atypical' and unlikely to be repeated. The rationale for registration was, if anything, the opposite; it was a serious typical offence and the offender was likely to do it again. As Liberty put it: 'Cautions are supposed to act as a salutary warning ... if cautions are being used for sexual offences deemed so serious that they merit notification, they should not be' (1997a: para. 1.5). The bill also departed from the consultation document on the question of qualifying offences. The document's original 32 offences in England and Wales were reduced in the bill to just 14. Omissions include bigamy, abduction, soliciting by a man, giving drugs to facilitate intercourse, incest by a woman, causing prostitution of a woman and others. Indecent exposure, which is a category of offence for which the Home Office keeps records, appeared neither in the consultation document nor the bill, even though some professionals believe it often to be a precursor to more serious sexual offending (see, e.g., Worrall 1997: 121; HMIP 1998a: para. 5.58).

A comparison of the qualifying offences in the consultation document and the bill is further confused by the fact that the former is directed only at England and Wales, whilst the bill is intent on registration requirements for the whole of the UK. This meant further lists of qualifying offences for Scotland and Northern Ireland had to be added to the bill because of the different laws in those two countries. In Scotland, the very age of criminal responsibility is two years below that in England, making registration a possibility for a Scottish child (aged 8 and upwards) whereas in England, a child of the same age, doing the same things, cannot even have committed an offence (the age of criminal responsibility being 10).

The parliamentary debate

The parliamentary committee discussions on the bill – Standing Committee D – made no reference to the qualifying offences left out from the consultation document. No reference was made to the decision to include cautions as well as convictions as criteria for registering (although that issue was raised earlier, outside the committee, on the main floor of the House (HC Debs, 27 January 1997, col. 60)). The debate did not consider the ways in which the police would ensure verification and compliance with requirements to register and whether or not they would be active in searching out defaulters and, if so, what extra resources they would need. It is, however, worth noting that right at the outset of discussions, the government announced an increase in the penalties that would apply for failing to register – the original £1,000 rising to £5,000 and one month in prison rising to six months in prison – and that this decision was made 'after receiving representations from the police ... to stop sex offenders from flouting the registration requirements' (Home Office 1997b; HC Debs, 27 January 1997, cols. 30–1).

In summary, the main criticisms aimed at the bill as it passed through the House of Commons were the facts that: 1) it was not retrospective; 2) it was unclear on how the police should use the information registered with them, and whether or not this might include public disclosure; and 3) in concentrating only on convicted sex offenders it was missing out thousands of other potentially dangerous people.

On the question of public disclosure or 'community notification' to let neighbourhoods know when a registered sex offender has moved into the area, the view was expressed that this was not appropriate for the UK even if it existed in the USA. The preferred option was that of 'controlled disclosure' that would possibly include disclosure to one or two particular members of the community, but not to everyone. In the main, information of this nature would remain for use by professionals and practitioners only. Alun Michael concluded that 'we may learn some lessons from the United States [but] ... our culture, law, police service and other services are different' (HC Debs, Standing Committee D, 4 February 1997, col. 58).

The debate was simultaneously carried on outside Parliament, and at one point Home Secretary Michael Howard looked willing to concede on community notification ('Howard set to name sex offenders', *Guardian*, 12 February 1997). The police, however, remained opposed to the idea and the Association of Chief Police Officers (ACPO) through its spokesperson, Tony Butler, Chief Constable of Gloucestershire, let it be known that notification on a wide scale would be 'fraught with dangers' and 'could drive offenders underground'. *The Times* believed:

> Last night's statement from ACPO is likely to thwart the mounting pressure on Michael Howard to allow neighbourhoods to be told when convicted child sex offenders move in. Mr. Howard, who said earlier this week that he was giving serious consideration to the idea, is unlikely to want to press ahead in the face of opposition from senior police officers ('Police chiefs oppose plan to advertise paedophiles', 15 February 1997).

A few years later Howard said it had never been his intention to allow public disclosure because it would be 'inviting vigilante activity' (cited in Silverman and Wilson 2002: 162).

Back within the confines of Parliament, attempts to amend the Sex Offenders Bill and introduce regulations and guidance on the use of information were unsuccessful. The status quo would remain, and existing channels of communication and areas of discretion were felt sufficient for the time being.

The Sex Offenders Act 1997

The Sex Offenders Act, s. 1 applied to all those convicted or cautioned of an offence outlined in Schedule 1 to the Act. It also applied to those with mental health problems where there has been no finding of guilt but a hospital order had been made under the Mental Health Act 1983 for reasons of insanity or being unfit to plead, and where an offence as listed in Schedule 1 would otherwise have been committed. The time period for which the Act applied is outlined in Table 9.1 (mirroring the Rehabilitation of Offenders Act 1974) and time periods commence from the day of conviction or caution, with subsequent time spent in custody of hospital being discounted. The Sex Offender Act 1997 was later subsumed into Part 2 of the Sexual Offences Act 2003, and Table 9.1 gives the slightly revised later version of time periods (as of 1 May 2004).

A restriction order attached to a hospital order usually implies the offence has been particularly serious, and means the restricted patient cannot be discharged from hospital by doctors without the consent of the Home Secretary; any discharge can also have conditions attached to it (Mental Health Act 1983, s. 41–2). Schedule 1 to the 1997 Act listed the offences to which the 'register' will apply and divided into three parts for 1) the law in England and Wales; 2) the law in Scotland; and 3) the law in Northern Ireland (now in Sexual Offences Act 2003, Sch. 3).

The 1997 Act set out the details which had to be given to the police within 14 days of conviction or change of address; these were simply the person's name, or any other used names, and address. Date of birth and address at the time of conviction or caution may be required for purposes of identification. The details could be given in person, by a visit to a police station or in writing. The police had also to be notified if the offender stayed at any other address for longer than two weeks in a 12-month period. Any failure to comply was punishable by a fine up to £5,000 and/or a period of imprisonment of up to six months.

For sex offenders below the age of 18, all registration periods were to be halved. The NSPCC was amongst those that thought young offenders should not be on the register at all and that alternative arrangements should have been devised (NSPCC 1997); the Sexual Offences Act 1993 had abolished the presumption that boys under the age of 14 were incapable of sexual intercourse, and enabled charges to be brought against them for the first time for rape and various forms of unlawful sexual intercourse.

When the register was later strengthened (see below) proposals were put forward to remove children and young people from the register altogether. One idea was to have a completely separate register for young people held by a welfare agency rather than the police (Home Office/Scottish Executive 2001: chap. Six). Many child care organisations were enthused by these proposals but were left disappointed by the resulting white paper which simply made no mention at all of the young sex offender except to increase the sanctions for non-compliance (Home

Table 9.1 Sexual Offences Act 2003 'registration' periods

Description of relevant offender	Notification period
A person who, in respect of the offence, is or has been sentenced to imprisonment for life or for a term of 30 months or more	An indefinite period beginning with the relevant date
A person who, in respect of the offence, has been made the subject of an order under s. 210F(1) of the Criminal Procedure (Scotland) Act 1995 (order for lifelong restriction)	An indefinite period beginning with that date
A person who, in respect of the offence or finding, is or has been admitted to a hospital subject to a restriction order	An indefinite period beginning with that date
A person who, in respect of the offence, is or has been sentenced to imprisonment for a term of more than 6 months but less than 30 months	10 years beginning with that date
A person who, in respect of the offence, is or has been sentenced to imprisonment for a term of 6 months or less	7 years beginning with that date
A person who, in respect of the offence or finding, is or has been admitted to a hospital without being subject to a restriction order	7 years beginning with that date
A person within s. 80(1)(d)	2 years beginning with that date
A person in whose case an order for conditional discharge or, in Scotland, a probation order, is made in respect of the offence	The period of conditional discharge or, in Scotland, the probation period
A person of any other description	5 years beginning with the relevant date

Office 2002b). This focus on non-compliance was even more surprising because the original consultation paper had put the compliance rate by 2001 as high as 97 per cent and 'steadily improving' and admitted that 'it is not currently possible to interrogate the [register] data ... to produce collated statistical information about particular groups of offenders, for example, the number of them below the age of 18 years' (Home Office/ Scottish Executive 2001: 11; see also Thomas 2003).

Implementing the Sex Offenders Act 1997

The Home Office published guidance on the new law for the police in England, Wales and Northern Ireland (Home Office 1997c) and the Scottish Office did the same for Scotland (Scottish Office 1997a; see also NIO 1997). The Home Office Police Research Group circulated information on how registers worked in the USA (Hebenton and Thomas 1997). Further guidance was sent to local authority social services and social work departments and to hospital managers (NHS Executive 1997; Scottish Office 1997b). The stated intention was that this initial guidance was to be considered as 'interim' in status whilst further work continued on drawing in other agencies, such as housing departments and schools (see also Department of Health 1998: para. 3.9).

The interim guidance of 1997 (Home Office 1997c) limited itself to taking practitioners through the Act and its implications and adding on an Appendix A entitled 'Managing Information Acquired under the Provisions of the Sex Offenders Act 1997'. The guidance had little to say on resource implications for the police, or exactly how they were supposed to ensure compliance and verification that addresses were being accurately notified. The guidance also skirted around another snag to implementation that had arisen: the new systems required the police to be given advance warning that a new name had been added to the register of those required to notify. Whilst the courts and prisons were happy routinely to advise the police each time a new name was added, the medical profession and health care professionals had been more reluctant. They interpreted the Act as putting duties and responsibilities on no one other than the offender and, therefore, it followed that the offender should consent to them notifying the police, and that they would only over-ride a withholding of consent if they judged it to be in the public interest. They disliked the idea of 'automatic' routine notifications. The NHS Executive could only say that it 'anticipated that the need to protect the public means that the balance will generally come down in favour of notification' (1997: Part A, para. 8). Later the Secretary of State would be given powers to regulate in this area to achieve greater consistency (Sexual Offences Act 2003, s. 96).

The follow-up to the interim guidance appeared in draft form in the summer of 1999 and was described as drawing 'upon the good practices established since the 1997 Act came into force' (Home Office PSTU 1999). This guidance reaffirmed the idea that information exchange between agencies was to be integrated into risk assessment and management systems, and was not to be seen as an end in itself. It also emphasised the principle that information sharing should 'be rooted in the powers and duties of any agency' (ibid.: para. 13) and not be exchanged just because another agency requested it; in other language this might be termed the 'need to know principle'. The police and other agencies were encouraged to draw up inter-agency protocols outlining how information would be shared (ibid.: paras. 17–18). At the time of writing this guidance is still only in draft form.

The register itself was, from the outset, to be held on the Police National Computer (PNC), which is available to all forces in the UK through 5,000 terminals from its operational headquarters in Hendon, north London. At the time of writing the police are developing ViSOR – the Violent and Sex Offender Register – as a new database to store more information on registrants in a way accessible to the police and probation services ('Visor makes a name for itself', *PITO News*, Summer 2003).

The sex offender register had come online on 1 September 1997, and despite some early concerns that offenders were not complying and were 'going to ground', and despite various pessimistic headlines from the press, by the end of the year, 88 per cent of offenders had reportedly notified the police of their whereabouts as requested ('Hundreds of violent sex offenders go to ground', *Sunday Telegraph,* 28 December 1997).

By February 1999, 8,161 individuals were recorded on the PNC as having notified the police in England and Wales of their details (HC Debs, 12 May 1999, col. 159 WA), and by March 2001 the figure was put at 'about 15,000' (Home Office/Scottish Executive 2001: 11).

On the first anniversary of the register, the professional social work journal *Community Care* conducted a survey of 200 social workers on their views of the register's usefulness. Most thought it had had a limited effect and had diverted public attention to the 'stranger danger', away from the much greater threat to children from their own immediate or extended families. Half the social workers were in favour of 'community notification', and a majority also thought that a register of suspects and those found 'guilty' in civil actions should be kept, as well as those convicted before September 1997 (Valios 1998).

Strengthening the 'register'

Since its inception the sex offender register has been strengthened in two identifiable phases. The first changes to the register came in 2000 when new legislation introduced a strengthening of the requirements placed on registrants. Initial reporting was to be within three days rather than fourteen and was in future to be in person at a prescribed police station, rather than by mail or email. The police were also given new powers to photograph and fingerprint offenders on initial reporting and the sanction for non-compliance was increased from a maximum six months' imprisonment to a possible five years. All these changes were contained in Schedule 5 of the Criminal Justice and Court Services Act 2000, which in turn amended the Sex Offenders Act 1997.

The changes were a direct response to the abduction and murder of 8-year-old Sarah Payne in July 2000, and Home Secretary Jack Straw said: 'We have I believe, recognised the very strong public concern which her murder has evoked. This has been brought home to us very strongly in the discussions we have had with Mr. and Mrs. Payne about how the law could be improved' (Home Office 2000e; see also Home Office 2002b: 34, Annex 1). The public concern at this time had also been expressed through the headlines of the *News of the World* newspaper, which started a campaign for public access to the register. Such access was refused (see below) and the changes to strengthen the register were arguably to deflect the demands for open access (see Thomas 2004).

At the same time as devising these changes the Home Office published its own commissioned evaluation of the working of the register. The report, entitled *Where Are They Now?*, found the police to be supportive of the register despite the extra work it gave them, and encouraged by the better multi-agency working it had created with the probation service (Plotnikoff and Woolfson 2000). They did have difficulties in getting information on new registrants within the fourteen days allowed, and sometimes sex offenders could turn up at a police station and be the first the police knew of it (ibid.: 21); how that now squared with reducing the initial reporting time from fourteen days down to three was never made clear.

One thing the evaluation report felt unable to comment on was the overall effectiveness of the register. Was it making communities any safer? The authors were pessimistic: 'forces had no agreed way of quantifying the contribution of sex offender monitoring to improving community safety ... no single measure of effectiveness emerged from this study as suitable for performance measurement' (ibid.: 50). It could safely be said that 94 per cent of those required to notify were doing so, but the success of the procedural operation of the register has to be distinguished from its overall effectiveness as an instrument of community safety.

One other innovation brought in by the Criminal Justice and Court Services Act 2000 was that of the Multi-agency Public Protection Panel or MAPPP. The MAPPP formalised the previously informal arrangements that had grown up between police, probation and sometimes other agencies like social services departments, since the advent of the register. The work of the MAPPP will be considered in more detail below.

The second phase of changes to the register was instigated by a Home Office formal review of its work. A consultation paper had been published in July 2001 outlining various options but premised on the idea that, once again, 'some aspects [of the register] could be strengthened' (Home Office/Scottish Executive 2001: 1). Views were sought on the range of offences that should lead to registration, the nature of the registration requirements, the position of sex offenders under 18, and the position of sex offenders who travelled abroad.

Proposals coming out of the review were contained in a chapter of the white paper on sexual offences that was to become the basis for the new Sexual Offences Bill. In keeping with the general theme the chapter was unequivocally entitled 'Strengthening the Sex Offenders Register' (Home Office 2002b: chap. One). It was now suggested that registrants be asked to notify all changes within three days – not just the initial reporting; be asked to report annually – in person – to a prescribed police station where they might be photographed and fingerprinted annually; finally, additional identification might be sought in the form of National Insurance numbers and biometric scanning of the iris (ibid.). Most of these changes were incorporated into the Sexual Offences Act 2003, Part II and implemented from 1 May 2004.

These exercises in strengthening the register and making notification requirements ever more onerous were carried out with a degree of apprehension by the Home Office. The fear was that the register might be losing its 'civil' status and becoming almost a punishment in its own right. The Home Office reported its fears: 'were the registration requirement to become more onerous, there could come a point at which the Act could no longer be seen as an administrative requirement' (Home Office/Scottish Executive 2001: 13).

Community notification

'Community notification' is the American terminology for the public disclosure of sex offender register information. As we have noted, such disclosures were debated during the parliamentary discussions on the bill, and any general right of access was precluded. Home Office guidance was, however, able to shed some more light on the public's right to know whether sex offenders were living amongst them.

Even before the register was implemented, the police had been giving information to the public about known sex offenders. Information on child sex offenders had been disclosed to schools in Hampshire ('Schools sent lists of local paedophiles', *Daily Telegraph*, 18 October 1996) and schools in Wales had duly passed such information on to parents when they had received it ('Teachers name paedophile in letter to parents',

Independent, 30 November 1996). The London Borough of Lewisham had also disclosed information it had on paedophiles to the general public living in the Forest Hill area of south London ('In the name of the children', *Independent*, 28 March 1997).

The community notification debate was fuelled by reports of 'Megan's Law' coming across the Atlantic from the USA. In 1994, a Federal law (the Jacob Wetterling Crimes against Children and Sexually Violent Offender Registration Act) had required all states of the USA to enact laws creating a sex offender register; many had already had them in place for a number of years, but now all were mandated to do so. In 1996, Megan's Law amended the Jacob Wetterling Act to require all states to allow public access to, or dissemination of, the registration information. The law was named after Megan Kanka, a 7-year-old girl from New Jersey who had been sexually assaulted and killed by a convicted sex offender living in the same street as his victim and her family.

In the summer of 1997, as the UK public debate on community notification continued, Megan's mother, Maureen Kanka, visited the UK to add her weight to the calls for the sex offender register to be public. Tabloid headlines became ever more strident (e.g. ' "I'll name the sex beasts" – Straw's pledge to parents as perverts head for freedom', *Daily Mirror*, 9 June 1997) and more controversy came with news of a book from Australia, based on press reports of court hearings, naming all that country's known sex offenders (Coddington 1997); an earlier version had covered New Zealand and now one was being promised for the UK ('This woman has named 600 child abusers in Australia. Now she plans a British list', *Independent*, 19 February 1997); no UK version ever appeared. When the North Wales Police disclosed information on two sex offenders to a local community in the summer of 1997, the two people concerned sought a judicial review of the police decision.

In July, the High Court judicial review ruled that the North Wales Police had acted properly in alerting people of the conviction record of their neighbours (*R* v. *Chief Constable of North Wales Police, ex p. AB* (1997) *Times*, 14 July). At the time, the police had actually used press cuttings of the offender's court appearance that had been kept on file to try to avoid accusations of improper disclosure; using press cuttings meant the information was already in the public domain.

The High Court stated that, as a general principle, and in terms of good public administration, the police should keep criminal record histories confidential, but if there was specific reason to disclose, then they could do so. The specific reason would normally be a risk to the public, and that risk should be carefully assessed before any such disclosure. The High Court cited the Home Office guidance to the police regarding criminal record disclosures for pre-employment screening purposes (see Chapter 8) and an earlier case in Derbyshire, when the police had been found to have acted properly in circulating a photograph of a convicted shoplifter to certain shopkeepers to enable them to take preventive action (*Hellewell* v. *Chief Constable of Derbyshire* [1995] 1 WLR 804).

The two people involved later unsuccessfully appealed against the decision. The Court of Appeal discussed the sensitive balance involved in disclosure, the problems of accommodating such offenders and the possibility of others being driven 'underground'. They also thought the police should discuss disclosures with offenders in advance of taking any action, but that ultimately the police had to adopt 'a proactive rather than a reactive policy for dealing with offenders who had committed offences against children in the past' (*R* v. *Chief Constable of North Wales Police, ex p. Thorpe* (1998) *Times*, 23 March).

An earlier judicial review, not referred to in the ruling but which arguably had some relevance, was that made in favour of Devon County Council when that local authority's Social Services Department was found to have been acting properly in disclosing information to the public about a man only *suspected* of having committed sex offences against children (*R* v. *Devon CC, ex p. L* [1991] 2 FLR; see Hayes 1992 for a critique of this ruling).

Although the North Wales case did not relate specifically to sex offender 'register' information – the Act was as yet unimplemented – the 1997 Home Office guidance was able to draw on the judgement – and indeed the *Devon* judgement – to give its interim guidance to the police on public disclosure from the register, whilst at the same time affirming its belief that authoritative statements on the law were for the courts and not the Home Office. The police were to make a risk assessment, involving other agencies as appropriate, make the information available to identified people and be prepared to give advice on how that information should be used (Home Office 1997c: Appendix A; see also Power 1999). The terminology used was that of 'controlled disclosure' as opposed to 'a right of public access'.

Not everyone was happy with this arrangement, and headteachers were one group who were confused by the idea of being given information by the police which they might then be unable to pass on to parents. Tony Butler, ACPO's then spokesperson on sex offending, did not see it so starkly. Teachers might acquire information as part of a risk management strategy with other agencies and to that extent they could be faced with moral dilemmas – unfortunately, that was simply 'the reality of this area' ('Heads attack guidelines on naming paedophiles',

Daily Telegraph, 12 August 1997); the National Association of Head Teachers and ACPO later agreed a protocol on how information disclosed to schools should be handled, with the police being given the 'guiding role' (NAHT/ACPO 1998).

As we have seen, the Home Office eventually produced a follow-up draft guidance on information disclosure and sex offenders to its interim 1997 version. This document covered inter-agency exchanges of information for risk analysis purposes, but also gave advice on disclosures to third parties including members of the public. Such disclosures were expected to be exceptional and only as part of an individual sex offender's risk management plan (Home Office PSTU, 1999: paras. 21–7).

Just how big the problems of disclosure were to be was revealed within a few weeks by the case of the 43-year-old discharged sex offender, Robert Oliver. Oliver was assessed as dangerous and as posing a continuing risk, and so his neighbours were duly notified. Oliver moved on to a series of addresses in Swindon, Manchester, Liverpool, Dublin, London and, finally, Brighton. Each time the community was notified of his whereabouts, he effectively became an 'outlaw'. Each time, he had to keep moving for his own safety and eventually sought protective custody with the East Sussex Police before moving on to 'secure accommodation' in a Midlands hospital. One mother in Brighton summed up the position: 'This man must go. I don't care where he goes to, as long as he goes away from here' ('Police keep watch on freed paedophile', *Independent,* 15 October 1997; see also Bowman *et al.* 1998 for a detailed account of the professional response to Oliver during his stay in East Sussex).

The same thing happened in April 1998, when Sydney Cooke, 71-year-old co-offender with Oliver, was released. He too started his return to the community living in a London police station and agreeing to voluntary supervision and voluntary electronic monitoring. Cooke soon moved to the West Country and, when word got out that he was in the Bristol area, a crowd of several hundred besieged the police station in the Knowle West area of the city. A peaceful protest deteriorated when bottles and stones were thrown and the police in riot gear had to be deployed. Similar spontaneous protests against Cooke had taken place in Bridgwater, Yeovil and Minehead in Somerset ('Riot police called in as paedophile protest turns violent', *PA News,* 24 April 1998).

Police would also be called out two years later in the summer of 2000 when more unrest broke out over paedophiles. The Sunday newspaper, the *News of the World,* led demands for community notification of sex offenders in the wake of the abduction and murder of 8-year-old Sarah Payne. In Paulsgrove near Portsmouth demonstrations lasted a week as a wave of 'paedophile panic' ran round the country (see Chapter 2).

At the moment the move towards any form of general public access to the UK sex offender register seems to have gone as far as it is going. The then Home Secretary David Blunkett reiterated the belief that 'we cannot open the register to the vigilantes who do not understand the difference between paediatricians and paedophiles' (2002). Blunkett was referring to an incident where vigilantes had vandalised the home of a paediatrician ('Doctor driven out of home by vigilantes', *Guardian*, 30 August 2000).

In Essex the police decided to name convicted adults (not sex offenders) and give them publicity over and beyond that accorded by the press to their court hearing. The exercise ended when a successful court application was made citing the European Convention on Human Rights, Article 8 (the right to privacy) (*R (Ellis)* v. *Chief Constable of Essex Police* (2003) EWHC Admin. 1321). On the other hand young people made the subject of anti-social behaviour orders *have* been given publicity including community notification by way of especially produced leaflets giving photographs, names and other details (see Grier and Thomas 2003, where examples of leaflets are reproduced).

Multi-agency Public Protection Panels (MAPPPs)

An unforeseen consequence of the Sex Offenders Act and the ruling in the North Wales decision that police could disclose information to the public on particularly dangerous sex offenders was the requirement now to set up mechanisms to help police decide when they actually had a dangerous offender on their hands. Risk assessments had to be made on all new entrants on the register if the police were to fulfil their newly acquired role of 'controlled disclosure' to inform the public. Risk assessment required information exchange and, as we have seen, draft guidance on how this should take place was produced in August 1999 (Home Office PSTU 1999).

Some police forces already had public protection panels where they met with other agencies, such as the probation service, to make multi-agency risk assessments of all kinds of dangerous offenders. Others were moving into the risk assessment business for the first time and wide variations were being noted:

> The most obvious example of lack of consistency was the way in which risk assessments were being undertaken. The speed with which the [Sex Offender] Act was introduced had led many forces to adopt their own risk assessment models drawing on the experience and expertise of specialists outside the police service (HMIC 1999: 5.10).

The Association of Chief Police Officers has moved in response to these criticisms and developed a standardised risk-assessment model, based on the good practice of various forces and the model used by the Home Office's Prison Department. By June 1999, it was reported that the model – MATRIX 2000 – had been sent to all forces and training needs were being determined ('Risk model approved to identify sex re-offenders', *Policing Today* 5 (2), 1999: 9).

An attempt to bring in further consistency came through the Criminal Justice and Court Services Act 2000 which put informal 'public protection panels' on to a statutory footing. Multi-agency Public Protection Panels, or MAPPPs, would in future be the forum whereby local agencies led by the police and probation service would keep an oversight of *all* adults in the area thought to be dangerous – not just those on the register. MAPPPs would look at three groups of offenders:

- registered sex offenders;
- violent and other sexual offenders;
- other offenders considered to pose a risk to the public (Criminal Justice and Court Services Act 2000, ss. 67–8)

and in so doing arrange to assess and manage any risks they might continue to pose; an annual report was to be published by each MAPPP on its work (although containing no identification of individuals) (see Bryan and Doyle 2003).

Although the police and probation service were the lead agencies, other agencies could join the MAPPP; the Criminal Justice Act 2003, s. 325(6) later listed the agencies that must co-operate:

- the local Youth Offending Team;
- government ministers responsible for social security, child support, war pensions, employment and training;
- the local education authority;
- the housing authority or social services authority;
- any registered social landlord responsible for accommodation in which someone subject to MAPPP arrangements may reside;

- an NHS health authority or strategic health authority;
- an NHS hospital trust or primary care trust (see also Hewitt 2004).

In December 2001 the Home Office announced its proposal to include lay members on MAPPPs to help give a general oversight at a strategic level. The announcement by Home Secretary David Blunkett was made in the Sunday newspaper, the *News of the World*, on 16 December as that newspaper renewed its campaign for open access to the register; the man responsible for the abduction and murder of Sarah Payne had been convicted on the 12 December (see 'He's done it before', *Daily Express*, 13 December 2001; 'Named, shamed', *News of the World*, 16 December 2001). Non-readers of the *News of the World* were informed by a Home Office press release dated 17 December 2001 (Home Office 2001c). Following some pilot schemes (Hebenton and Thomas 2004) the Home Office began recruiting lay people in April 2004 (Home Office 2004b) by which time the necessary law was in place (Criminal Justice Act 2003, s. 326(3)).

An evaluation of MAPPPs remains to be completed, but concerns about their resourcing have already been aired (NSPCC 2002). Whether or not the inclusion of lay members will be of long-term value or was just a short-term measure to head off more calls for community notification also remains to be seen.

The sex offender order

The sex offender order was partly created to allay fears about the register not being retrospective. One estimate from the Home Office put the number of convicted sex offenders in the community at over 100,000 (Marshall 1997). The vast majority of these would not be on the register simply because their offences had been committed too early for inclusion; they were not 'in the system' – in custody or under supervision – at the time of implementation on 1 September 1997. The problem had been raised during parliamentary discussion on the Sex Offenders Bill, but once the Act was in place it was seen as something still requiring resolution.

The Home Office responded with its consultation paper on the 'Community Protection Order' (Home Office 1997d), later renamed as sex offender orders. These orders were designed to rein in all those convicted sex offenders in the community who were not required to keep their details up to date on the register. The sex offender would not automatically be required to start registering, but if a so-called 'trigger event' was spotted by the police, such as a person acting suspiciously near a playground or school, and the police knew they had previous convictions for sex offences against children, an application could be made to a court for a sex offender order. The order would not only initiate a requirement on the person concerned to register, but also could lay down activities they must desist from and areas of the community which they could not enter because of the risk they posed to children. Failure to comply was a criminal office (Crime and Disorder Act 1998, ss. 2–4 (covering England and Wales) and ss. 20–2 (covering Scotland) (see Home Office 1998d); the Criminal Justice (NI) Order 1998, Articles 6-7 extended the Sex Offender Order to Northern Ireland).

The Greater Manchester Police were reportedly the first force to apply for a sex offender order. The courts made an order on a 35-year-old man, requiring him to keep out of much of the southern part of Manchester between the hours of 10 pm and 7 am for a period of eight years. The man had previously served a custodial sentence for rape after breaking into student bed-sits, and the trigger behaviour involved being seen by police peering through bed-sit windows at night before running away ('Bed-sit rapist becomes subject of first legal exclusion order', *Independent*, 24 December 1998). By June 2002, the Home Office was aware of 170 orders having been applied for with a success rate in the courts of around 94 per cent (Home Office 2002d); overall the police were finding them to be useful instruments to help manage sex offenders (Knock 2002).

In 2003 the sex offender order was replaced by the sexual offences prevention order (see below).

The restraining order

Restraining orders were introduced by the Criminal Justice and Court Services Act 2000 (s. 66 and Schedule 5). The restraining order was made on a sex offender at the point of sentencing at the discretion of the court; no one had specifically to apply for it (see, e.g., 'Paedophile's life ban on child contact', *Daily Telegraph*, 28 March 2003). The court had to be satisfied that the order was needed to prevent risk of serious harm to the general public or to an individual; the latter would most likely be the victim of the crime. As with the sex offender orders, the restraining order could only make 'negative' requirements for an offender to desist from certain activities and not 'positive' requirements that they do something. The order could be for a specific time or for an indefinite period, and breach of the order would be dealt with as a criminal matter with sanctions of imprisonment or fines. Like the sex offender order the restraining order has now been replaced by the sexual offences prevention order.

The sexual offences prevention order

The Sexual Offences Act 2003, ss. 104–13 introduced the sexual offences prevention order (SOPO) which effectively replaced and combined the earlier sex offender order and restraining order. The SOPO was applied for by the police on anyone with a history of convictions who was demonstrating the 'trigger' activities as outlined for sex offender orders, and it could also be made on an offender at the time of conviction. The SOPO contains prohibitions on a person's activities in order to protect the public or any particular members of the public from serious sexual harm from the defendant, and requires registration as a sex offender if that requirement does not already exist. Failure to comply is a criminal offence. The first SOPO was reportedly made in Bristol ('Sex offender banned from all contact with children', *Guardian*, 7 May 2004).

The foreign travel order

Amendments were made to the Sexual Offences Bill as it passed through Parliament to tackle 'sex tourism' in a more robust manner. A brief consultation paper was published by the Home Office (Home Office 2003f) and the necessary sections added to the Sexual Offences Act 2003 (ss. 114–22) to prevent certain sexual offenders – the 'qualifying offenders' – from travelling abroad.

The foreign travel order is applied for by the police and lasts for six months. During this time the subject of the order is unable to leave the UK for either a specified country or indeed anywhere in the world. Failure to comply is a criminal offence.

The notification order

The notification order came into effect on 1 May 2004 along with most of the other provisions of the Sexual Offences Act 2003. The notification order could be applied for by the police on anyone known to have committed relevant sexual offences in another country and who was considered a risk to the public; the subject of a notification order could be a British national returning to the UK having offended overseas, or a foreign national taking up residence here. There had been a great deal of hostility aimed at the Home Secretary for the boxer Mike Tyson's two visits to the UK within five months when he had convictions for sexual offences at home in the USA ('Anger as Tyson is granted visa for Glasgow fight', *Independent*, 19 May 2000). The new notification orders meant the subject had to be on the UK sex offender register and abide by all its requirements (Sexual Offences Act 2003, ss. 97–103).

The risk of sexual harm order

One troubling aspect of sexual offending for legislators was the practice of 'grooming' a child for sexual activity by lengthy befriending and often deception. Sex offenders had long been thought to do this but the use of the Internet and 'chatrooms' whereby adult men could anonymously pretend to be of the same age as their intended victims made the problem more urgent. A former US marine – Toby Studabaker – triggered an international search when he abducted an English girl met this way; he was eventually found in Germany ('Abductor of girl, 12, jailed', *Guardian*, 3 April 2004). The proposed answer was the risk of sexual harm order (RSHO) introduced by the Sexual Offences Act 2003 (ss. 123–9). The police can apply for these orders if they see a pattern developing and there is an identifiable sexual component to the behaviour. Fines or imprisonment can be imposed for breach of the order.

Summary

The civil law has increasingly been turned to as a means of protection from sex offenders. A raft of civil measures has now been put into place to help regulate the activities of the sex offender – not as a punishment – but in the interests of greater community protection. Starting with the sex offender 'register' in 1997 as a way of knowing where convicted sex offenders are living at any one time, we now have notification orders, sexual offences prevention orders, foreign travel orders, and risk of sexual harm orders which all place restrictions of various kinds on the sex offender. The common feature of all of them is that failure to comply brings the individual subjected to them into the criminal courts where they will be dealt with as an offender.

Chapter 10

Conclusions

As we complete this survey of sexual offending and the social responses being made to it, a number of recurring themes keep emerging: the relative nature of sexual offending and how we define it; the need to hold 'personal information' in various databases in order to identify the otherwise 'invisible' sex offender; and the need to use that personal information to carry out risk assessment and thereby achieve better 'risk management' on those who pose a threat to us.

Risk and dangerousness revisited

We first encountered risk and dangerousness in Chapter 1 and have bumped into both concepts at frequent intervals thereafter. The assessment and management of the risk posed by sexual offenders have become an all-consuming task for the police, prisons, probation service, social services departments and those health care professionals who come across these offenders.

In its wider context, 'risk' has taken on a greater significance in all areas of life, and we are now told we live in the 'risk society'. The risk being described is invariably a negative one in terms of crime or where there is some kind of deficit and something may happen to us; risk does have a positive side where taking a risk can lead on to greater things, but in terms of crime reduction that is not the side we are looking at.

As the world grows more complex, and some would say more fragmented, so the areas of unfamiliarity in life increase. In so doing, they increase the perceived risks of life which it is then incumbent upon us to try to reduce. In so far as sexual offenders pose a risk, we need to identify them and have information about them to calculate the risk or degree of danger they pose in order then to manage that risk. In turn, we are making 'calculations' of an almost actuarial nature to determine who is or is not a risk. Some practitioners literally use the calculus of 'tick-boxes' to record the information on a sex offender which then becomes part of their risk assessment.

The wider social theories of risk and risk society are beyond the brief of this book (see, e.g., Beck 1992; Young 1999), and the degree to which risk work now predominates in the 'social care' field has been noted by writers such as Parton (1996a).

The role of law enforcement in the risk society has, in turn, started to reshape our very understanding of what policing means. Ericson and Haggerty describe the move from traditional policing to a policing that is more about information production and dissemination. The police have become just part of a network of agencies that move information around to the most appropriate location for risk assessment or risk management to take place (Ericson and Haggerty 1997).

This new form of policing challenges the police to develop new skills of information management and to use the new tools of information technology. At its most simple, it is the opening up of police-held criminal records to organisations like the Criminal Records Bureau in order that the pre-employment screening of child care workers can take place. Twenty years ago, there were no such disclosures and criminal records were used mainly by the police themselves and the courts; today, millions of applications for disclosures of this kind are made to the CRB every year.

In the case of sex offenders, other examples arise as information rebounds between the police, the courts, the prisons, local authorities, the probation service and others as we try to get the right information to the right person at the right time for him or her to do his or her job; in many instances that 'job' is part of a risk analysis.

Peter Neyroud, the Assistant Chief Constable of the West Mercia Police, believes it is leading to fundamental changes:

The nature of the new skills and the requirement to work across agency boundaries raises the question as to whether the current 'pillared' structure of independent agencies – each with its own operational independence – is the best way of protecting the public. It certainly challenges the old professional model and creates an argument for a new cross-agency discipline of risk management (1999).

Whether or not risk assessment – the prediction of the future behaviour of others – can ever be an exact science remains debatable. For some critics, it will only ever be a haphazard 'guessing game' that will inevitably draw in and label people who would never go on to be a risk to anyone. Advocates of risk assessment believe otherwise and have faith in their abilities to refine their techniques and make ever better predictions, but some people will inevitably be wrongly assessed and punished or constrained for crimes they would never have committed in the future, and we have to ask if this does not conflict with our notion of justice.

Risk analysis also needs information, and it especially needs personal information about identifiable people.

The central role of personal information

As risk assessment and management moves to centre stage in law enforcement and crime reduction, it drags with it the role of personal information to inform those risk analysis tasks. Personal information, information technology and the information 'superhighways' are all familiar terms in the information society. But what actually is 'personal information'?

Personal information relates to a particular individual and includes all that information we might expect to be considered private or personal, such as information about health, sexual matters or family. It would include all that information about which the community at large has no particular interest, because it holds no significance for the community. According to the academic Raymond Wacks, we might define it as follows:

> 'Personal information' consists of those facts, communications, or opinions which relate to the individual and which it would be reasonable to expect him (or her) to regard as intimate or sensitive and therefore want to withhold or at least to restrict their collection, use, or circulation (1989: 26).

The individual sex offender would probably subscribe to this definition. His intentions are personal to him, his activities carried out in private and his victims – especially children – are asked or threatened to keep 'the secret'. Within feminist analysis, wider cultural forces (male) may support this 'containing' of information, narrowing of the definition of a sexual offence and refusal to take the victims' views seriously.

The role of the law enforcement and other public protection agencies has been to move this personal information on the sex offender from the private to the public domain. In this instance, public domain is only the various agencies who have a 'need to know' in order to identify, track and intervene in the sex offender's activities as appropriate. As the sex offender seeks to restrict the 'collection, use or circulation' of personal information about him, so these agencies are trying to do the exact opposite by collecting, using and circulating that same information.

To this end, we have seen the creation of the sex offender 'register', the promotion of 'intelligence-led' policing, the build-up of the NCIS Serious Sexual Offences Unit database and the more active use of the national collection of criminal records and their routine dissemination to other agencies to help them make their risk assessments. Elsewhere, we have seen the upgrading of the Department of Health Consultancy Service Index and the 'List 99' into statutory units and the creation of the Protection of Vulnerable Adults list; we have seen the upgrading of the Forensic Science Services National DNA Database, and the Bichard Inquiry Report call for a National Intelligence Service. All these initiatives put personal information at the centre of activities to combat the sex offender.

This personal information is not being collated for its own sake, but is increasingly being actively used and also exchanged between agencies charged with law enforcement or public protection. As we have seen, this inter-agency work seeks to get the right information to the right agency at the right time to enable them to do their job.

At one time, police-held criminal record repositories were for the police alone, to help them do their work and for the police to produce them in court (as antecedents) to help sentencers make appropriate decisions. Today, police-held criminal records are available to numerous other agencies throughout the criminal justice system and beyond. The national criminal record collection was renamed as PHOENIX and computerised in 1995, when, significantly, it took on the subtitle 'The Criminal Justice Record Service' to reflect the changing priorities.

Personal information becomes the 'currency' that all agencies value, and personal information thereby facilitates the overall interactions that make up inter-agency work. To use another metaphor, personal information is the oil that keeps the cogs of the inter-agency machine working. Traditional frictions and 'turf-wars' are reduced as personal information is put into circulation to make manifest the old cross-discipline cliché that 'at the end of the day we are all working to the same end'.

The circulation of personal information has been furthered by changes in the law (see, e.g., the Crime and Disorder Act 1998, s. 115, implemented 30 September 1998) and by information technology which gives real-time information exchange rather than the old index cards, microfiche and telephone.

Traditional ideas of 'confidentiality' and 'privacy' are breaking down as 'serious crime' demands the production and exchange of personal information. Data Protection Acts offer some safeguards, but exceptions exist for investigating crimes and protecting children (see, e.g., Department for Constitutional Affairs 2003). Worrall has expressed pessimism about any future positive work with sex offenders: 'the debate on working with sex offenders in the community has been virtually foreclosed ... official government discourse now rejects the language of rehabilitation in favour of the language of surveillance and control through information' (1997: 125). Much of this information exchange is to allow agencies to intervene appropriately; to make an arrest, remove a child from a harmful situation, make a sentencing decision, make an employment selection decision or a housing decision. All these interventions are made on the basis of the information in question being used for risk assessment and risk management.

The rights of the sex offender

In general terms, the aim of penal policy is to identify and punish those who break the criminal law. Punishment, in turn, involves a degree of censure, containment and attempts to circumscribe and reduce the activities of the offender. At one end of the line is the custodial sentence and at the other the community sentence, which still tries to delimit and reduce the offenders' activities. Since the early 1970s, there has been a retreat from sentences designed to reform or rehabilitate the offender in favour of sentences commensurate with the seriousness of the crime and which deliver 'just deserts'. This retreat has been accompanied by a questioning of the value of treatment – 'what works?' – the rediscovery and renaissance of dangerousness and the rise of the 'victim movement', which prefers to see some direct redress for the victim rather than help for the offender. The 'law and order' political lobby has been able to mobilise these features to argue for longer sentences, electronic tagging, more active databases, extended supervision and indeterminate sentences. The Criminal Justice Act 2003 has given us the concept of imprisonment for the public protection. The sex offender has been a prime candidate for all these measures.

More recently, these moves to commensurate punishments have been complemented by new forms of 'regulation' to ensure sufficient degrees of public protection and safeguards are in place to reduce the risk posed by offenders. As with punishment, regulation seeks to contain and circumscribe the activities of offenders. Registers tell us where they are and DNA databases confirm their identity. 'Paedophile enclaves' may not yet exist, but electronic tagging, sexual offences prevention orders and pre-employment screening all help to reduce the risk they pose by circumscribing their activities.

The detection and prosecution of sex offenders and the measures of protection from them have, none the less, to accept that the offenders concerned are still entitled to the 'due process' of law and other rights enjoyed by all citizens. However awful the crimes, and however much we give priority to the rights of the victims or potential victims – especially children – the residual rights of the sex offender remain. Freedom of movement, for example, is usually considered a fundamental right, even if not always spelt out in statutory form. Sex offenders may find their freedom of movement curtailed in the UK by conditions attached to supervisory arrangements, electronic tagging or sexual offences prevention orders that require them to stay away from certain localities.

Privacy is held to be another basic right and is enshrined in Article 8 of the European Convention on Human Rights (Council of Europe 1950; now incorporated into the Human Rights Act 1998). From privacy has emerged the additional right to 'information privacy' and 'data protection' when that information – personal information – is held on computer (Council of Europe 1980) and most industrialised countries now have data protection legislation. In turn, this legislation becomes qualified when it comes to the 'suppression of criminal offences' (ibid.: art. 8(2)), and separate recommendations may be made on law enforcement-held information (see, e.g., Council of Europe 1988). A balance must be struck between the need to 'know' and the individual's right to privacy.

The right to rehabilitation or to be accepted back into society after a period of punishment – custodial or non-custodial – is another 'right' that is not clearly defined. The old adage that once you have 'paid your debt to society' you are a free man or woman again has been stated more fully: 'Rehabilitation implies the action of re-establishing a degraded person in a former standing with respect to rank and legal rights, and to attempt to ensure that those rights are maintained over time' (McWilliams and Pease 1990). The sex offender thought to be 'once a paedophile always a paedophile' and hounded out of his home by vigilante crowds and newspaper reporting, may find this statement has a somewhat hollow ring to it.

What McWilliams and Pease are saying is that the ending of a period of punishment, whether or not the offender is 'reformed', should still be marked by that offender's 'rehabilitation' to society in terms of the restoration of all his civic and legal rights and duties. In this sense, rehabilitation serves as a means of limiting the extent of the punishment to that time period decreed by the court; without it the punishment continues.

The offender, having to submit to a pre-employment criminal record check years after the end of his sentence, might argue that his punishment continues. The sex offender subject to regular home visits by probation officers or social workers or required to 'register' for life might feel the same way. The argument that these community interventions are still less of an imposition than a custodial sentence, or that certain activities are for purposes of 'regulation' rather than 'punishment', might not lessen the degree of grievance they believe they are experiencing (see also von Hirsch 1990).

An international problem

The phenomenon of sex offending is an international one. The United Nations describes the sexual exploitation of children as a 'global phenomenon', to be found in both developing and developed countries and becoming increasingly complex due to its transnational scope (UN 1996). The International Labour Organisation (ILO) has described prostitution in South East Asia as growing so rapidly in recent decades that the sex industry has assumed the dimensions of a commercial sector, contributing substantially to employment and national income in the region (ILO 1998).

In Europe, the Council of Europe has asked its member states to review their legislation and practice better to protect children (Council of Europe 1991) and the European Union has made the same demand of its members following the massive public demonstrations in the streets of Brussels against child kidnap and murder in Belgium (EU Joint Action 97/1 54 JHA) and more recently in its 2001 Council Framework decision on combating the sexual exploitation of children and child pornography (Thomas 2001c). The European Parliament has passed its own resolution (12 December 1997) calling for better integration of agencies' efforts to protect children (*Official Journal C.20*, 20 January 1997); for a further exposition of European initiatives, see Thomas *et al.* (1999), Hebenton and Thomas (1999) and Council of Europe (2003).

Closer to home, we can see almost a domino effect in social responses to sex offenders. When the UK sex offender register came into being in September 1997, stories began emerging of offenders in Northern Ireland moving over the border to the Republic of Ireland to avoid having to register ('Paedophiles go South to avoid sex register', *The Sunday Times*, 7 December 1997). These newspaper allegations were officially refuted (see Houses of the Oireachtas – Official Report, 9 December 1997), but it started a debate in the republic on the need for a sex offender register of its own. A discussion paper put the arguments for and against (Department of Justice, Equality and Law Reform 1998: chap. 10) and eventually a newly drafted Sex Offenders Bill appeared (10 January 2000), containing provisions for not only a register but also for a sex offender order (comparable to the UK's), more post-release supervision and a ban on sex offenders seeking work with children (see Thomas 2000); the Irish register eventually came online in 2001.

Meanwhile, the European Parliament has called for a Europe-wide register (*Official Journal C.20*, 20 January 1997), and some politicians have even suggested a worldwide register ('Mitchell argues for world-wide register of paedophiles', *Irish Times*, 26 April 1996). Such wide-ranging registers would seem to be completely impractical at this point in time, not least because of the different definitions of a sex offence in different countries, but the idea certainly demonstrates the centrality of personal information databases in the regulation of sex offenders, and the seriousness accorded the problem by politicians.

References

Ackroyd, S., Harper, R., Hughes, J., Shapiro, D. and Soothill, K. (1992) *New Technology and Practical Police Work*. Milton Keynes: Open University Press.

ACOP (Association of Chief Officers of Probation) (1996) *Community Based Interventions with Sex Offenders Organised by the Probation Service – A Survey of Current Practice*. London: ACOP.

ACOP (Association of Chief Officers of Probation)/Victim Support (1996) 'The release of prisoners: informing, consulting and supporting victims – joint statement', July, London.

ACPO (Association of Chief Police Officers) (2002a) *SIO Handbook: the Investigation of Historic Institutional Child Abuse* (March). London: ACPO.

ACPO (Association of Chief Police Officers) (2002b) *Code of Practice for Data Protection* (3rd edn). London: ACPO.

Adams, C. and Horrocks, C. (1999) 'The location of child protection in relation to the current emphasis on core policing', in the Violence against Children Study Group (eds) *Children, Child Abuse and Child Protection*. Chichester: Wiley.

Adler, Z. (1987) *Rape on Trial*. London: Routledge & Kegan Paul.

Adler, Z. (1991) 'Picking up the pieces', *Police Review*, 31 May: 1114–15.

Alexander, S., Meuwese, S. and Wolthuis, A. (2000) 'Policies and developments relating to the sexual exploitation of children: the legacy of the Stockholm conference', *European Journal on Criminal Policy and Research*, 8 (4): 479–501.

AMA (Association of Metropolitan Authorities) (1995) *Social Services Circular 95/1995*. London: AMA.

Anna, T. (1988) 'Feminist responses to sexual abuse: the work of the Birmingham Rape Crisis Centre', in M. MaGuire and J. Pointing (eds) *Victims of Crime – A New Deal*. Milton Keynes: Open University Press.

Apex Trust (1990) *Realising the Potential: The Recruitment of People with a Criminal Record*. London: Apex Trust.

Atkins, S. and Hoggett, B. (1984) *Women and the Law*. Oxford: Blackwell.

Bagshaw, M. (1997) 'Inside track', *Policing Today*, 3 (4): 20–2.
Bailey, V. (ed.) (1981) *Policing and Punishment in Nineteenth-century Britain*. London: Croom Helm.
Bailey, V. and Blackburn, S. (1979) 'The Punishment of Incest Act: a case study of law creation', *Criminal Law Review*, 708–18.
Bancroft, J. (1974) *Deviant Sexual Behaviour: Modification and Assessment*. Oxford: Clarendon Press.
Barker, M. and Morgan, R. (1993) *Sex Offenders: A Framework for the Evaluation of Community Based Treatment* (March). London: Home Office.
Barnardos (1998) *Whose Daughter Next? Children Abused through Prostitution*. London: Barnardos.
Bartley, P. (2000) *Prostitution: Prevention and Reform in England, 1860–1914*. London: Routledge.
Bartrip, P.W.J. (1981) 'Public opinion and law enforcement: the ticket of leave scares in mid-Victorian Britain', in V. Bailey (ed.) *Policing and Punishment in Nineteenth-century Britain*. London: Croom Helm.
Beattie, J.M. (1986) *Crime and the Courts in England 1660–1800*. Oxford: Clarendon Press.
Beck, U. (1992) *Risk Society*. London: Sage.
Beckett, R. (1994) 'Cognitive-behavioural treatment of sex offenders', in T. Morrison *et al.* (eds) *Sexual Offending against Children: Assessment and Treatment of Male Abusers*. London: Routledge.
Beckett, R., Beech, A., Fisher, D. and Fordham, A.S. (1994) *Community-based Treatment for Sex Offenders: An Evaluation of Seven Treatment Programmes* (August). London: Home Office.
Beech, A., Fisher, D., Beckett, R. and Scott-Fordham, A. (1998) *An Evaluation of the Prison Sex Offender Treatment Programme. Research Findings 79*. London: Home Office Research, Development and Statistics Directorate.
Benyon, J., Turnbull, L., Wilks, A., Woodward, R. and Beck, A. (1993) *Police Cooperation in Europe: An Investigation*. Leicester: Centre for the Study of Public Order, University of Leicester.
Better Regulation Task Force (1999) *Fit Person Criteria* (May). London: Cabinet Office.
Bichard Inquiry Report (2004) HC 653. London: HMSO.
Bilton, M. (2003) *Wicked beyond Belief: The Hunt for the Yorkshire Ripper*. London: Harper Collins.
Blunkett, D. (2002) 'Fighting crime and disorder at core of social justice' (speech), 2 October.
Booth, W. (1890) *In Darkest England and the Way Out*. Pamphlet.
Bosanquet, H. (1914) *Social Work in London 1869–1912*. London: John Murray.
Bottoms, A.E. (1977) 'Reflections on the renaissance of dangerousness', *Howard Journal of Penology and Crime Prevention*, 16 (2): 70–96.

Bottoms, A.E. (1995) 'The philosophy and politics of punishment and sentencing', in C. Clark and R. Morgan (eds). *The Politics of Sentencing Reform*. Oxford: Clarendon Press.

Bowman, A., Buller, P., Lewis, M. and Smith, G. (1998) 'Practical difficulties encountered by police, probation and social services; the key issues for inter-agency working within the Sex Offenders Act 1997', in S. Hayman (ed.) *Child Sexual Abuse: Providing for Victims Coping with Offenders*. London: Institute for the Study and Treatment of Delinquency.

Brackenridge, C. (1997) ' "He owned me basically ..." – women's experiences of sexual abuse in sport', *International Review for the Sociology of Sport*, 32 (2): 115–30.

Brackenridge, C. (1998) 'Casting a shadow: the dynamics and discourses of sexual abuse in sport.' Paper presented at the Leisure Studies Association international conference, *The Big Ghetto: Gender, Sexuality and Leisure*, Leeds Metropolitan University, July.

Bristow, E.J. (1977) *Vice and Vigilance*. Dublin: Gill & Macmillan.

Brongersma, E. (1988) 'A defence of sexual liberty for all age groups', *Howard Journal of Criminal Justice*, 27 (1): 32–43.

Brown, A. and Barrett, D. (2002) *Knowledge of Evil: Child Prostitution and Child Sexual Abuse in Twentieth Century England*. Cullompton: Willan Publishing.

Brown, D. (1997) *PACE Ten Years On: A Review of the Research. Research Study* 155. London: Home Office Research and Statistics Directorate.

Brown, M. and Pratt, J. (eds) (2000) *Dangerous Offenders: Punishment and Social Order*. London: Routledge.

Brown, W. (1993) 'DNA fingerprinting back in the dock', *New Scientist*, 6 March.

Brownlee, I. (1998) *Community Punishment; A Critical Introduction*. London: Longman.

Bryan, T. and Doyle, P. (2003) 'Developing multi-agency public protection arrangements', in A. Matravers (ed.) *Sex Offenders in the Community: Managing and Reducing Risks*. Cullompton: Willan Publishing.

Burn, G. (1985) *Somebody's Husband, Somebody's Son*. London: Pan Books.

Cabinet Office/Home Office (1999) *Living without Fear; an Integrated Approach to Tackling Violence against Women* (June). London: The Women's Unit.

Cameron, D. and Frazer, E. (1987) *The Lust to Kill*. Cambridge: Polity Press.

Cann, J., Falshaw, L. and Friendship, C. (2004) 'Sexual offenders discharged from prison in England and Wales: a 21-year reconviction study', *Legal and Criminological Psychology*, 9: 1–10.

Carr, J. (2003) *Child Abuse, Child Pornography and the Internet*. London: NCH.

CCPAS (Churches Child Protection Advisory Service) (1998) *Protecting Children and Appointing Children's Workers: Guidance to Churches* (9th edn). Swanley, Kent: CCPAS.

Chamberlain, L. (1993) 'Valuable young', *Community Care*, 19 August: 7.

Chambers, G. and Millar, A. (1983) *Investigating Sexual Assault. Scottish Office Central Research Unit Study*. Edinburgh: HMSO.

Chief Secretary to the Treasury (2003) *Every Child Matters* (Cm 5860). London: HMSO.

Clark, C. and Morgan, R. (eds) (1995) *The Politics of Sentencing Reform*. Oxford: Clarendon Press.

Clark, H. and Johnston, D. (1994) *Fear the Stranger*. Edinburgh and London: Mainstream Publishing.

Clark, P. and Erooga, M. (1994) 'Groupwork with men who sexually abuse children', in T. Morrison *et al.* (eds) *Sexual Offending against Children: Assessment and Treatment of Male Abusers*. London: Routledge.

Cleveland Report (1988) *Report of the Inquiry into Child Abuse in Cleveland 1987* (Cm 412). London: HMSO.

Clyde Report (1992) *The Report of the Inquiry of the Removal of Children from Orkney in February 1991*. Edinburgh: HMSO.

Cobbe, F.P. (1992) 'Wife torture in England', in J. Radford and D. Russell (eds) *Femicide: The Politics of Woman Killing*. Milton Keynes: Open University Press.

Coddington, D. (1997) *The Australian Paedophile and Sex Offender Index*. Sydney: The Mount View Trust.

Coggan, G. and Walker, M. (1982) *Frightened for my Life: An Account of Deaths in British Prisons*. London: Fontana.

Cohen, S. (1972) *Folk Devils and Moral Panics*. London: MacGibbon & Kee.

Coker, J.B. and Martin, J.P. (1985) *Licensed to Live*. Oxford: Blackwell.

Collins, P. (1999) 'Operation Osprey', *Cross Border Control*, 11: 44–8.

Coombes, R. (2003) 'Adolescents who sexually abuse', in A. Matravers (ed.) *Sex Offenders in the Community: Managing and Reducing the Risks*. Cullompton: Willan Publishing.

Corby, B. (1998) *Managing Child Sexual Abuse Cases*. London: Jessica Kingsley.

Council of Europe (1950) *European Convention on Human Rights*. Strasbourg.

Council of Europe (1980) *Convention for the Protection of Individuals with Regard to Automatic Processing of Personal Data*. Strasbourg.

Council of Europe (1988) *The Use of Personal Data in the Police Sector. Recommendation* R (87) 15. Strasbourg.

Council of Europe (1991) *Sexual Exploitation, Pornography and Prostitution of, and Trafficking in, Children and Young Adults. Recommendation* R(91) 11. Strasbourg.

Council of Europe (2003) *Child Sexual Abuse in Europe*. Strasbourg.

Council of the European Union (1997) *Council Resolution on the Exchange of DNA Analysis Results* (97/C 193/02). Brussels.

Cox, B., Shirley, J. and Short, M. (1977) *The Fall of Scotland Yard*. Harmondsworth: Penguin Books.

CPS (Crown Prosecution Service) (n.d.) *Code for Crown Prosecutors*. London: CPS.

CPS (Crown Prosecution Service) (1994) *Code for Crown Prosecutors* (June). London: CPS.

CPS (Crown Prosecution Service) (1996) *An Explanatory Memorandum for Use in Connection with the Code for Crown Prosecutors* (June). London: CPS.

CPS (Crown Prosecution Service) (2003) *CPS Consultation on the Handling of Rape Cases*. London: CPS.

CPSI (Crown Prosecution Service Inspectorate) (1998) *Cases Involving Child Witnesses. Thematic Report* 1/98 (January). London: CPSI.

Crane, P. (1983) *Gays and the Law.* London: Pluto Press.

Criminal Law Revision Committee (1984) *Sexual Offences* (15th report) (Cmnd 9213). London: HMSO.

Critchley, T.A. (1967) *A History of Police in England and Wales.* London: Constable.

Cullen Report (1996) *The Public Inquiry into the Shootings at Dunblane Primary School on 13 March 1996* (Cm 3386). London: HMSO.

Daley, H. (1986) *This Small Cloud: A Personal Memoir.* London: Weidenfeld & Nicolson.

D'Arcy, M. and Gosling, P. (1998) *Abuse of Trust: Frank Beck and the Leicestershire Children's Homes Scandal.* London: Bowerdean.

Davies, G., Williams, C., Mitchell, R. and Milson, J. (1995) *Video Taping Children's Evidence: An Evaluation.* London: Home Office.

DENI (Department of Education, Northern Ireland) (1990) *Disclosure of Criminal Background of Persons with Access to Children. Circular* 28/1990. Belfast: DENI.

Departmental Committee (1925) *Sexual Offences against Young Persons* (Cmd 2561). London: HMSO.

Departmental Committee (1926) *Sexual Offences against Children and Young Persons in Scotland* (Cmd 2592). London: HMSO.

Department for Constitutional Affairs (2003) *Public Sector Data Sharing* (November). London.

Department of Health (1991a) 'The Children Act 1989: guidance and regulations', *Independent Schools, Vol. 5.* London: HMSO.

Department of Health (1991b) 'The Children Act 1989 – guidance and regulations', *Residential Care. Vol. 4.* London: HMSO.

Department of Health (1991c) *Children in the Public Care – A Review of Residential Child Care.* London: HMSO.

Department of Health (1994a) 'Introduction of supervision registers for mentally ill people from 1 April 1994', *HSG,* (94) 5.

Department of Health (1994b) 'The Child, the Court and the Video', *SSI.* London.

Department of Health (1995) *Annual Reports of Area Child Protection Committees 1993/4.* London.

Department of Health (1997) *Family Law Act 1996: Part IV Family Homes and Domestic Violence. Circular* LAC (97) 15. London.

Department of Health (1998) *Working Together to Safeguard Children: New Government Proposals for Inter-agency Co-operation.* Consultation Paper (February). London.

Department of Health (1999) *Working Together to Safeguard Children.* London: HMSO.

Department of Health (2000a) *Reforming the Mental Health Act* (Cm 5016–1). London.

Department of Health (2000b) *The Protection of Children Act 1999 – A Practical Guide to the Act for all Organisations Working with Children* (September). London.

Department of Health (2002) *Draft Mental Health Bill* (Cm 5538–1). London.

Department of Health (2003) 'Government cracks down on those who abuse vulnerable adults' (11 December). Press release, London.

Department of Health, Home Office, Department for Education and Employment, National Assembly for Wales (2000) *Safeguarding Children Involved in Prostitution* (May). London.

Department of Justice, Equality and Law Reform (1998) *The Law on Sexual Offences – A Discussion Paper* (May). Dublin.

DFEE (Department for Education and Employment) (2001) 'Free checks to keep criminals out of voluntary sector' (7 February). Press release, London.

DFES (Department for Education and Skills) (2002) *Child Protection: Preventing Unsuitable People from Working with Children and Young Persons in the Education Service. Circular 0278/2002* (May). London.

DHSS (Department of Health and Social Security) (1974) *Non-accidental Injury to Children: Area Review Committees. Circular LASSL (74) 13.* London.

DHSS (Department of Health and Social Security) (1975) *Report of the Committee of Inquiry into the Provision and Coordination of Services to the Family of John George Auckland.* London: HMSO.

DHSS (Department of Health and Social Security) (1976) *Non-accidental Injury to Children: The Police and Case Conferences. Circular LASSL (76) 26.* London.

DHSS (Department of Health and Social Security) (1978) *Release of Prisoners Convicted of Offences against Children in the Home. Circular LAC (78) 22.* London.

DHSS (Department of Health and Social Security) (1980) *Child Abuse: Central Register Systems. Circular LASSL (8) 4.* London.

DHSS (Department of Health and Social Security) (1988) *Working Together: A Guide to Arrangements for Inter-agency Cooperation for the Protection of Children from Abuse.* London: HMSO.

DHSS (Department of Health and Social Services) (NI) (Northern Ireland) (1978) *Release of Prisoners Convicted of Offences against Children.*

DHSS (Department of Health and Social Services) (NI) (Northern Ireland) (1989) *Cooperating to Protect Children.* Belfast: DHSS.

DHSS (Department of Health and Social Services) (NI) (Northern Ireland) (1993) *An Abuse of Trust: The Report of the SSI Investigation into the Case of Martin Huston.* Belfast: DHSS.

DHSS (Department of Health and Social Services) (NI) (Northern Ireland) (1995) *Review of the DHSS Pre-employment Consultancy Service (PECS)* (May). Belfast: DHSS.

DHSS (Department of Health and Social Services) (NI) (Northern Ireland) (1996a) *Interagency Guidance on the Movement of the Persons Charged, Held or Cautioned in Connection with Certain Offences against Children or Young People under the Age of 17. Circular HSS (CC) 3/1996,* as revised. Belfast: DHSS.

DHSS (Department of Health and Social Services) (NI) (Northern Ireland) (1996b) *Making the Right Choice: A Guide to Using the Pre-employment Consultancy Service (PECS).* Belfast: DHSS.

DHSS (Department of Health and Social Services) (NI) (Northern Ireland) (1996c) *Our Duty to Care*. Belfast: DHSS.

Donnelly, L. (1999) 'Dangerous precedent', *Health Service Journal*, 25 February.

Dovaston, D. and Burton, C. (1996) 'Vital new ingredient', *Policing Today*, April: 44–8.

Drew, B. (1997) 'On paedophile patrol in the Philippines', *Nexus*, 4 (July): 16–17 (internal NCIS bulletin).

East, W.N. and Hubert, W.H. (1939) *Report on the Psychological Treatment of Crime*. London: HMSO.

Eldridge, J., Kitzinger, J. and William, K. (1997) *The Mass Media and Power in Modern Britain*. Oxford: Oxford University Press.

Emsley, C. (1991) *The English Police: A Political and Social History*. Cambridge: Harvester Wheatsheaf.

Ericson, R.V. and Haggerty, K.D. (1997) *Policing the Risk Society*. Oxford: Clarendon Press.

Europol Convention (1995) *Convention Based on Article K3 of the Treaty on European Union, on the Establishment of a European Police Office*. Brussels.

FA (Football Association) (1997) *A Charter for Quality: Football Education for Young Players* (October). London: FA.

Fennell, P. (1988) 'Sexual suppressants and the Mental Health Act', *Criminal Law Review*, 660–76.

Fennell, P. (1996) *Treatment without Consent*. London: Routledge.

Ferris, D. (1977) *Homosexuality and the Social Services*. London: National Council for Civil Liberties.

Finkelhor, D. (1986) *A Source Book on Child Sexual Abuse*. London: Sage.

Foot, P. (1996) 'Sir, the sadist', *Guardian*, 4 September.

Franklin, B. (1997) *Newszak and News Media*. London: Arnold.

Gallagher, B. (1998) *Grappling with Smoke: Investigating and Managing Organised Child Sexual Abuse – A Good Practice Guide*. London: NSPCC.

Gallagher, B., Bradford, M. and Pease, K. (2002) 'The sexual abuse of children by strangers', *Children and Society*, 16: 346–59.

Gallagher, J. (1999) *Violent Times: TUC Report on Violence at Work*. London: Trades Union Congress.

Garland, D. (2001) *The Culture of Control: Crime and Social Order in Contemporary Society*. Oxford: Clarendon Press.

Geis, R., Wright, R. and Geis, G. (1978) 'Police surgeons and rape – a questionnaire survey', *The Police Surgeon*, 14: 7–14.

Gibbons, S. (1997) 'Catching the killers', *International Police Review*, July/August: 32–3.

Glidewell Report (1998) *The Review of the Crown Prosecution Service – A Report* (Cm 3960). London: HMSO.

Gosling, M. (2002) 'Dangerous people with severe personality disorders', *Justice of the Peace*, 166: 592–3.

Grace, S., Lloyd, C. and Smith, L.J.F. (1992) *Rape: From Recording to Conviction. Research and Planning Unit Paper* 71. London: Home Office.

Greenlees, L.T. (1991) 'Washington State's Sexually Violent Predators Act: model or mistake?', *American Criminal Law Review,* 29 (35): 107–32.

Gregory, J. and Lees, S. (1999) *Policing Sexual Assault.* London: Routledge.

Grier, A. and Thomas, T. (2003) 'Out of order', *Young People Now,* 16–22 July.

Grover, C. and Soothill, K. (1995) 'Miscarriages of justice: sex crime appeals in the news', *Police Journal,* April: 120–8.

Grubin, D. (1998) 'Sex offending against children: understanding the risk', in *Police Research Series Paper* 99: *Policing and Reducing Crime.* London: Home Office.

Guy, E. (1992) *The Prison Services' Strategy in (PRT).* London: Prison Reform Trust.

Hague, G. and Malos, E. (1998) *Domestic Violence: Action for Change.* Cheltenham: New Clarion Press.

Harris, J. and Grace, S. (1999) *A Question of Evidence: Investigating and Prosecuting Rape in the 1990's. Home Office Research Study* 196. London: Home Office.

Hawton, K. (1983) 'Behavioural approaches to the management of sexual deviations', *British Journal of Psychiatry,* 143: 248–55.

Hayes, M. (1992) '*R v Devon County Council ex p. L:* bad practice, bad law and a breach of human rights?', *Family Law,* 22 June: 245–57.

Hayman, S. (ed.) (1998) *Child Sexual Abuse: Providing for Victims Coping with Offenders.* London: Institute for the Study and Treatment of Delinquency.

Hebenton, B. and Thomas, N. (2004) *Introducing Lay People into Multi-agency Public Protection Panels: Pilot Study of Eight Areas.* London: Home Office.

Hebenton, B. and Thomas, T. (1993) *Criminal Records: State, Citizen and the Politics of Protection.* Aldershot: Avebury.

Hebenton, B. and Thomas, T. (1997) *Keeping Track? Observations on Sex Offender Registers in the US. Crime Detection and Prevention Series Paper* 83. *Police Research Group.* London: Home Office.

Hebenton, B. and Thomas, T. (1999) 'Capacity building against transnational crime: European measures to combat sexual offenders', *European Journal of Crime, Criminal Law and Criminal Justice,* 7 (2): 150–63.

Heilbron Committee (1975) *Report on the Advisory Group on the Law on Rape* (Cmnd 6352). London: HMSO.

Heim, N. and Hursch, C.J. (1979) 'Castration for sex offenders: treatment or punishment? A review and critique of recent European literature', *Archives of Sexual Behaviour,* 8 (3): 281–304.

Henham, R. (1998) 'Sentencing sex offenders: some implications of recent criminal justice policy', *Howard Journal of Criminal Justice,* 37 (1): 70–81.

Hewitt, D. (2004) 'An added duty of risk assessment, *New Law Journal,* 23 January: 87–8.

Heywood, J.S. (1959) *Children in Care.* London: Routledge & Kegan Paul.

Hill, B. and Fletcher-Rogers, K. (1997) *Sexually Related Offences.* London: Sweet & Maxwell.

Hill, C. (1996) *Liberty against the Law*. London: Penguin Books.

Hilliard, B. and Casey, C. (1993) '800 women officers sexually assaulted by colleagues', *Police Review*, 12 February.

HMCPSI/HMIC (HM Crown Prosecution Service Inspectorate/HM Inspectorate of Constabulary) (2002) *A Report on the Joint Inspection into the Investigation and Prosecution of Cases involving Allegations of Rape* (April). London.

HMIC (Her Majesty's Inspectorate of Constabulary) (1997) *The National Criminal Intelligence Service Inspection Report*. London.

HMIC (Her Majesty's Inspectorate of Constabulary) (1999) *Child Protection* (Thematic Inspection Report). London: Home Office.

HMIC (Her Majesty's Inspectorate of Constabulary) (2000) *Under the Microscope – Thematic Inspection Report on Scientific and Technical Support* (July). London.

HMIP (Her Majesty's Inspectorate of Probation) (1995) *Dealing with Dangerous People: The Probation Service and Public Protection* (Report of a Thematic Inspection). London: Home Office.

HMIP (Her Majesty's Inspectorate of Probation) (1998a) *Exercising Constant Vigilance: The Role of the Probation Service in Protecting the Public from Sex Offenders* (Report of a Thematic Inspection). London: Home Office.

HMIP (HM Inspectorate of Probation) (1998b) *Evidence Based Practice: A Guide to Effective Practice*. London: Home Office.

HM Prison Service (1989) *Suicide Prevention*. Circular 20/1989. London.

HM Prison Service (1991) *Treatment Programmes for Sex Offenders in Custody: A Strategy* (Directorate of Inmate Programmes) (July). London.

HM Prison Service (1994) *Release of Prisoners Convicted of Offences against Children or Young Persons under the Age of 18, Guidance Notes to Instruction to Governors 54/1994*. London.

HM Prison Service (1996) *The Treatment of Imprisoned Sex Offenders – Programme Development* (February). London.

HM Prison Service (1998) *The Prison Service Sex Offender Treatment Programme* (Offending Behaviour Programmes Unit) (June). London.

Hobbs, C.J. and Wynne, J.M. (1986) 'Buggery in childhood – a common syndrome of child abuse', *The Lancet*, 4 October: 792–6.

Hobbs, C.J. and Wynne, J.M. (1987) 'Child sexual abuse – an increasing rate of diagnosis', *The Lancet*, 10 October: 837–41.

Home Office (1954) *Convictions on Teachers*. Circular 151/1954. London.

Home Office (1959) *Street Offences Act 1959*. Circular 109/1959. London.

Home Office (1963) *Preventive Detention: Report of the Advisory Council on the Treatment of Offenders*. London: HMSO.

Home Office (1964) *Children and Young Persons Act 1963: Parts I and II*. Circular 22/1964. London.

Home Office (1983) *Investigation of Offences of Rape*. Circular 25/1983. London.

Home Office (1986a) *Violence against Women*. Circular 69/1986. London.

Home Office (1986b) *Protection of Children: Disclosure of Criminal Background of those with Access to Children*. Circular 44/1986. London.

Home Office (1986c) *Police Reports on Convictions and Related Information. Circular* 45/1986. London.

Home Office (1987) *The Use of Video Technology at Trials of Alleged Child Abusers* (8 May). London.

Home Office (1988) *The Investigation of Child Sexual Abuse. Circular* 52/1988. London.

Home Office (1990a) *Crime, Justice and Protecting the Public* (Cm 965). London: HMSO.

Home Office (1990b) *Domestic Violence. Circular* 60/1990. London.

Home Office (1990c) *Criminal Records, the Government Reply to the Third Report from the Home Affairs Committee Session 1989–90* (Cm 1163). London: HMSO.

Home Office (1991) *Misuse of Witness Statements in Sexual Offences Cases: A Consultation Paper.* London: HMSO.

Home Office (1993a) *Protection of Children: Disclosure of Criminal Background of those with Access to Children. Circular* 47/1993. London.

Home Office (1993b) *Disclosure of Criminal Records for Employment Vetting Purposes* (Cm 2319). London: HMSO.

Home Office (1994a) *The Cautioning of Offenders. Circular* 18/1994. London.

Home Office (1994b) *Protection of Children: Disclosure of Criminal Background to Voluntary Sector Organisations. Circular* 41/1994. London.

Home Office (1994c) *Safe from Harm?: Code of Practice for Safeguarding the Welfare of Children in Voluntary Organisations in England and Wales.* London.

Home Office (1995a) 'DNA database goes live' (10 April). Press release, London.

Home Office (1995b) *Probation Service Contact with Victims. Probation Circular* 61/1995. London.

Home Office (1996a) *Sentencing and Supervision of Sex Offenders – A Consultation Document* (Cm 3304). London.

Home Office (1996b) *Review of Extra-territorial Jurisdiction – Steering Committee Report* (Sentencing and Offences Unit) (July). London.

Home Office (1996c) *Protecting the Public: The Government's Strategy on Crime in England and Wales* (Cm 3190). London: HMSO.

Home Office (1996d) *On the Record: The Government's Proposals for Access to Criminal Records for Employment and Related Purposes in England and Wales* (Cm 3308). London: HMSO

Home Office (1997a) 'Electronic monitoring – the future of community punishment' (12 November). Press release, London.

Home Office (1997b) 'Sex offenders to face tougher penalties – MacLean' (27 January). Press release, London.

Home Office (1997c) *Sex Offenders Act 1997. Circular* 39/1997. London.

Home Office (1997d) *Community Protection Order: A Consultation Paper* (November). London.

Home Office (1998a) *Speaking up for Justice* (June). London.

Home Office (1998b) 'Joyce Quinn commends rigorous supervision of sex offenders in the community' (28 April). Press release, London.

Home Office (1998c) *Effective Practice Initiative: A National Implementation Plan for the Effective Supervision of Offenders. Probation Circular* 35/1998. London.

Home Office (1998d) *The Crime and Disorder Act – Sex Offenders Orders: Guidance.* London.

Home Office (1999a) 'Sex offences review: terms of reference announced' (25 January). Press release, London.

Home Office (1999b) *Managing Dangerous People with Severe Personality Disorder: Consultation Document* (19 July). London.

Home Office (1999c) *The Work of the Probation Services with Sex Offenders* (Probation Unit) (March). London.

Home Office (1999d) '32 probation "Pathfinder" projects to reduce re-offending' (14 July). Press release, London.

Home Office (1999e) 'Criminal Records Bureau – outcome of timetable review' (16 December). Press release, London.

Home Office (1999f) *Report of the Interdepartmental Working Group on Preventing Unsuitable People from Working with Children and Abuse of Trust* (25 January): London.

Home Office (1999g) 'Tough measures to weed out child abusers' (29 July). Press release, London.

Home Office (1999h) *Disclosure to the Employment Service of Restrictions that Should be Placed on the Employment of Potentially Dangerous Offenders. Probation Circular* 48/1999. London.

Home Office (2000a) 'Recorded crime statistics England and Wales October 1998–September 1999', *Statistical Bulletin* 1/00, 18 January.

Home Office (2000b) *Setting the Boundaries: Reforming the Law on Sex Offences* (Vols 1 and 2) (July). London.

Home Office (2000c) *Domestic Violence: Revised Circular to the Police. Circular* 19/2000. London.

Home Office (2000d) 'Pilot project to assess dangerous personality disorder announced by Home Office' (10 February). Press release, London.

Home Office (2000e) 'Government proposals better to protect children from sex and violent offences' (15 September). Press release, London.

Home Office (2001a) *Government Reply to the Second Report from the Home Affairs Committee* (Session 2000, Criminal Records Bureau, HC 467). London.

Home Office (2001b) 'Fees for criminal records check announced' (2 April). Press release, London.

Home Office (2001c) 'Statement from the Home Secretary' (18 December). Press release, London.

Home Office (2002a) *Achieving Best Evidence in Criminal Proceedings: Guidance for Vulnerable or Intimidated Witnesses, including Children.* London.

Home Office (2002b) *Protecting the Public: Strengthening Protection against Sex Offenders and Reforming the Law on Sexual Offences* (Cm 5668). London.

Home Office (2002c) *National Standards for the Supervision of Offenders in the Community.* London.

Home Office (2002d) 'Research into sex offender orders published' (19 June). Press release, London.

Home Office (2003a) *Safety and Justice: The Government's Proposals on Domestic Violence* (Cm 5847) (June). London.

Home Office (2003b) *The Conduct of Investigations into Past Cases of Abuse in Children's Homes* (Cm 5799) (April). London.

Home Office (2003c) 'Home Secretary announces independent inquiry into Soham case' (17 December). Press release, London.

Home Office (2003d) 'New fee structure as CRB extends checks after doubling capacity in nine months' (5 June). Press release, London.

Home Office (2003e) 'New fee structure and registered body proposals to further improve the CRB' (1 December). Press release, London.

Home Office (2003f) *Sexual Offences Bill: Government Proposals on the Issue of Sex Offenders who Travel Abroad* (March). London.

Home Office (2004a) 'New UK-wide Organised Crime Agency pooling expertise to track down the crime bosses' (9 February). Press release, London.

Home Office (2004b) 'Public to play vital role in managing sex and violent offences in community' (15 April). Press release, London.

Home Office/Department of Health (1992) *Memorandum of Good Practice.* London: HMSO.

Home Office/Department of Health (2002) *Complex Child Abuse Investigations: Inter-agency Guidance* (May). London.

Home Office, Department of Health, Welsh Office (1995) *National Standards for the Supervision of Offenders in the Community* (2nd edn). London.

Home Office, Department of Health, DES and Welsh Office (1991) *Working Together: A Guide to Arrangements for Inter-agency Co-operation for the Protection of Children from Abuse.* London: HMSO.

Home Office/DHSS (Department of Health and Social Security) (1985) *Disclosure of Criminal Convictions of those with Access to Children: First Report* (July). London.

Home Office/DHSS (Department of Health and Social Security) (1987) *Mental Health Act 1983: Supervision and After-care of Conditionally Discharged Restricted Patients – Notes for the Guidance of Social Supervisors.* London.

Home Office/Lord Chancellor's Department (1996) *Stalking – the Solutions. Consultation Paper* (July). London.

Home Office PSTU (Police Science and Technology Unit) (1999) *Draft Guidance on the Disclosure of Information about Sex Offenders who may Present a Risk to Children and Vulnerable Adults* (31 August). London.

Home Office/Scottish Executive (2001) *Consultation Paper on the Review of Part 1 of the Sex Offenders Act 1997* (July).

Home Office/Scottish Executive (1997) *Sex Offenders: A Ban on Working with Children. Consultation Paper* (January). London.

Home Office/Youth Justice Board (2002) *Final Warning Scheme: Guidance for the Police and Youth Offending Teams* (November). London.

House of Commons (1984) *Children in Care. Second Report from the Social Services Committee* (Session 1983–1984, HC 360-351). London: HMSO.

House of Commons (1990) *Criminal Records. Third Report of the Home Affairs Committee* (Session 1989–90, HC 285). London.

House of Commons (1998) *Children Looked after by Local Authorities. Health Committee Second Report* (Session 1997–1998, HC 319 II). London: HMSO.

House of Commons (2001) *Criminal Records Bureau. Second Report of the Home Affairs Committee* (Session 2000–1, HC 227). London.

House of Commons (2002) *The Conduct of Investigations into Past Cases of Abuse in Children's Homes. Fourth Report of the Home Affairs Committee* (Session 2001–2, HC 836–1). London.

Howard League (1985) *Unlawful Sex: Offences, Victims and Offenders in the Criminal Justice System of England and Wales.* London: Waterlow.

Hucklesby, A. (1994) 'The use and abuse of conditional bail', *Howard Journal of Criminal Justice*, 33 (3): 258–70.

Hughes, B., Parker, H. and Gallagher, B. (1996) *Policing Child Sexual Abuse: The View from Police Practitioners* (Police Research Group). London: Home Office.

Human Rights Watch (HRW) (1997) *To Serve without Favour: Policing, Human Rights, and Accountability in Northern Ireland.* Helsinki: Human Rights Watch.

Hunt Report (1994) *Report of the Independent Inquiry into Multiple Abuse in Nursery Classes in Newcastle upon Tyne.* Newcastle upon Tyne: City Council of Newcastle Upon Tyne.

ICBA (Irish Catholic Bishop's Advisory Committee) (1996) *Child Sexual Abuse: Framework for a Church Response.* Dublin: Veritas.

Ignatieff, M. (1978) *A Just Measure of Pain.* London: Penguin.

ILO (International Labour Organization) (1998) *The Sex Sector: The Economic and Social Bases of Prostitution in South East Asia.* Geneva.

Interpol (1997) *Handbook on Good Practice for Specialist Officers Dealing with Crimes against Children* (November). Lyon.

Interpol – General Secretariat (1995) 'Interpol and the struggle to combat offences against minors', *International Criminal Police Review*, 452–3.

IOM (International Organisation for Migration) (1998) *Analysis of Data and Statistical Resources Available in the EU Member States on Trafficking in Humans, Particularly Women and Children for the Purposes of Sexual Exploitation.* Geneva.

Jackson, L.A. (2000) *Child Sexual Abuse in Victorian England.* London: Routledge.

Janus, E. (2000) 'Civil commitment as social control: managing the risk of sexual violence', in M. Brown and J. Pratt (eds) *Dangerous Offenders: Punishment and Social Order.* London: Routledge.

Jenkins, P. (1994) *Using Murder: The Social Construction of Serial Homicide.* New York: Aldine de Gruyter.

Jones, D. (1982) *Crime, Protest, Community and Police in 19th Century Britain.* London: Routledge & Kegan Paul.

Jones, D.J.V. (1992) *Crime in Nineteenth Century Wales.* Cardiff: University of Wales Press.

Kane, J. (1998) *Sold for Sex*. Aldershot: Arena.

Kelly, L. (1988) *Surviving Sexual Violence*. Cambridge: Polity Press.

Kelly, L. (1996) 'Weasel words: paedophiles and the cycle of abuse', *Trouble and Strife*, 33 (Summer): 44–9.

Kelly, L. (2002) 'Journeys of jeopardy: a commentary on current research on trafficking of women and children for sexual exploitation within Europe.' Paper presented at European Conference, *Preventing and Combating Trafficking in Human Beings: Global Challenge for the 21st Century*, Brussels, 18–20 September.

Kelly, L. and Radford, J. (1990–91) ' "Nothing really happened": the invalidation of women's experiences of sexual violence', *Critical Social Policy*, 30 (Winter): 39–53.

Kemshall, H. and McIvor, G. (eds) (2004) *Managing Sex Offender Risk*. London: Jessica Kingsley.

Kent Report (1997) *Children's Safeguards Review*. Edinburgh: Social Work Services Inspectorate for Scotland.

Kilbrandon Report (1964) *Children and Young Persons: Scotland* (Cmnd 2306). Edinburgh: HMSO.

King, D. (1999) *In the Name of Liberalism*. Oxford: Oxford University Press.

Knock, K. (2002) *The Police Perspective on Sex Offender Orders: A Preliminary Review of Policy and Practice. Police Research Series Paper 155*. London: Home Office.

Labour Party (1996) *Protecting our Children* (September). London.

La Fontaine, J.S. (1994) *The Extent and Nature of Organised and Ritual Abuse: Research Findings*. London: HMSO.

La Fontaine, J.S. (1998) *Speak of the Devil*. Cambridge: Cambridge University Press.

Laing, J.M. (2002) 'Detaining the dangerous: legal and ethical implications of the government's proposals for high-risk individuals', *The Journal of Criminal Law*, 66 (1): 64–83.

Laming Report (2003) *The Victoria Climbié Inquiry*. Norwich: HMSO.

Laurence, A. (1994) *Women in England 1500–1760*. London: Wiedenfeld & Nicolson.

Law Commission (1992) *Family Law, Domestic Violence and Occupation of the Family Home* (No. 207). London: HMSO.

Law Commission (1995) *Consent in the Criminal Law – A Consultancy Paper* (No. 139). London: HMSO.

Lee, M. and O'Brien, R. (1995) *The Game's Up: Redefining Child Prostitution*. London: Children's Society.

Lees, S. (1997) *Carnal Knowledge: Rape on Trial*. Harmondsworth: Penguin Books.

Levy, A. and Kahan, B. (1991) *The Pindown Experience and the Protection of Children*. Stoke-on-Trent: Staffordshire County Council.

LGA (Local Government Association) (1998) 'Don't apply sun lotions to children, LCA warns' (13 August). Press release, London.

Liberty (1996) *Response to the Home Office Consultation Paper on Sentencing and Supervision of Sex Offenders* (August). London.

Liberty (1997a) *Briefing on the Sex Offenders Bill* (January). London.

Liberty (1997b) *Response to the Home Office Consultation Paper, Sex Offenders: A Ban on Working with Children* (May). London.

Liberty (2002) *Briefing on the 'Criminal Justice Bill' – 2nd Commons Reading* (November). London.

Linebaugh, P. (1991) *The London Hanged: Crime and Civil Society in the Eighteenth Century.* London: Allen Lane.

London Rape Crisis Centre (1984) *Sexual Violence: The Reality for Women. The Women's Press Handbook Series.* London: Women's Press.

MacLean, N.M. (1979) 'Rape and false allegations of rape', *The Police Surgeon*, 15 (April): 29–40.

MacLeod, M. (1996) *Talking with Children about Child Abuse.* London: Childline.

Maguire, M. and Norris, N. (1992) *The Conduct and Supervision of Criminal Investigations Research Study No. 5. Royal Commission on Criminal Justice.* London: HMSO.

Mair, G. and Mortimer, E. (1996) *Curfew Orders with Electronic Monitoring. Home Office Research Study* 163. London: HMSO.

Marshall, P. (1997) *The Prevalence of Convictions for Sexual Offending. Research Finding* 55. London: Home Office Research and Statistics Directorate.

Matravers, A. (ed.) (2003) *Sex Offenders in the Community: Managing and Reducing the Risks.* Cullompton: Willan Publishing.

McAlinden, A.H. (2001) 'Indeterminate sentences for the severely personality disordered', *Criminal Law Review*, 108–23.

McGowen, R. (1995) 'The well-ordered prison: England 1780–1865', in N. Morris and D.J. Rothman (eds) *The Oxford History of the Prison: The Practice of Punishment in Western Society.* Oxford: Oxford University Press.

McLeod, N. (1991) 'English DNA evidence held inadmissible', *Criminal Law Review*, 583–90.

McWilliams, M. and Spence, L. (1996) *Taking Domestic Violence seriously: Issues for the Civil and Criminal Justice System.* Belfast: HMSO.

McWilliams, W. and Pease, K. (1990) 'Probation practice and an end to punishment', *Howard Journal of Criminal Justice*, 29 (1): 14–24.

Mearns, A. (1883) *The Bitter Cry of Outcast London* (pamphlet). London.

Mental Health Alliance (2002) *Briefing on Proposed Mental Health Act Reforms* (August). London.

Meyers, D.W. (1970) *The Human Body and the Law.* Edinburgh: Edinburgh University Press.

Morris, A., Giller, H., Szwed, E. and Geach, H. (1980) *Justice for Children.* London: Macmillan.

Morrison, T., Erooga, M. and Beckett, R.C. (eds) (1994) *Sexual Offending against Children: Assessment and Treatment of Male Abusers.* London: Routledge.

Mrazek, P.J., Lynch, M.A. and Bentovim, A. (1983) 'Sexual abuse of children in the United Kingdom', *Child Abuse and Neglect*, 7 (2): 147–53.

NACRO (National Association for the Care and Resettlement of Offenders) (1996a) *Sentencing and Supervision of Sex Offenders – NACRO's Response to the Consultation Document*. London.

NACRO (National Association for the Care and Resettlement of Offenders) (1996b) *Disclosing Convictions*. London.

NAHT (National Association of Head Teachers)/ACPO (Association of Chief Police Officers) (1998) *Protocol Regarding Sex Offenders Act 1997* (July). Haywards Heath.

NAO (National Audit Office) (2004a) Criminal Records Bureau: delivering safer recruitment (press release) 12 February.

NAO (National Audit Office) (2004b) Criminal Records Bureau: delivering safer recruitment HC 266 2003–4.

Nash, M. (1999) *Police, Probation and Protecting the Public*. London: Blackstone Press.

NCCL (National Council for Civil Liberties) (1988) 'NCCL urges reform of police checks system' (26 September). Press release, London.

NCF (National Coaching Foundation)/NSPCC (National Society for the Prevention of Cruelty to Children) (1995) *Protecting Children: A Guide for Sports People*. London.

NCIS (National Criminal Intelligence Service) (1995) 'Child sex tourism comes under scrutiny' (20 November). Press release, London.

Neyroud, P. (1999) 'Danger signals', *Policing Today*, 5 (2): 10–15.

NHS (National Health Service) Executive (1997) *Guidance to Hospital Managers and Local Authority Social Services Departments on the Sex Offenders Act 1997. Circular* HSG (97) 37. London.

NIO (Northern Ireland Office) (1997) *The Sex Offenders Act 1997 – Introductory Guide for Northern Ireland* (August). Belfast.

NIO (Northern Ireland Office) (1999) *Tackling Violence against Women: A Consultation Paper* (April). Belfast.

NI (Northern Ireland) Working Party (1988) *Disclosure of Criminal Background of Persons Seeking Access to Children* (interdepartmental, March). Belfast.

NSPCC (National Society for the Prevention of Cruelty to Children) (1997) 'NSPCC concerned re inclusion of juvenile offenders on sex offenders register' (24 October). Press release, London.

NSPCC (National Society for the Prevention of Cruelty to Children) (2002) 'MAPPPs will fail without support says NSPCC' (22 July). Press release, London.

Nuttall, J. (1970) *Bomb Culture*. London: Paladin.

Oates, T. (1998) 'The difficulties encountered when investigating abuse that has taken place in the past', in S. Hayman (ed.) *Child Sexual Abuse: Providing for Victims Coping with Offenders*. London: Institute for the Study and Treatment of Delinquency.

O'Carroll, T. (1980) *Paedophilia: The Radical Case*. London: Peter Owen.

O'Mahony, P. (1996) *Criminal Chaos: Seven Crises in Irish Criminal Justice*. Dublin: Round Hall Sweet & Maxwell.

Parker, T. (1970) *The Frying Pan: A Prison and its Prisoners*. London: Hutchinson.

Parris, M. (1997) 'All-party witch-hunt', *The Times*, 24 January.

Parry, N., Rustin, M. and Satyamurti, C. (eds) (1979) *Social Work, Welfare and the State*. London: Edward Arnold.

Parsloe, P. (1979) 'After-custody: supervision in the community in England, Wales and Scotland', in H. Parker (ed.) *Social Work and the Courts*. London: Edward Arnold.

Parton, N. (1991) *Governing the Family*. London: Macmillan.

Parton, N. (1996a) 'Social work, risk and the blaming system', in N. Parton (ed.) *Social Theory, Social Change and Social Work*. London: Routledge.

Parton, N. (ed.) (1996b) *Social Theory, Social Change and Social Work*. London: Routledge.

Pattullo, P. (1984) *Judging Women*. London: National Council for Civil Liberties.

Petrow, S. (1994) *Policing Morals: The Metropolitan Police and the Home Office 1870–1914*. Oxford: Clarendon Press.

Phoenix, J. (2004) 'Re-thinking youth prostitution: national provision at the margins of child protection and youth justice', *Youth Justice*, 3 (3): 152–68.

Pickover, E. (2001) 'A sample of common sense', *Police Review*, 2 February.

Pigot Report (1989) *Report of the Advisory Group on Video Evidence*. London: Home Office.

Pinchbeck, I. and Hewitt, M. (1973) *Children in English Society. Volume II*. London: Routledge & Kegan Paul.

Plotnikoff, J. and Woolfson, R. (1998) *Policing Domestic Violence: Effective Organisational Structures. Police Research Series Paper* 100. London: Home Office Policing and Reducing Crime Unit.

Plotnikoff, J. and Woolfson, R. (2000) *Where are they Now? An Evaluation of Sex Offender Registration in England and Wales. Police Research Series Paper* 126. London: Home Office.

Policy Advisory Committee on Sexual Offences (1981) *Report on the Age of Consent in Relation to Sexual Offences* (Cmnd 8216). London. HMSO.

Porter, R. (ed.) (1984) *Child Sexual Abuse within the Family* (The Ciba Foundation). London: Tavistock.

Porter, R. (1985) 'Rape – does it have a historical meaning?', in S. Tomaselli and R. Porter (eds) *Rape*. Oxford: Blackwell.

Potter, K. (1997) 'The right to know', *Police Review*, 21 February: 18–19.

Power, H. (1999) 'Sex offenders, privacy and the police', *Criminal Law Review*, 3–16.

Prochaska, J. and Di Clemente, C. (1986) 'Towards a comprehensive model of change', in W.R. Miller and N. Heather (eds) *Treating Addictive Behaviours: Processes of Change*. New York: Plenum Press.

PRT (Prison Reform Trust) (1992) *Beyond Containment: The Penal Response to Sex Offending*. London: PRT.

PRT (Prison Reform Trust) (1995) 'A suitable case for treatment?' (briefing paper) (August). London.

Radford, J. and Russell, D. (eds) (1992) *Femicide: The Politics of Woman Killing*. Milton Keynes: Open University Press.

Radzinowicz, L. (1948) *A History of English Criminal Law. Volume 2*. London: Stevens & Sons.

Radzinowicz, L. and Hood, R. (1990) *The Emergence of Penal Policy in Victorian and Edwardian England*. Oxford: Clarendon Press.

Rafferty, E. (1986) 'The Kincora casualties', *Social Work Today*, 10 February.

Ranyard, R., Hebenton, B. and Pease, K. (1994) 'An analysis of a guideline case as applied to the offence of rape', *Howard Journal of Criminal Justice*, 33 (3): 203–17.

Ravenscroft, L. (1997) 'The need to decriminalise child prostitution', *Childright*, 141 (November): 16.

RCCJ (Royal Commission on Criminal Justice) (1993) (Cm 2263). London: HMSO.

RCHWC (Royal Commission on the Housing of the Working Classes) (1885) (C (2nd series) 4402-1). London: HMSO.

RCP (Royal College of Psychiatry) (2001) *Working Party on the Reform of the Mental Health Act 1983: A Response from the College's Mental Health Sub-committee* (June): London.

Report of the Street Offences Committee (1928) (Cmd 3231). London: HMSO.

Ross, E. (1982) '"Fierce questions and taunts": married life in working class London 1870–1914', *Feminist Studies*, 8 (2).

Sampson, A. (1994) *Acts of Abuse: Sex Offenders and the Criminal Justice System*. London: Routledge.

SAP (Sentencing Advisory Panel) (2002) *Rape: The Panel's Advice to the Court of Appeal* (May). London.

SAP (Sentencing Advisory Panel) (2004) *Sentencing Guidelines on Sexual Offences: Consultation Paper* (February). London.

Scottish Office (1979) *Release of Inmates Convicted of Offences against Children in the Home. Circular* 14/1979 (Criminal). Edinburgh.

Scottish Office (1989a) *Effective Intervention: Child Abuse – Guidance on Cooperation in Scotland*. Edinburgh.

Scottish Office (1989b) *Protection of Children: Disclosure of Criminal Convictions of those with Access to Children: Local Authorities. Circular* SW9/1989. Edinburgh.

Scottish Office (1990) *Investigation of Complaints of Domestic Assault. Circular* 3/1990. Edinburgh.

Scottish Office (1994) *Child Protection: The Imprisonment and Preparation for Release of Offenders Convicted of Offences against Children. Circular* SWSG 11/1994. Edinburgh.

Scottish Office (1996) *On the Record in Scotland: Proposals for Improved Access to Criminal Records* (June). Edinburgh.

Scottish Office (1997a) *Sex Offenders Act 1997 Guidance on Implementation. Circular* HD 12/1997 2154. Edinburgh.

Scottish Office (1997b) *Implementation of the Sex Offenders Act 1997 – Implications for Local Authorities. Circular* SWSG 11/1997. Edinburgh.

Scottish Office (1998a) *Preventing Violence against Women: A Scottish Office Action Plan*. Edinburgh.

Scottish Office (1998b) 'Child protection to be strengthened with introduction of criminal record checks – McLeish' (14 December). Press release, Edinburgh.

Scottish Office (1999) *The MacLean Consultation Paper*. Edinburgh.

Sennett, R. (1974) *The Fall of Public Man*. Cambridge: Cambridge University Press.

Seven, P. (1991) 'Treating sex offenders in prison', *Journal of Forensic Psychiatry*, 2 (1): 8–9.

SFCRC (Support Force for Children's Residential Care) (1997) *Code of Practice for the Employment of Residential Child Care Workers*. London: Department of Health.

Sheridan Report (1982) *Homes and Hostels for Children and Young Persons in Northern Ireland*. Belfast: DHSS.

Silverman, J. and Wilson, D. (2002) *Innocence Betrayed: Paedophilia, the Media and Society*. Cambridge: Polity Press.

Skidmore, P. (1995) 'Telling tales: media power, ideology and the reporting of child sexual abuse in Britain', in D. Kidd-Hewitt and R. Osbourne (eds) *Crime and the Media: The Post-modern Spectacle*. London: Pluto.

Smith, J. (1998) 'How consistent are social services departments in appointing children and family social workers?', *Childright*, 144 (March): 9–10.

Smith, J. (1999) 'Prior criminality and employment of social workers with substantial access to children: a decision board analysis', *British Journal of Social Work*, 29: 49–68.

Soothill, K., Francis, B. and Ackerley, E. (1998) 'Paedophilia and paedophiles', *New Law Journal*, 12 June: 882–3.

Soothill, K. and Walby, C. (1991) *Sex Crime in the News*. London: Routledge.

Sparks, R., Bottoms, A. and Hay, W. (1996) *Prisons and the Problem of Order*. Oxford: Clarendon Press.

SWSG (Social Work Services Group) (1985) *Disclosure of Criminal Convictions of those with Access to Children: Consultation Paper* (November). Edinburgh.

Temkin, J. (1993) 'Sexual history evidence – the ravishment of Section 2', *Criminal Law Review*, 1: 3–20.

Temkin, J. (1999) 'Reporting rape in London: a qualitative study', *Howard Journal of Criminal Justice*, 38 (1): 17–41.

Temkin, J. (2002) *Rape and the Legal Process* (2nd edn). Oxford: Oxford University Press.

The Boston Globe (2002) *Betrayal: The Crisis in the Catholic Church*. Boston: Little, Brown.

Thomas, T. (2000) 'Protecting the public: some observations on the Sex Offender Bill, 2000', *Irish Criminal Law Journal*, 7 (2): 150–63.

Thomas, T. (2001a) 'Sex offenders, the Home Office and the Sunday papers', *Journal of Social Welfare and Family Law*, 23 (1): 103–8.

Thomas, T. (2001b) 'The national collection of criminal records: a question of data quality', *Criminal Law Review*, 886–96.

Thomas, T. (2001c) 'Child sexual abuse and the EU: recent policies and initiatives', *Childright*, 180: 5–6.

Thomas, T. (2002) 'Employment screening and the Criminal Records Bureau', *Industrial Law Journal*, 31 (1): 55–70.

Thomas, T. (2003) 'The Sex Offender Register: the registration of young people', *Childright*, 194: 10–11.

Thomas, T. (2004) 'Sex offenders: registers and monitoring', in H. Kemshall and G. McIvor (eds) *Managing Sex Offender Risk*. London: Jessica Kingsley.

Thomas, T., Katz, I. and Wattam, C. (1999) *CUPICSO: The Collection and Use of Personal Information on Child Sex Offenders*. London: NSPCC.

Tomaselli, S. and Porter, R. (eds) (1985) *Rape*. Oxford: Blackwell.

UN (United Nations) (1948) *Universal Declaration of Human Rights*. New York.

UN (United Nations) (1996) *Sexual Exploitation of Children. Study Series 8*. Geneva: Centre for Human Rights.

Unell, J. (1992) *Criminal Record Checks within the Voluntary Sector: An Evaluation of the Pilot Schemes*. Volunteer Centre.

Unsworth, C. (1979) 'The balance of medicine, law and social work in mental health legislation 1889–1959', in N. Parry *et al.* (eds) *Social Work, Welfare and the State*. London: Edward Arnold.

Utting Report (1997) *People Like Us: Report of the Review of the Safeguards for Children Living Away from Home*. Department of Health/Welsh Office.

Valios, N. (1998) 'Social workers warn register is flawed', *Community Care*, 27 August–2 September.

Valios, N. (1999) 'Mental health groups angered by Straw's plans for indefinite detention', *Community Care*, 18–24 February.

Violence against Children Study Group (1999) *Children, Child Abuse and Child Protection*. Chichester: Wiley.

von Hirsch, A. (1990) 'The ethics of community-based sanctions', *Crime and Delinquency*, 36 (1): 162–73.

VSWGSO (Voluntary Sector Working Group on Sex Offenders) (1997a) *Sex Offenders in the Community*. Belfast: NIACRO.

VSWGSO (Voluntary Sector Working Group on Sex Offenders) (1997b) *Sex Offenders in the Community – Conference Report* (19 February). Belfast: NIACRO.

Wacks, R. (1989) *Personal Information: Privacy and the Law*. Oxford: Clarendon Press.

Walkowitz, J.R. (1992) *City of Dreadful Delight*. London: Virago.

WAR/LAW (Women against Rape/Legal Action for Women) (1995) *Dossier: The Crown Prosecution Service and the Crime of Rape*. London: Crossroads.

Warner Report (1992) *Choosing with Care: Report of the Committee of Enquiry into the Selection, Development and Management of Staff in Children's Homes.* London: HMSO.

Waterhouse, L., Dobash, R. and Carnie, J. (1994) *Child Sexual Abusers.* Edinburgh: HMSO.

Waterhouse Report (2000) *Lost in Care – Report of the Tribunal of Inquiry into the Abuse of Children in Care in the Former County Council Areas of Gwynedd and Clwyd since 1974* (Summary) (HC 201). London: HMSO.

Webster, R. (1998) *The Great Children's Home Panic.* Oxford: Orwell Press.

Webster, R. (1999) 'How the police trawl the innocent', *New Statesman,* 19 July.

Whitfield, D. (1997) *Tackling the Tag: The Electronic Monitoring of Offenders.* Winchester: Waterside Press.

Williams, B. (1999) *Working with Victims of Crime.* London: Jessica Kingsley.

Wilson, E. (1983) *What is to be Done about Violence against Women?.* Harmondsworth: Penguin Books.

Wohl, A. (1978) 'Sex and the single room: incest among the Victorian working classes', in A. Wohl (ed.) *The Victorian Family.* London: Croom Helm.

Wolfenden Report (1957) *Report of the Committee on Homosexual Offences and Prostitution* (Cmnd 247). London: HMSO.

Worrall, A. (1997) *Punishment in the Community – The Future of Criminal Justice.* London: Longman.

Wyre, R. (1996) 'The mind of the paedophile', in P.C. Bibby (ed.) *Organised Abuse: The Current Debate.* Basingstoke: Arena.

Young, J. (1999) *The Exclusive Society.* London: Sage.

Index

women victims, court hearings 84
Women's Aid 130
women's movement 62
Wookey, James 49
workhouses 41
Working Together to Safeguard Children 127, 129

X v. Chief Constable of West Midlands Police [2004] EWHC Admin. 61 148

Yorkshire Evening Post 2, 11, 23, 27

Yorkshire Post 23, 78
Yorkshire Ripper 21, 61
young offenders
   cautions 71
   custodial facilities 54
   early treatment 34
   registration periods 158
young people, protection of 123–7
youth clubs, unlawful sexual intercourse 5
Youth Justice and Criminal Evidence Act (1999) 86, 89
Youth Offending Teams 98